MW00779753

Partners in deterrence

Manchester University Press

Partners in deterrence

US nuclear weapons and alliances in Europe and Asia

Stephan Frühling and Andrew O'Neil

MANCHESTER UNIVERSITY PRESS

Published by Manchester University Press

Oxford Road, Manchester M13 9PL

www.manchesteruniversitypress.co.uk

British Library Cataloguing-in-Publication Data

A catalogue record for this book is available from the British Library

ISBN 978 1 5261 5072 1 hardback
ISBN 978 1 5261 7185 6 paperback

First published 2021
Paperback published 2023

Typeset by Newgen Publishing UK

Contents

Preface

In this book we explain how and why key decisions have been taken regarding nuclear weapons in US alliances in Europe and Asia. Nuclear weapons have been central to the US alliance system since the 1950s, yet there are very few detailed studies of the topic. This is both curious and unfortunate. It is curious because nuclear assurances via extended deterrence remain at the heart of US security commitments to allies; it is unfortunate because the influence of US allies on American nuclear policy has tended to be overlooked in much of the literature. This book attempts to fill these gaps while making an original contribution to existing scholarship and providing lessons for policymakers.

This book is the product of a shared fascination with the dynamic interrelationship between alliance management and nuclear deterrence. In surveying the secondary literature, we were unsettled by the lack of comparative analysis of European and Asian experiences and struck by the absence of theoretical frameworks beyond traditional realism to explain complex phenomena. The book aims to furnish an account that is theoretically informed, empirically rigorous, and has relevance for contemporary policymakers. In many respects, this is the 'holy trinity' of academic scholarship and we leave it to readers to judge whether or not we have succeeded in this quest.

Since this project began in 2016, we have accumulated many debts along the way. We would especially like to thank those who have provided valuable research assistance: Helen Taylor, Emily Robertson, and Kate Grayson deserve particular acknowledgement. Ben Wilson provided valuable help in preparing the final index. We would also like to thank Karoline Gårdsmoen for providing an extensive English summary of Kjetil Skogrand and Rolf Tamnes, *Fryktens likevekt: Atombomben, Norge og verden, 1945–1970*.

Thanks are due to Hylke Dijkstra for organising a round-table debate in *Contemporary Security Policy* in 2017 on our article 'Nuclear Weapons, the United States, and Alliances in Europe and Asia: An Institutional

Perspective', vol. 38, no. 1 (DOI: 10.1080/13523260.2016.1257214). The very thoughtful reactions to our piece from Van Jackson, Alexander Lanoszka, and Jeffrey Knopf helped shape a number of key ideas in this book. Chapters 1 and 6 draw on our article 'Institutions, Informality and Influence: Explaining Nuclear Cooperation in the Australia–US Alliance', which appeared in 2020 in the *Australian Journal of Political Science*, vol. 55, no. 2 (DOI: 10.1080/10361146.2019.1697199).

At Manchester University Press, we were very fortunate to collaborate with a team that provided first-class support from the commissioning to the production cycle. Jon De Peyer provided early encouragement of the proposal, and Rob Byron and Lucy Burns were critical in ensuring continuity throughout the process. We are very grateful for the detailed feedback from the MUP anonymous reviewers and their time and commitment. We also thank Sarah Green at Newgen Publishing UK for her support in finalising the proofs.

We gratefully acknowledge the financial support provided by Australian Research Council Grant DP140101478.

Finally, Frühling would like to thank Mary, and O'Neil would like to thank Jo for their support and forbearance, including for many of the working weekends this book required.

Abbreviations

ACM	Alliance Coordination Mechanism
ADM	atomic demolition munition
AFNORTH	Allied Forces Northern Europe
AMF	Allied Mobile Force
ANZUS	Australia, New Zealand, and United States (security treaty)
ASEAN	Association of Southeast Asian Nations
AUSMIN	Australia–US Ministerial (meeting)
CDU	Christian Democratic Union
CFC	Combined Forces Command
CINCNORTH	Commander-in-Chief Northern Europe
DDPR	Deterrence and Defence Posture Review
DMZ	Demilitarized Zone
DPC	Defence Planning Committee
EDC	European Defence Community
EDD	Extended Deterrence Dialogue
EDPC	Extended Deterrence Policy Committee
EDSCG	Extended Deterrence Strategy and Consultation Group
ERW	enhanced radiation weapon
GLCM	ground-launched cruise missile
HLG	high-level group
ICBM	intercontinental (range) ballistic missile
INF	intermediate (range) nuclear forces
INTERFET	International Force East Timor
JDA	Japanese Defence Agency
LRTNF	long-range theatre nuclear forces
MC	Military Committee
MLF	Multilateral Force
MRBM	medium-range ballistic missile
MST	Mutual Security Treaty
NAC	North Atlantic Council

NATO	North Atlantic Treaty Organisation
NDPG	National Defense Program Guidelines
NDPO	National Defense Program Outline
NPG	Nuclear Planning Group
NPR	Nuclear Posture Review
NPT	Non-Proliferation Treaty
NSC	National Security Council
OPCON	operational control
PoC	Program of Cooperation
RAAF	Royal Australian Air Force
ROK	Republic of Korea
SAC	Strategic Air Command
SACEUR	Supreme Allied Commander Europe
SACLANT	Supreme Allied Commander Atlantic
SALT	Strategic Arms Limitation Treaty
SCC	Security Consultative Committee
SCM	Security Consultative Mechanism/Meeting
SDF	Self-Defense Force
SDI	Strategic Defense Initiative
SEATO	Southeast Asia Treaty Organisation
SHAPE	Supreme Headquarters Allied Powers Europe
SIGINT	signals intelligence
SIOP	Single Integrated Operational Plan
SLOC	sea lines of communication
SNOWCAT	support of nuclear operations with conventional attacks
SPD	Social Democratic Party
SPNFZ	South Pacific Nuclear-Free Zone
SSBN	subsurface ballistic nuclear (submarine)
THAAD	terminal high-altitude area defence
TLAM – N	Tomahawk land attack missile – nuclear
TNW	tactical nuclear weapon
USAF	US Air Force

Introduction

During Donald Trump's term as US President, doubts began to emerge about whether his administration would deliver on established US commitments to defend its allies around the world. Trump's fixation on the 'cost' of allies, coupled with his cavalier approach to alliance management, stoked concern in allied capitals that the US was beginning to backtrack on its extended deterrence commitments. Yet, by the time Trump left office in January 2021, many of the strategic reassurance initiatives put in train under the Obama administration, such as missile defence deployments to South Korea and the enhanced forward presence of the North Atlantic Treaty Organization (NATO), had been implemented. Indeed, if one compares the Trump administration's rhetoric with US actions where it counts – on the ground in Europe and Asia – it is clear that in a number of important respects the US has, in fact, reinforced its capacity to defend allies against threats from adversaries.[1] In the case of NATO, although the Trump administration decided in its last year to draw down US troop levels in Germany, this distracted from the continuing reinforcement of the US military presence in eastern Europe and the Baltic states.[2]

While conventional force commitments under extended deterrence remain of key importance to US alliance management, a major source of US global leadership is Washington's agreement to protect its allies by extending the nuclear umbrella to a number of European and Asian countries. As Mira Rapp-Hooper has argued, extended deterrence became fundamental to the logic underlying US alliances in Europe and Asia after 1945.[3] The US signed a range of multilateral and bilateral treaties under which it pledged to defend smaller allies in Western Europe, Northeast Asia, and Australasia. Nuclear weapons were central to this development that shapes the international security order to this day. The US advantage over the Soviet Union in nuclear weapons during the two decades after 1945 gave it the confidence to enter into these new alliance commitments as a basis for deterring Communist attack and coercion. Nuclear deterrence was central to America's Cold War strategy and most US allies continue to regard it as a core benefit of their alliance with the US, despite predictions in the two decades after the Cold War that the nuclear umbrella would gradually become redundant. The most recent US Nuclear Posture Review notes that 'the US extends deterrence to over 30 countries with different views about the threat environment and the credibility of US security commitments'.[4] Today, buoyant demand for extended nuclear deterrence among US allies is seen by many disarmament advocates as one of the primary obstacles to achieving the elimination of nuclear weapons.

At a strategic level, the nuclear umbrella is embedded in US commitments to defend NATO allies, and in bilateral alliances with Japan, South Korea, and Australia. In practical terms, these commitments are demonstrated through a combination of the following: US and joint statements with allies; material preparations for US nuclear operations that include high-profile deployments of nuclear-capable systems and, in the case of the NATO alliance, 'sharing' of US nuclear weapons; and consultation arrangements that accord US allies structured insights and influence on American nuclear policy. Extended nuclear deterrence is most institutionalised in the case of NATO, where allies have sought to create what David Yost describes as 'a presumption of concerted action in the event of a crisis'.[5]

The extent to which nuclear weapons have become ingrained in interactions between the US and its allies has, however, varied significantly over time and space. During the Cold War, the US stationed nuclear warheads in Europe and on the Korean Peninsula, and transited nuclear weapons regularly through Japan, but not Australia. In Europe, from the 1960s, the Nuclear Planning Group became the forum for detailed discussion, analysis, and development of NATO's nuclear posture and strategy. No similar forum emerged in Asia, and only in the last decade have there been concrete steps to embed policy discussions on extended deterrence in formal alliance institutions in Northeast Asia. In Europe, the US openly provided nuclear warheads for use by its allies, while in Asia even the existence of US nuclear-armed forces on sovereign territory of allies remained secret for decades. Norway, despite being a frontline state during the Cold War, refused to participate in many of the practical aspects of nuclear weapons cooperation that West Germany and others saw as being central to NATO's deterrence strategy. New Zealand, for its part, even accepted the end of its alliance with the US in the mid-1980s as a price worth paying for dissociating itself from US nuclear strategy. And while the nuclear aspect of extended deterrence lost some of its lustre after the Cold War as the Soviet threat disappeared, it was only in 1993 that Australia began to refer publicly to the nuclear umbrella as a security pay-off through its alliance with the US.

This book addresses timely, yet fundamental, questions about the role of nuclear weapons in relations between the US and its non-nuclear allies: What is the role of nuclear weapons in US alliances? And what explains the differences in the way in which nuclear weapons cooperation takes place in US alliances?

After the end of the Cold War, some analysts argued that technological advances, especially precision guidance, made it possible to substitute conventional forces for US nuclear weapons.[6] From this flowed the suggestion that conventional forces could substitute for nuclear forces in deterrence and extended deterrence, and that the US should therefore work towards nuclear disarmament.[7] This argument assumed that nuclear weapons are ultimately relevant for reasons of the military power they convey, and that this power is ultimately fungible between conventional and nuclear weapons. Yet, when it comes to nuclear weapons, the focus of US allies is often less on 'hard' measures of power than on what extended nuclear deterrence really signifies regarding the depth of US security commitments overall. NATO has for some time emphasised the political significance of its nuclear forces,[8] and the relatively small material importance of the US forward-based B-61 nuclear warheads in Europe is probably the one point on which proponents and opponents of NATO strategy can agree.

Despite the centrality of nuclear weapons to US security policy since 1945, the role they play in different alliances has received scant systematic attention. Many of the most influential works on alliances and US strategy, such as Henry Kissinger's classic *Nuclear Weapons and Foreign Policy*,[9] date from the early Cold War and are most interested in the pressing policy and strategic issues of the day. The same is true of those works that discuss US alliances and highlight the role of nuclear weapons, such as Robert Osgood's *NATO: The Entangling Alliance.*[10] The literature on the historical development of US nuclear strategy, such as Lawrence Freedman and Jeffrey Michaels' classic *The Evolution of Nuclear Strategy*[11] and Matthew Kroenig's *The Logic of American Nuclear Strategy*[12] have an (understandable) bias towards discussing those alliances and alliance decisions of specific relevance to the nuclear powers. In more recent times, the difference between the way nuclear weapons capabilities and strategy are formally integrated in the NATO alliance, and the comparatively looser arrangements in Asia, has been highlighted by several authors.[13] However, like Brad Roberts in his book, *The Case for US Nuclear Weapons in the 21st Century*,[14] these authors all share a primary interest in informing current policy and the future of US alliances, nuclear weapons, and deterrence. How US nuclear weapons became embedded in alliance arrangements, and what factors explain this, are largely unanswered questions with important implications for our understanding of the long-term dynamics of alliances.

Unlike existing historical accounts of US alliances, this book's country-focused case studies include NATO allies and US allies in Asia in equal measure. The book draws insights from bilateral and multilateral alliances confronting very different security challenges and historical legacies in the Cold War era as well as since the end of the Cold War. Using a framework that balances realist and institutionalist perspectives on the role of nuclear weapons in alliances, the book seeks to enrich the theoretical literature on alliances as well as contribute to policy debates about nuclear weapons and US alliance management in Europe and Asia.

This book focuses on pinpointing the drivers of nuclear cooperation by using six analytic frames to investigate structured cooperation involving nuclear weapons: threat assessment and prioritisation; policy objectives regarding cooperation on nuclear weapons; nuclear strategy; domestic factors; the importance of the ally for US security; and access to information regarding nuclear weapons and US nuclear planning. The book begins by arguing that there are two basic theoretical approaches to explaining nuclear cooperation in alliances: realism and institutionalism. We develop two distinctive hypotheses around these theories that form the basis for explaining the drivers of nuclear weapons cooperation in US alliances with NATO, Japan, South Korea, and Australia.

Realism focuses on the role of power in international affairs, evaluates the value (and limitations) of nuclear weapons from a mainly military perspective, and assesses alliances and alliance credibility with primary reference to the international balance of power. By contrast, institutionalism emphasises the political and practical importance of nuclear weapons for building alliance coherence and credibility, and of organisational structures that are created for cooperation on nuclear weapons, which are in turn designed to create trust and the basis for common action between allies.

Based on these critical distinctions, realism and institutionalism explain nuclear weapons cooperation in US alliances in different ways. Realism, for its part, sees such cooperation as being dominated by the US and motivated by narrow national aims, including preventing allies from acquiring the bomb, deterring adversaries, and a desire to exercise a degree of control over allies. For realists, alliances are evanescent because shared interests are temporary rather than enduring; nuclear weapons cooperation is therefore based on short-term considerations informed exclusively by security and insecurity. Realists are largely silent when it comes to explaining change in alliances over time. In contrast, institutionalism regards nuclear cooperation in alliances in the context of the broader benefits that states accumulate from security cooperation. As institutions that operate independently from narrow balance-of-power considerations, alliances endure after the initial threat that led to their formation has dissipated. Seen in this context, nuclear weapons cooperation can be regarded as exemplifying depth of commitment within an alliance based on shared political, as well as strategic, objectives.

US nuclear weapons, alliances, and extended deterrence

Realism and institutionalism draw on very different theoretical and conceptual foundations. While realism and institutionalism are present in the academic and policy debate, the literature on nuclear weapons and alliances has been dominated by realist assumptions about state behaviour and motivations. Indeed, for realists, policy choices regarding the nuclear umbrella are usually analysed exclusively through the prism of extended deterrence and the conditions for successful deterrence.[15]

Deterrence is the prevention of an action through threats of unacceptable counteraction. As a strategy, a deterrer can seek to convince a deterree not to undertake unwanted action by threats of punishment, or by threats of denying the success of the action.[16] But deterrence is ultimately a state of mind of the potential aggressor, and rests on the deterree's judgement of the deterrer's cost–benefit calculation.[17] This calculation is all the more difficult to assess in cases of extended deterrence, where the US seeks to deter threats not to itself, but to close allies. This logic is challenging enough given the mere presence of nuclear weapons, but as Lieber and Press argue, 'in a world where both sides have secure retaliatory arsenals ... [t]hreats to use nuclear weapons to defend allies from conventional attack appear even more irrational and incredible'.[18]

Whether US signalling and threats on behalf of allies 'works' against adversaries and, in the case of the nuclear umbrella, how adversaries perceive the credibility or otherwise of US signalling and threats, has received major academic attention over the years. However, testing for what does or does not work in terms of deterrence is challenging methodologically,[19] and the evidence from quantitative studies regarding the deterrent value of alliances and nuclear weapons remains ambiguous. While Walt argues that 'the presence of a formal agreement often says relatively little about the actual degree of commitment',[20] Leeds contends – on the basis of a data set spanning 1816 to 1944 – that formal alliance commitments are important in underpinning the credibility and success of extended deterrence.[21] In contrast, Danilovic argues that empirical evidence strongly points to the importance of the 'intrinsic interest' of the major power in its protégé's security.[22]

Huth and Russett tested an expected utility model of deterrence on a set of cases of extended immediate deterrence from 1900 to 1980, and found that success was most often associated with close economic and political–military ties between the defender and its protégé and a favourable local military balance, but not the presence of an alliance or nuclear weapons.[23] In contrast, Weede found empirical support in his data for the hypothesis that extended nuclear deterrence substantially reduced the risk of war and military conflict between states.[24] In a different study, Huth found that the extended deterrent value of nuclear weapons, at least in situations not characterised by an adversary possessing a secure second-strike retaliatory capability, seemed to arise from fear of a low probability, but highly costly, threat of nuclear use.[25] In a more recent analysis, McManus finds that visible commitment from individual US leaders serves to reinforce the credibility of extended deterrence and reduce the possibility of US allies being targeted in disputes with adversaries.[26]

During the Cold War especially, the forward stationing of nuclear weapons on or near allied territory was perceived as an important means of enhancing the credibility of assurances. Huth concluded as follows: 'Alliance ties are not likely to enhance the credibility of extended-general deterrence unless peace-time military cooperation between the allies includes the deployment of forces from the stronger power on the territory of the weaker power.'[27] However, Fuhrmann and Sechser found that, based on data spanning 1950 to 2000, defence pacts with nuclear weapon states increase the extended deterrence effect, but that nuclear deployments or forward basing on allied territory does not.[28] Nonetheless, it is commonly argued that the value of extended deterrence for many non-nuclear allies lies in the deployment of American nuclear weapons on their territory and the demonstration of resolve that these deployments convey.[29] Involvement of non-nuclear allies in the policy, planning, and employment of US nuclear weapons in this context confirms a desire to become further integrated into the process of extended nuclear deterrence.

This approach has been encouraged by two distinctive sets of analysts.[30] On the one side are academic and think tank experts who are concerned with the nuts and bolts of nuclear policy and strategy, and on the other side are advocates of nuclear disarmament who regard the nuclear umbrella as a major obstacle to the abolition of nuclear weapons. Both of these schools, however, are united in focusing on the nuclear umbrella as something supplied by the US, as the security guarantor, to satisfy the demands for deterrence and assurance on the part of anxious allies. For the nuts and bolts experts, demand for US nuclear assurances underscores the need to retain and modernise America's nuclear arsenal, whereas for disarmament advocates it highlights the need for US leadership to wean allies off their nuclear addiction. Formal alliances may ebb and flow in terms of strategic cooperation, and officials come and go, but the fundamental demand–supply paradigm in the analysis of extended deterrence has proved to be enduring.

The demand–supply directionality assumed to be inherent in this relationship is problematic, however, for understanding the nature of the day-to-day cooperation on nuclear weapons between the US and its allies. Although the US owns and controls the nuclear warheads, almost all aspects of nuclear weapons cooperation in an alliance require the consent and contribution (often involving significant political and financial costs) of the non-nuclear allies. States that host American nuclear weapons usually bear major financial costs (through host nation support), military opportunity costs (for forces required to guard or employ the warheads, such as Dual Capable Aircraft in NATO), and diplomatic costs (if the cooperation attracts criticism from other states). Moreover, civilian casualties would be substantial if these weapons were targeted by adversaries. This fact alone has created strong domestic pressures that matter for the role of nuclear weapons in US alliances because, as Robert Putnam has argued, 'central decision makers strive to reconcile domestic and international imperatives simultaneously'.[31] For policymakers, balancing the costs and benefits of nuclear weapons cooperation thus often involves a two-level game, with many allied populations more sceptical than their governments about the value of nuclear weapons for safeguarding national security.

So far, only New Zealand has been unwilling to bear the costs of the nuclear umbrella. In 1984, with a strong eye to public opinion, the newly elected Lange Labour government demanded assurances from the US that its navy vessels would not bring nuclear weapons into New Zealand harbours. Upholding its 'neither confirm nor deny' policy, the Reagan administration refused, and subsequently moved to suspend the US security commitment to New Zealand under the ANZUS (Australia, New Zealand, and United States) treaty.[32] While the New Zealand case is unique, other US allies have also sought to limit in practice their interaction with the nuclear umbrella. This even included West Germany, whose defence benefited most from NATO's nuclear posture. In the late 1970s, the Schmidt government rebuffed proposals that the *Bundeswehr* should operate nuclear-armed, ground-launched cruise missiles and that it should be the only country in NATO to host these systems.[33] Analogously, despite being a frontline NATO member, during the Cold War, Norway actively sought to screen its engagement in the nuclear umbrella by refusing permanent basing of NATO forces and specifically rejecting the participation of nuclear-capable aircraft in exercises on its territory.

Influence and intra-alliance bargaining

What, then, do allies seek to achieve through the way they cooperate with the US on nuclear weapons? It is widely accepted that alliances are built on a series of bargains about the anticipated benefits for each party.[34] However, analysis of how and why alliances operate once they are established – including how bargains are struck between the stronger and weaker alliance members – is less common.[35] While the influence of small states in international relations has received growing coverage in the academic literature, there remains little comparative analysis of the influence of these states in alliance relationships,[36] including on the subject of nuclear weapons cooperation from the vantage point of junior partners.

Most accounts assume that the outcome of intra-alliance bargaining will simply reflect the power asymmetries inherent in individual alliances; indeed, this is a core assumption of realism. Bargaining power within alliances is often assumed to arise from the intersection between the parties' dependence on the alliance; their degree of commitment to the alliance; and the parties' stake in the specific issue about which they are negotiating.[37] Viewed through the demand–supply prism, there is little reason to expect significant allied influence on US policy regarding extended nuclear deterrence. Non-nuclear allies of the US have seemingly little to bargain with to elicit credible nuclear security assurances.[38]

Yet, the type of contribution made by individual allies tends to evolve. As Tongfi Kim notes, '[a]lthough members of alliance agreements typically have some form of military commitments in formality, the real contribution of many alliance members lies outside the provision of military force'.[39] The relative material strength of a state is not necessarily a reliable indicator of how much influence or leverage it enjoys in particular situations.[40] In the US security alliance context, it is notable that intra-alliance bargaining has not always resulted in Washington getting its way on major policy issues. For example, Thomas Risse-Kappen outlines how European and Canadian NATO allies had far greater influence on US foreign policy during the early Cold War than basic power differentials would suggest.[41]

America's global position and influence rests in large part on its ability to address the security concerns and demands of its allies, as well as the ability to create unity and consensus on international security issues. Washington's reputation for successful alliance management is itself a factor in promoting US leadership credentials worldwide. Implicit in US leadership of its alliances is, to some extent, the need to find consensus on alliance purpose, priorities and strategies. As Kenneth Waltz has observed: 'Alliance strategies are always the product of compromise since the interest of allies and their notions of how to secure them are never identical.'[42]

The need for consensus in an alliance context thus raises a series of questions – from relative influence, to the nature of bargains struck, and their reliability and endurance. Most examinations of allied consensus focus on NATO as an integrated alliance, but often reach conclusions of questionable generality. In a wide-ranging examination of allied cooperation on alliance decisions on nuclear policy, arms control, out-of-area operations and strategy spanning several decades, Chernoff sought to explain cooperation within NATO. In his study, Chernoff defined cooperation as reaching policy accord despite initial differences, and satisfaction across the alliance with the policy compromise. Chernoff also tested for the influence of several variables drawn from both institutionalist and realist theory: quality of information available to all allies, the experience national leaders have had with similar decisions, support from the hegemonic power, and perception of a common threat. Concluding that no single variable is either sufficient or indispensable for cooperation, Chernoff argued that it is attainable through any combination of the factors he examined.[43]

Charles Kupchan found that public fallout from NATO's 'out-of-area' debate during the early 1980s was avoided largely due to 'European compromise because they perceived a growing need to secure their political link to the United States',[44] but that political agreement did not always translate into material contributions. In formulating policy over Bosnia during the 1990s, the Bush and Clinton administrations 'typically compromised with or accommodated the Europeans' in an effort to preserve alliance unity, but Papayanou finds little clear support for neorealism or neoliberal institutionalism in explaining bargaining behaviour in this case, highlighting the importance of domestic factors.[45] Studying allied negotiations over NATO defence planning and strategy in the 1950s and 1960s, however, Christian Tuschhoff found that the existence of NATO military integration shaped the preferences and cost–benefit calculations of the member states by increasing trust, transparency and calculability of allied behaviour, in turn highlighting the importance of institutional factors.[46]

Outline of this book

The academic literature discussed above has identified a range of significant factors that shape nuclear weapons cooperation between the US and its allies, but power and institutions are both recurring themes around which most of these factors can be grouped. Quantitative studies of deterrence success test and highlight, to varying and not always consistent degrees, the existence of nuclear weapons, formal treaties, the strength of political–military links, and forward basing. The practical importance of allied contributions to extended nuclear deterrence points to the allies' interest in US power, as well as having a broader influence on US policy as part of reassurance. The literature on alliance bargaining and consensus, finally, highlights the importance both of relative power and institutional factors as important potential explanations of alliance decisions.

In this book we are concerned with explaining the drivers of nuclear weapons cooperation in US alliances and what allies seek to achieve in their cooperation on nuclear weapons. Unlike existing studies on the topic, our focus traverses Europe and Asia and provides insights into bilateral and multilateral alliances confronting very different security challenges and historical legacies. Through detailed and diverse country-focused case studies spanning the Cold War and post-Cold War eras, the book's research design aims to yield explanations that have a degree of applicability across time and space. The book is therefore designed to make a dual contribution to the theoretical literature on alliance cooperation, as well as policy debates about nuclear weapons and US alliance management in Europe and in Asia.

The analysis begins in Chapter 1, where we outline the key differences between realism and institutionalism when it comes to assessing security alliances. Realists are inherently sceptical about the value of alliances as entities in their own right and argue they simply formalise the dominance of major powers over junior partners. Institutionalists maintain that alliances operate as independent variables in international relations and, in addition to providing formal mechanisms for structured interaction between states, have the effect of influencing the behaviour of decision makers. Realism and institutionalism therefore provide distinctive explanations of how nuclear weapons cooperation occurs in alliances over time. With this in mind, the book tests two hypotheses:

Hypothesis 1: Nuclear weapons cooperation reflects the external balancing and power asymmetries between the US and its ally.
Hypothesis 2: Nuclear weapons cooperation reflects the structured interaction and organised practices inherent in individual alliances.

To test these respective hypotheses, the empirical analysis contained in the case study chapters is filtered through six analytic frames that encompass international, state-level, and sub-state level factors. These frames capture the objectives of allies and the sources of influence between allies in relation to nuclear weapons cooperation.

Within this overall framework, Chapters 2 and 3 focus on the evolution of nuclear weapons cooperation in the NATO alliance. Chapter 2 examines the development of NATO nuclear strategy and cooperation, focusing specifically on the case of (West) Germany as the single most important non-nuclear ally for the US within NATO. Chapter 3 examines the case of Norway, which, like West Germany, was a frontline state but had a markedly different relationship with the US and also in relation to NATO nuclear posture.

Chapters 4 to 6 discuss nuclear weapons cooperation in three of America's Asian alliances. Chapter 4 examines Japan, including the role of US nuclear operations from Okinawa during the Cold War, Japan's declared anti-nuclear stance, and its growing interest in formalised exchanges with the US on nuclear weapons policy after 2010. Chapter 5 investigates

US–South Korean nuclear weapons cooperation, which was almost completely absent before the 1970s and since then has only developed incrementally in the context of broader concerns about the rise of a nuclear-armed North Korea. Chapter 6 examines the case of Australia, which remains one of America's closest allies but also the one with the least institutionalised alliance mechanisms. Australia's relative disinterest in nuclear guarantees since the 1970s contrasts with the country's strong interest in greater institutional cooperation with the US during the 1950s and 1960s, including on nuclear deterrence.

Chapter 7 draws the key conclusions from the case studies and what these mean for the hypotheses, the theoretical implications of these conclusions, as well as the policy implications of the book's findings. The book's analysis reveals four major findings. First, the US has often deliberately used its nuclear weapons to shore up confidence about its strategic commitment to allies' security in general and to promote alliance consensus. Second, the enhancement of institutional depth in nuclear weapons cooperation has promoted reassurance among US allies, which in turn has allowed closer political and operational integration among allies. Third, all US allies examined in the book have either reduced or declined at some point cooperation that would have more explicitly linked US nuclear weapons to their security. Finally, contrary to realist arguments, US allies are, in fact, capable of exercising a significant degree of agency and influence when it comes to issues of substance regarding nuclear weapons cooperation.

Notes

1 A. Lanoszka, 'Alliances and Nuclear Proliferation in the Trump Era', *The Washington Quarterly*, 41:4 (2019), 96.

2 The Trump administration increased its budget request to Congress to support the US military in Europe to $6.5 billion in fiscal 2019 from $4.7 billion in 2018. This has been complemented by a steadily growing tempo of joint US exercises with NATO allies. R. Emmott and J. Chalmers, 'Trump Troop Pullout Would Still Leave Hefty US Footprint in Europe', *Reuters*, 9 June 2020, www.reuters.com/article/us-usa-germany-military-analysis/trump-troop-pullout-would-still-leave-hefty-u-s-footprint-in-europe-idUSKBN23F29P

3 M. Rapp-Hooper, *Shields of the Republic: The Triumph and Peril of America's Alliances* (Cambridge, MA: Harvard University Press, 2020), especially chapter 2.

4 Office of the Secretary of Defense, *Nuclear Posture Review* (2018) https://media.defense.gov/2018/Feb/02/2001872886/-1/-1/1/2018-NUCLEAR-POSTURE-REVIEW-FINAL-REPORT.PDF

5 D. Yost, 'The US Debate on NATO Nuclear Deterrence', *International Affairs*, 87:6 (2011), 1411.
6 D. Gormley, 'Securing Nuclear Obsolescence', *Survival* 48:3 (2006), 127–148.
7 G. Shultz, W. Perry, H. Kissinger, and S. Nunn, 'A World Free of Nuclear Weapons', *Wall Street Journal*, 4 January 2007.
8 M. Chalmers and S. Lunn, *NATO's Tactical Nuclear Dilemma*, RUSI Occasional Paper (London: Royal United Services Institute, 2010), 6–7.
9 H. Kissinger, *Nuclear Weapons and Foreign Policy* (New York: Harper, 1957).
10 R. Osgood, *NATO: The Entangling Alliance* (Chicago, IL: University of Chicago Press, 1962).
11 L. Freedman and J. Michaels, *The Evolution of Nuclear Strategy*, 4th edition (Houndmills: Palgrave Macmillan, 2019).
12 M. Kroenig, *The Logic of American Nuclear Strategy: Why Strategic Superiority Matters* (Oxford: Oxford University Press, 2018).
13 D. Yost, 'US Extended Deterrence in NATO and North-East Asia', in B. Tertrais (ed.), *Perspectives on Extended Deterrence*, recherches & documents 03/2010, (Paris: Fondation pour la recherche stratégique, 2010), 15–36; and M. Tsuruoka, 'The NATO vs. East Asian Models of Extended Nuclear Deterrence? Seeking a Synergy Beyond Dichotomy', *Asan Forum*, 4:3 (2016).
14 B. Roberts, *The Case for U.S. Nuclear Weapons in the 21st Century* (Stanford, CA: Stanford University Press, 2016).
15 For example, they are discussed in detail by W. Kaufmann (ed.), *Military Policy and National Security* (Princeton, NJ: Princeton University Press, 1956); T. Schelling, *The Strategy of Conflict* (Cambridge, MA: Harvard University Press, 1960); and F. Zagare, 'Rationality and Deterrence', *World Politics*, 42:2 (1990), 238–260.
16 G. Snyder, *Deterrence by Denial and Punishment*, Research Monograph (1) (Princeton, NJ: Center of International Studies, Woodrow Wilson School, Princeton University, 1959).
17 K. Payne, *Deterrence in the Second Nuclear Age* (Lexington, KY: The University Press of Kentucky, 1996); and P.M. Morgan, *Deterrence Now* (Cambridge: Cambridge University Press, 2003).
18 K. Lieber and D. Press, *The Myth of the Nuclear Revolution: Power Politics in the Atomic Age* (Ithaca, NY: Cornell University Press, 2020), 97.
19 P. Huth and B. Russett, 'Testing Deterrence Theory: Rigor Makes a Difference', *World Politics*, 42:4 (1990), 466–501.
20 S. Walt, 'Why Alliances Endure or Collapse', *Survival*, 39:1 (1997), 157.
21 B. Leeds, 'Alliance Reliability in Times of War: Explaining State Decisions to Violate Treaties', *International Organization*, 57:4 (2003), 801–827.
22 V. Danilovic, 'The Sources of Threat Credibility in Extended Deterrence', *Journal of Conflict Resolution*, 45:3 (2001), 341–369.
23 P. Huth and B. Russett, 'What Makes Deterrence Work? Cases from 1900–1980', *World Politics*, 36:4 (1984), 496–526.
24 E. Weede, 'Extended Deterrence by Superpower Alliance', *Journal of Conflict Resolution*, 27:2 (1983), 231–254.

25 P. Huth, 'The Extended Deterrent Value of Nuclear Weapons', *Journal of Conflict Resolution,* 34:2 (1990), 270–290.
26 R. McManus, 'Making It Personal: The Role of Leader-Specific Signals in Extended Deterrence', *The Journal of Politics*, 80:3 (2018), 982–995.
27 P. Huth, *Extended Deterrence and the Prevention of War* (New Haven, CT: Yale University Press, 1988), 215.
28 M. Fuhrmann and T. Sechser, 'Signalling Alliance Commitments: Hand-Tying and Sunk Costs in Extended Nuclear Deterrence', *American Journal of Political Science,* 58:4 (2014), 919–935.
29 D. Trachtenberg, 'US Extended Deterrence: How Much Strategic Force is Too Little?' *Strategic Studies Quarterly,* 6:2 (2012), 62–92; and J. Fearon, 'Signalling Foreign Policy Interests: Tying Hands Versus Sinking Costs', *Journal of Conflict Resolution,* 41:1 (1997), 68–90.
30 K. Payne, 'US Nuclear Weapons and Deterrence: Realist Versus Utopian Thinking', *Air and Space Power Journal* (July–August 2015), 63–71.
31 R. Putnam, 'Diplomacy and Domestic Politics: The Logic of Two Level Games', *International Organization,* 42:3 (1988), 460.
32 See S. McMillan, *Neither Confirm Nor Deny: The Nuclear Ships Dispute Between New Zealand and the United States* (Sydney: Allen and Unwin, 1987).
33 K. Spohr Readman, 'Conflict and Cooperation in Intra-Alliance Nuclear Politics: Western Europe, the United States and the Genesis of NATO's Dual-Track Decision, 1977–79', *Journal of Cold War History,* 13:2 (2011), 74–86.
34 See S. Walt, *The Origins of Alliances* (Ithaca, NY: Cornell University Press, 1987).
35 For a notable exception, see T. Christensen, *Worse than a Monolith: Alliance Politics and Problems of Coercive Diplomacy in Asia* (Princeton, NJ and Oxford: Princeton University Press, 2011).
36 For exceptions, see R. Rothstein, *Alliances and Small Powers* (New York: Columbia University Press, 1968); and E. Reiter and H. Gärtner (eds), *Small States and Alliances* (Heidelberg and New York: Physica-Verlag, 2001).
37 G. Snyder, *Alliance Politics* (Ithaca, NY: Cornell University Press, 1997), 166–172.
38 S. Quackenbush, *Understanding General Deterrence: Theory and Application* (New York: Palgrave Macmillan, 2011), 75–78.
39 T. Kim, *The Supply Side of Security: A Market Theory of Military Alliances* (Stanford, CA: Stanford University Press, 2016), 28.
40 T. Sechser, 'Goliath's Curse: Coercive Threats and Asymmetric Power', *International Organization*, 64:4 (2010), 627–660.
41 T. Risse-Kappen, *Cooperation Among Democracies: The European Influence on US Foreign Policy* (Princeton, NJ: Princeton University Press, 1995).
42 K. Waltz, *Theory of International Politics* (Long Grove, IL: Waveland Press, 1979), 166.
43 F. Chernoff, *After Bipolarity: The Vanishing Threat, Theories of Cooperation, and the Future of the Atlantic Alliance* (Ann Arbor, MI: University of Michigan Press, 1995).

44 C. Kupchan, 'NATO and the Persian Gulf: Examining Intra-Alliance Behavior', *International Organization*, 42:2 (1988), 336.
45 P. Papayoanou, 'Intra-Alliance Bargaining and U.S. Bosnia Policy', *Journal of Conflict Resolution*, 41:1 (1997), 92.
46 C. Tuschhoff, *Deutschland, Kernwaffen und die NATO 1949–1967* (Baden-Baden: Nomos, 2002).

1

Realism, institutionalism, and nuclear weapons cooperation

Formal security commitments that entail obligations for parties to use, or consider using, force are an enduring feature of modern international relations. Typically portrayed as transactional arrangements of convenience, much of the scholarship on alliances has focused on the formal security treaties in Europe among major and less powerful states that were a standard feature of the nineteenth century. These alliances were purpose built to counter specific threats and had a limited shelf-life that was dependent on the longevity of perceived security threats. Sustained by the imperative of balancing against states that threatened to dominate the European continent, these alliances were dominated by great power interests. Nineteenth- and early twentieth-century alliances were fluid, underpinned by crude balance-of-power imperatives, and lacking in institutional depth. In many key respects, they bore all the hallmarks of 'counterbalancing coalitions', as distinct from the highly structured institutional arrangements that have evolved since the Second World War.[1]

Together with the UN Security Council, bilateral and multilateral alliances formed by the US during the Cold War constitute the most resilient security institutions in contemporary international relations. Created in response to specific Cold War threats, US alliances have endured in spite of significant changes to the external threat environment of their member states. In marked contrast to the rapid tempo of alliance formation (and dissolution) before 1945, US alliances have not only endured, they have been progressively strengthened by increasing operational integration and political cooperation. While these arrangements have been asymmetric in the sense that the US has remained the dominant partner, they have nonetheless become more democratic in terms of decision making. The depth and breadth of alliance consultation and joint decision making in NATO is unparalleled historically, but America's Asian alliances have also become less overtly hierarchical and focused increasingly on genuine information sharing and joint planning.

The prospect of using military force in unison with other states to achieve common goals lies at the heart of alliances. As Paul Schroeder writes, 'whether offensive or defensive, limited or unlimited, equal or unequal, bilateral or multilateral, alliances must involve some measure of commitment to use force to achieve a common goal'.[2] These commitments are enshrined in treaties that constitute the alliance initially, but they are often reaffirmed subsequently in more detailed and operationally focused language. One of the prominent features of Cold War US alliances was that this reaffirmation was embedded in the institutionalisation of alliance structures that streamlined security cooperation in an operational sense, while at the same time giving expression to deeper political and ideological commitment between the US and its allies. Reflecting practice in NATO, the US–Japan and US–Republic of Korea (ROK) alliances have created various consultative committees in the twenty-first century tasked with addressing defence cooperation, strategic policy coordination, weapons procurement, and status of force negotiations. In addition, these consultative committees have been supplemented by less formal working groups and routine consultations between mid-level officials. 'Everyday' alliance interactions create and reinforce inter-subjective understandings between the US and its partners that, mostly, serve to strengthen overall cooperation.[3]

This chapter outlines the primary differences between realist and institutionalist perspectives on alliances and provides the theoretical background that frames the two hypotheses outlined in the Introduction. We argue that realism and institutionalism are distinctive, even if they are not necessarily exclusive of each other, and they arrive at quite different conclusions about the relevance of formal cooperation arrangements within alliances. In general, realists treat alliances as epiphenomenal and are dismissive of the role of junior allies in shaping outcomes within alliances. They are also sceptical about the influence of domestic factors in alliance relationships and focus almost exclusively on external security threats as the primary causal factor shaping alliance behaviour. Given the pronounced power differential between the US and its junior partners, and because nuclear weapons are regarded by major powers as the jewel in the crown of their military capabilities, realist theory would predict that an alliance has negligible influence over the nature of nuclear weapons cooperation.

By contrast, institutional theory sees alliances as independent phenomena that shape not only the structures within which states operate, but also the behaviour of these states. From this perspective, alliances are themselves institutions, but how they function is influenced by the formal and informal institutions within them where officials from both sides meet and work. As is the case for institutions generally, within alliances, 'agents and institutions interact dialectically and are mutually constitutive'.[4] For institutionalists, alliances empower smaller states by formalising structured avenues for accessing information and influencing policy outcomes. Nuclear weapons cooperation is no exception to this.

Realism and institutionalism provide the theoretical foundation for the two competing hypotheses about the drivers of nuclear weapons cooperation in US alliances. Against this background, the chapter is organised as follows. First, it defines the key differences between realism and institutionalism. Second, it outlines how realism and institutionalism seek to explain the existence and endurance of alliances. Third, the chapter describes realist and institutionalist views on how allies interact over time. Fourth, it explores realist and institutionalist perspectives on deterrence and reassurance in alliances, which remain at the core of nuclear weapons cooperation. Fifth and finally, the chapter outlines a series of frames that are used in the book's empirical case studies to capture the objectives of allies and the sources of influence with respect to nuclear weapons cooperation.

Realism and alliances

Dominated by realist theory, early international relations scholarship characterised alliances as a by-product of the balance of power. As the balance of power shifted over time among states, so too did alliances, as they were based on shared interests in the balance of power, rather than shared interests per se. As the doyen of neorealism Kenneth Waltz observed, 'alliances are made by states that have some but not all of their interests in common. The common interest is ordinarily a negative one: fear of other states'.[5]

As a paradigm, realism incorporates a number of theories designed to explain how the international system works. However, as Benjamin Frankel has argued, all realists agree on six key assumptions: that states are the central unit of analysis; that the international system is anarchic; that, because of this, states seek to maximise their power or security; that the international system, as distinct from domestic politics, is largely responsible for state conduct in international relations; and that the utility of force is regarded as the major currency by states.[6]

Traditional realism seeks to explain the behaviour of states in an anarchical international system on the basis of one fundamental variable, power, which is both the means and aim of state behaviour. Robert Dahl defines power as 'A having power over B to the extent that he can get B to do something that B would not otherwise do',[7] but power can also be manifest as a more diffuse influence on social relations.[8] Neorealism presents an alternative theory, and sees countries seeking security rather than power for its own sake. This leads to consideration of structure in the international system insofar as countries' security is influenced by their relative position. Neoclassical realism emphasises that decisions about the use of power in international affairs and perceptions of security arise from the domestic context of states, meaning that the behaviour of states cannot be explained solely by their external environment; internal factors of political systems, norms and elite perceptions, and access to resources also need to be taken into account. All variants of realism, however, have in common that they see the international system as fundamentally anarchic, that states act first and foremost in their own interest, and that these states are ultimately responsible for their own security.

For realists, alliances are merely the sum of their parts, as distinct from constituting independent entities in international relations. Alliances are epiphenomenal because they do not in themselves exert influence over specific events but are instead dependent on what states parties, in particular major powers, permit them to do. As Jeremy Pressman argues, 'institutional aspects of the alliance provide mechanisms for the powerful ally to flex its muscles if it so chooses'.[9] From this perspective, alliances in the form of institutions have a negligible independent effect on states' behaviour; at most, they impose sporadic constraints on the actions of sovereign states. Realists believe that, everything being equal, states would much prefer to remain separate from multilateral or bilateral entanglements and make do in life with their own capabilities.

However, in a world where material power capabilities are anything but equal, realists acknowledge that weaker states are attracted to the major power protection they receive under alliance arrangements. Indeed, for realists, alliances exist because of the insecurity felt by smaller states in international relations. These states want protection from actual and potential adversaries, and they seek to achieve this at minimum cost. For major powers, alliances help to formally co-opt like-minded states into regional and global spheres of influence. As one analyst notes, 'a minor power is concerned mostly with direct threats to its security, whereas a great power must also consider the security of those proximate and overseas territories and countries instrumental to the security of its homeland and national interests'.[10] While even those most sceptical of international institutions acknowledge that 'great powers sometimes find institutions – especially alliances – useful for maintaining or even increasing their share of world power',[11] there is a sense in which realists believe alliances can be attributed to major powers indulging the demands of smaller, insecure states. It is no coincidence that some of the most vocal critics of America's 'entangling' global alliance commitments (and proponents of offshore balancing) have been drawn from the ranks of realist thinkers.[12]

Alliances are therefore seen as something of a public good dispensed by major powers, which are usually but not always in the interests of the latter, who may not have incentives to abide by their own commitments, and who are wary of the relative distribution of gains. For realists, alliances, like institutions more generally, provide a 'hard test' of commitment, and most maintain that, on key issues, states will either formally disengage from or disregard alliances altogether if their preferences cannot be met.[13] Once alliances lose their original purpose for existing, which for realists is fundamentally predicated on the nature and scale of threat perceptions, their future viability is seriously eroded. Yet, this perspective overlooks the persistence of most US alliances beyond the historical Cold War context in which they were created. The persistence of NATO after the demise of the Soviet threat is the most prominent example of this, with several realists wrongly predicting the alliance would slide into irrelevance.[14]

Institutionalism and alliances

While realism has long dominated the field of international relations, institutionalism in its various guises has acquired major importance in the study of alliances. In general terms, institutionalism is concerned with the existence and effect of institutions, as organisations or as coordinated behaviour, and how they influence their members at both the domestic and international levels. Political science was almost synonymous with the analysis of institutions until the 1950s, until the discipline shifted in the 1960s and 1970s to theories that sought to explain actors' behaviour more directly. From the 1980s onwards, a synthesis emerged in the form of the 'new institutionalism', comprising a range of blended approaches. Common to all of these approaches is an interest in rules of behaviour rather than formal organisations alone.[15] Two leading theorists in the field, James March and Johan Olsen, provide the most succinct definition of an institution as 'a relatively enduring collection of rules and organized practices, embedded in structures of meaning and resources that are relatively invariant in the face of turnover of individuals and relatively resilient to the idiosyncratic preferences and expectations of individuals and changing external circumstances'.[16]

Hence, new institutionalism is interested in structured as well as unstructured, sometimes emergent, rules. A central topic in this context is collective action: the incentive to 'free-ride' on the efforts of others, and the institutional mechanism of how this can be managed or overcome.[17] Although institutionalism includes a variety of theoretical approaches that illuminate different aspects of the relationship between actors and institutions, institutional literature in practice is often characterised by an eclectic approach.[18] Particularly important are 'analytical narratives' that combine the historical narrative central to historical institutionalism with an analytical framework to structure different case studies.[19]

In the international relations literature, institutions have traditionally been identified as an intervening variable between state interests and policy outcomes. Like realists, many institutionalists regard states as the single dominant actor in international relations and see material power as a critical influence shaping the behaviour of states. Nonetheless, for institutionalists such as Robert Keohane, 'state actions depend to a considerable degree on prevailing institutional arrangements'.[20] Some like David Lake have argued that institutions can themselves 'have an independent effect on world politics'.[21] As Robert Keohane and Lisa Martin observe, 'institutions are important "independently" only in the ordinary sense used in the social sciences: controlling for the effects of power and interests, it matters whether they exist'.[22]

Institutionalists argue that the uncertainty about other countries' interests, capabilities, and intentions, which realists see as the source of perpetual mistrust between states, can be reduced through structured cooperation, and that states are more focused on absolute rather than relative gains in their relationships.[23] This does not mean that material power concerns are unimportant. It merely means that institutions can mitigate the more egregious effects of anarchy by structuring cooperation between states. Security institutions, as is the case with institutions more broadly, 'can provide information, reduce transaction costs, make commitments more credible, establish focal points for coordination, and in general facilitate the operation of reciprocity'.[24]

One important hallmark of formal arrangements within an alliance is transaction costs, which can be minimised through governance structures that facilitate the transfer of information, help formulate agreements, and enforce compliance.[25] Richard Higgott points out that 'the power to mold understandings, articulate organisational norms, and act as mediators in disputes between members can give organizations considerable operational autonomy', regardless of their formal power and authority.[26] Formal organisation of international institutions has specific advantages for its members, such as the ability to speak 'with a single voice to dispense politically significant approval and disapproval of the claims, policies, and actions of states'.[27]

Centralisation of activities in an alliance organisation provides efficiency, and access to resources for weaker members that they could not otherwise obtain. Organisations also help members to link different issues, including through leveraging internal rules.[28] Different aspects of alliance institutions may thus have different functions and benefits for members, and institutions are often analysed through the concept of 'complementarity' – the idea that their components fit with each other, leading to distinct identifiable shapes. However, this complementarity is ultimately the result of human agency, and Colin Crouch comments that 'the stability of institutions and their complementarities is the stability of the person riding a bicycle, not that of the person standing still'.[29]

Although realist and institutionalist perspectives on alliances are not necessarily in conflict, they do emphasise different factors in relation to basic questions about how alliances deter and reassure, and how allies can find agreement to act in common – both of which are crucial to understanding the role that nuclear weapons play in US alliances.

How do alliances deter and reassure?

With its focus on the role of power, force, and threats, the concept of deterrence is a natural fit for a realist view of international affairs, and a key reason why realists assume states seek alliances in the first place. As Robert Jervis has noted, '[b]ecause most American scholars accepted Realism, it is not surprising that they found deterrence theory congenial'.[30] Patrick Morgan points out that

> classic balance of power systems were based on deterrence ... many alternative structures, such as a hegemonic system, a great power concert or a collective security system, have involved security sought and maintained by deterrence – power accumulated by actors singly or collectively (usually in alliances) to threaten serious harmful consequences so as to ward off attacks or other noxious behaviour or, when used, to demonstrate those harmful consequences for the edification of potential opponents.[31]

Realist literature on alliances and deterrence regards extended deterrence as a relationship defined by a major power supplying assurances based on its national interest, and smaller allies requesting such assurances in accordance with their insecurity stemming from weaker relative power. As with realist views on alliances overall, this perspective on extended deterrence assumes that the outcomes of bargaining between allies regarding security guarantees will simply mirror prevailing power asymmetries. Extended deterrence from this perspective is a function of US supply, and it serves to underscore the asymmetry inherent in US alliance relationships where recipient allies have little bargaining power or agency. Consequently, for realists, a declining US commitment to alliances will translate into weaker extended deterrence commitments and an inevitable dilution in the credibility of US security assurances. Extended deterrence is essentially a one-way street in terms of supply; hence its credibility is only ever as robust as the strength of commitment on the part of the US.

The appropriation of deterrence as a quintessentially realist concept has proved too narrow, however, for a genuine understanding of deterrence in practice. Frank Zagare asks the following question:

> Is deterrence theory a structural or a decision-theoretic construct? The answer is that it is, and must be, both. It is well appreciated that deterrence is a type of power relationship, and power is obviously a critical determinant of system structure. But deterrence is also, in part, a psychological relationship, which implies that it must also be understood in decision theoretic terms. To look at deterrence, then, as strictly a structural problem is to miss a core aspect of the problem.[32]

From this position, it is only a small step to more explicit consideration of the context within which decisions about deterrence are taken, both in terms of the adoption of deterrence as a strategy in the first place, to decisions about the implementation of deterrence threats, and adversaries' as well as allies' perspectives on the credibility of such promises. Here, institutional and relational factors are widely recognised in the literature as important for deterrence and assurance. James Wirtz, for example, writes that '[t]he credibility of assurances is important but is not necessarily conveyed by any specific tactic such as signing a legally binding agreement. Instead, credibility emerges more from a process of engagement that demonstrates the importance of the relationship between assurance providers and recipients'.[33]

Consequently, deterrence and reassurance cannot be seen as two sides of the same coin, because deterrence is about the perception of the alliance as a collective actor by the adversary, whereas reassurance relates to intra-allied relations, with the alliance (organisation) being the forum within which those perceptions are developed and influenced. David Yost has highlighted the importance of institutional factors in assurance within NATO, writing that '[t]he elements of assurance in US extended deterrence in NATO appear to include the following factors: confidence in the reliability of the US; openness of the US to allied influence; the US military presence in Europe; the US nuclear weapons presence in Europe as a link to US strategic nuclear forces; allied roles in the nuclear posture; and agreed strategic policy'.[34] Although NATO's arrangements are identified as exemplifying how institutions can promote reassurance, US alliances in Asia – particularly those with Japan and South Korea – have increasingly embraced greater institutional depth regarding mechanisms of reassurance.

In general, there is widespread recognition of how institutions can embed key understandings and promote transparency and trust about commitments; how they promote high-level interpersonal relationships critical to streamlining communication between allies, including in crisis situations; how institutions can help overcome asymmetry of information; and how they can change interests through physical commitment of forward-based forces. However, differences exist in the literature about the relative importance of these factors, and particularly the importance of forward-based nuclear forces for maintaining credibility and assurance. As Elaine Bunn's 'wedding ring' analogy demonstrates, extended nuclear deterrence and assurance is very much socially constructed: 'Nuclear weapons are kind of like the wedding ring of the marriage – there are those in cultures that don't wear wedding rings who are perfectly committed to their spouses, and others who wear them who don't really have much of a commitment at all. But once you start wearing one, it means something entirely different to be seen without it than it does for someone who never wore one.'[35]

How do allies agree over time?

Realists cast alliances in terms of risks to given interests, and are particularly persuasive in explaining the difficulties of finding agreement among allies. In general, the assumption that alliances reflect transitory interests linked to the balance of power encourages the expectation that allies will find it difficult to act with common purpose once they find themselves moving beyond the initial circumstances that led to the creation of the alliance.

A major theme in realist thinking regarding intra-alliance bargaining is Glenn Snyder's concept of 'the alliance security dilemma'.[36] Instead of focusing on the benefits that accrue to weaker powers in alliances with major powers, the alliance security dilemma highlights the inherent risks in alliance relationships for both sides, stemming from the dual hazards of entrapment and abandonment. The more dependent a weaker ally is for its security on an alliance with a major power, and the less the major ally's security depends on that of the junior ally, the more vulnerable the weaker ally will feel to being abandoned. As a result, the weaker ally will feel pressure to demonstrate loyalty to the major power and will therefore possess commensurately weaker leverage. The dilemma is that if the junior ally demonstrates excessive loyalty to avoid abandonment, it risks being entrapped in the major ally's policy agenda, including potentially going to war, but if it seeks excessive autonomy, it risks abandonment.

For major powers too, becoming entrapped in a conflict initiated by the junior ally is a risk. A strong theme in realist analysis of US alliance commitments is the supposed danger of entrapment, which articulates closely with the view that the costs of upholding US primacy are excessive, and taps into long-standing apprehension in US foreign policy tradition regarding the costs of 'entangling alliances'.[37] This perspective favours a shift to so-called 'offshore balancing', in which the US scales back its overseas-based force commitments while upholding alliances by pressuring allies to take on more of the burden of defending their own interests. As Michael Beckley observes, the fear of entanglement derives from the assumption that 'alliances rope states into conflicts by placing states' reputations on the line, by socialising leaders into adopting allied interests and norms, and provoking adversaries and emboldening allies'.[38] This perception of entrapment risk, itself highlighting some aspects of institutional effects, has been evident in empirical examples. Victor Cha, for example, shows that the preference of the US for a bilateral hub-and-spokes alliance system in Asia after 1945 was motivated in large part by a desire to exercise control over its allies and mitigate (if not eliminate altogether) the risk of entrapment.[39]

In contrast, Robert Keohane observed in relation to America's post-war security relationships in Europe and Asia that 'alliances have in curious ways increased the leverage of the little in their dealings with the big'.[40] Institutionalists argue that smaller allies can exert significant agency because they have the ability to influence norms, principles, rules, and decision-making criteria within alliances.[41] In a variety of contexts, the ability to veto or change decisions can provide a better explanation of the relative influence of actors or groups within institutions than their initial strength.[42] Within a formal or informal network, the degree to which actors are likely to broker between different groups can also be a source of influence.[43] Institutional scholarship has thus highlighted the importance of personal networks that exist within and across more formal organisational structures.[44] In a multilateral setting, the 'agency slack' accorded to supranational bodies in international organisations can help this further as it 'allows them to perform certain functions more effectively than individual or even groups of states', including through their non-partisan status.[45]

A key theoretical insight into international institutions is the importance of trust arising from multilateral cooperation over time and, in particular, the willingness of the strongest member to be bound by agreed rules.[46] Rules that shape behaviour within institutions reduce flexibility and variability, but are followed because 'they are seen as natural, rightful, expected, and legitimate'.[47] In alliances, this is particularly the case, as operative rules governing relations and cooperation between the allies are ultimately derivative and support the contingent rules underpinning the common defence commitment.[48] Institutionalists point out that in a historical process, all actors are generally 'rule-makers' and 'rule-takers' at different times. As Gregory Jackson argues, '[a]ctors may be strategic, but define their goals in a historically situated fashion based on prevailing and contingent interpretations of social situations, including institutionalized values, norms and power configurations'.[49]

While a distinction is often drawn between formal institutions and inter-subjective understanding among members (i.e. norms), institutions themselves can play an important role in shaping and embedding shared norms in social contexts. This is certainly relevant in the case of security alliances. As Kirsten Rafferty points out, 'the conjunction of constitutive norms and effective alliance performance produces a situation in which states are expected to broaden the purpose, functions and/or scope of the alliance's activities to transplant the norm into other issue areas'.[50] In Europe and Asia, US alliances have been transformed beyond their original intent (i.e. to protect geopolitically important countries from being dominated by major power adversaries) in favour of a much broader mission. 'Global' humanitarian and peacekeeping operations both within and outside regional alliance areas are the most notable examples, but others include democracy promotion and sponsoring regional forums that deal with security and non-security issues. Indeed, US alliances have over time embedded normative values that serve to strengthen commitment among members over and above the transactional benefits they see as important. Trust and longevity of alliances thus enables division of labour, and states seek absolute rather than relative gains which means that not every transaction requires reciprocity.[51]

The importance of path dependence for institutional change over time is now widely recognised. This raises the question of how actors' preferences and goals change over time, and the role of ideas and interests therein.[52] Different institutional scholars have emphasised inherent stability, the dramatic nature of change between different equilibria, or evolutionary processes. An emerging synthesis across different disciplines highlights the importance of evolutionary shifts that lead to significant and consequential change over time.[53] Constructivists, for instance, argue that participation in institutions can change members' policy preferences, including through strengthening vested interests and the creation of complementary domestic rules.[54] In combination, the willingness to tolerate the uneven distribution of gains, the importance of alliances as focal points for demonstrating resolve, the role of domestic interest groups, the efficiency dividends of formal organisation, and the emergence of ideational security communities through cooperation in alliances can explain why alliances endure even though their original raison d'être is long gone.[55]

There is, therefore, '[n]o one-to-one relationship between an institution and its meaning in a specific situation', and '[a]ctors may interpret or utilise institutions in different ways, stretching their boundaries, adapting them to new contingencies, or avoiding them through deviant behaviour'.[56] Changes in resource allocation can influence the capacity 'to follow and enforce' rules within the institution,[57] altering the bargains and perceptions of interest underpinning the established order within it. Even so, institutions can be ambiguous, with different meanings depending on the situational context.[58] Indeed, in the NATO alliance, 'constructive ambiguity' about commitments and strategy has often been a part of many alliance compromises. Similarly, the US and its Asian allies are often ambiguous about how they frame forward commitments, including most recently in regard to their role in any potential conflict with China. Institutionalists argue that it is exactly because institutions are complex, heterogenous and partially incoherent that members can 'use them as enabling bits and pieces, as toolkits' in influencing change and adaptation. Members are embedded in their institutional context, but this context allows for a recombination or bricolage of institutional elements to adapt an alliance over time and find new ways of cooperation.[59]

Tracing nuclear weapons cooperation in alliances

Hypotheses provide competing explanations of the outcomes and processes of specific cases under investigation.[60] In order to identify the drivers of nuclear weapons cooperation in US alliances, we trace six frames through the case studies that are designed to test the following hypotheses:

Hypothesis 1: Nuclear weapons cooperation reflects the external balancing and power asymmetries between the US and its ally.
Hypothesis 2: Nuclear weapons cooperation reflects the structured interaction and organised practices inherent in individual alliances.

Taken together, the six frames capture the objectives of allies and the sources of influence between allies in relation to nuclear cooperation. The two hypotheses predict different dynamics within each frame, which we test through detailed empirical case studies in Europe and Asia that span the Cold War and post-Cold War eras.

Threat assessment and prioritisation

For realists, the perception of threats remains the single most salient factor underpinning the logic of alliances. The core function of an alliance is to defend parties against threats, so achieving convergence among members about ranking priorities in threat assessments is a key pillar of effective alliance management. An important consideration for deterrence and reassurance is whether a threat to an ally is direct or more indirect, and whether it is immediate or more remote in time. However, allies may differ in their assessment of the capabilities or intentions of the same adversary, and they may also prioritise the same threats differently depending on their overall security interests. Differences between allies in prioritisation of immediate threats will increase entrapment fears on the part of the United States, and abandonment fears on the part of junior allies.

For institutionalists, threat perception is moderated through the alliance as an institution and members as an epistemic community. Achieving consensus on what the main threats are and, crucially, whether they have been addressed sufficiently in the alliance requires the exchange of credible and timely information as well as policy preferences. In addition, it requires the ability to commit credibly to the common defence, including through the use of nuclear weapons, which needs to be communicated and demonstrated between allies.

Policy objectives regarding cooperation on nuclear weapons

Although alliances are founded on a convergence of interests, allies can and often do diverge on important policy questions. In relation to nuclear weapons in particular, the potential cost of nuclear use for different allies will be a key point of difference. In general, however, realists would assume that both the US and its allies seek security from specific adversaries, and that their objectives regarding cooperation on nuclear weapons would be focused exclusively on deterrence of the adversary, and the (material) cost and benefit of nuclear deterrence for respective allies.

For institutionalists, however, institutions evolve over time as members adjust to changing circumstances, and objectives are partly endogenous and negotiated through the institution. Policy objectives in nuclear cooperation will thus reflect the aims of the alliance overall, which may move beyond a focus on immediate threats to any single party and include the value of the alliance in its own right.

Nuclear strategy

Nuclear deterrence rests on assumptions about how and when nuclear weapons would be used, and what their role is in relation to conventional military capabilities. In practice, such considerations are contained in both formal strategic guidance and operational plans. They are also captured in more informal understandings about the role of nuclear weapons and the circumstances in which they would be used.

For realists, US and allied preferences regarding nuclear strategy will reflect the perceived consequences of that strategy for their own immediate security through deterrence, as well as the consequences of nuclear use. Insofar as strategy translates capability into power, allies will avoid ambiguity and focus on the effect of nuclear strategy on the adversary. In contrast, institutionalists would focus on the role of nuclear strategy as an interpretive, ideational framework that gives (political) meaning to physical nuclear capabilities. That meaning can encompass a wider range of objectives than operational outcomes, insofar as the objectives of the alliance are partly endogenous to the institution.

Domestic factors

While classic realism discounts domestic factors in general, the behaviour of allies is shaped by domestic-level variables, including public opinion and domestic politics. In relation to the deployment of nuclear systems on the territory of an ally and the integration of the latter into US nuclear war-fighting plans, there is often a gap between elite and public opinion. Although it acknowledges the influence of such domestic factors, realism still sees them as factors extraneous to the operation of alliances.

For institutionalists, formal alliance cooperation will reinforce broader elite cooperation and bolster domestic support for nuclear cooperation among elites. Alliance cooperation will make national elites more resistant to domestic pressures on nuclear issues through the 'linkage' of issues and the formation of perceptions within the alliance institution. In general, even if the sole objective of alliances remains the immediate security of its member states, national leaders need to balance national security against other domestic objectives, and hence domestic politics can operate both as a constraint and as an influence on the way in which those leaders seek consensus with other allies, and the objectives they define for alliance cooperation.

Importance of the ally for US security

For realists, the currency of international affairs is hard power. The US will seek to avoid increases in the relative power of its allies (including nuclear proliferation to allies). This concern will increase with the absolute power of the ally. At the same time, more powerful junior allies will be more influential, because they bring greater capability to bear in the alliance, but are also less dependent on the alliance at the same time. Although power is generally measured in military capabilities, for mainly geographic reasons, some allies matter more than others for the direct security of the US. If an ally's importance for the US in this respect is high, the ally's fear of abandonment will be low, and avoiding entrapment will be of relatively low priority for Washington, as it shares the ally's concerns for its security.

For institutionalists, the influence of states is not based on hard power (or geography) alone, but also on the ability to shape collective decisions. Multilateral alliance institutions requiring consensus decision making will increase the opportunities for influence by small allies regardless of their hard power. Materially weaker allies can thus leverage mechanisms of cooperation, and their importance to the US – and hence the US incentive to compromise with them, including on questions relating to nuclear weapons – arises from the institutional framework and the role they play. A perception of high value will lead to greater confidence in the enduring nature of the alliance overall, which will encourage closer cooperation and mutual dependence between the US and its ally.

Access to information

Different abilities and priorities in the collection of information about adversaries, as well as different national capabilities, mean that allies will differ in their access to information about adversaries as well as the practicalities of nuclear warfare. Moreover, US allies will not automatically have information regarding US capabilities, plans, and political intentions (or vice versa). Asymmetric access to information is especially important in the nuclear sphere, given the political and military imbalance of capabilities between nuclear and non-nuclear allies and the latter's dependence on US national decisions.

In general, realism accords little relevance to such factors, as it considers national interest and power the main (and self-evident) factors determining state behaviour. Access to information by smaller states in alliances with major powers is a peripheral consideration because major alliance partners can convert their power into influence and control over alliance policy. Information is a source of influence, and the US will seek to impose strict limits on the release of information concerning its own nuclear plans and capabilities to further its own interests vis-à-vis its allies.

Institutionalism devotes much greater attention to the importance of information sharing. Formal organisation inevitably involves a greater level of information sharing than informal arrangements due to the reduced transaction costs of sharing information and the structured as well as informal communication channels promoted by institutions. Hence, formal institutionalisation undermines the US monopoly on nuclear weapons information in the alliance. On the flip side, allies' lack of consistent and credible information regarding US plans and thinking will erode trust, and raise fears of abandonment, increasing the incentive for the US to share information, including on nuclear weapons, as part of its overall bargaining strategy in the alliance.

***

Taken together, these frames are not exhaustive, but they do provide a comprehensive analytical tool for identifying the nature and sources of nuclear cooperation across time and space. The frames allow us to trace empirically the role of nuclear weapons within US alliances and test the hypotheses outlined above. This has significant relevance for US and allied policymakers who continue to grapple with questions about the nuclear umbrella and its relationship to the credibility of security assurances; how allies codify nuclear weapons cooperation in this context is of fundamental importance.

Nuclear weapons have retained a central place in US alliances for over seventy years, and so much of what can be gleaned about nuclear weapons cooperation within alliances stems from detailed historical experience. Yet, conveying a chronology of key developments can only tell part of the story. In this book, we argue that institutionalism provides a rich supplement to standard realist accounts that have dominated the literature on nuclear weapons and alliances. Bringing institutionalist perspectives into focus in an archetypically realist area of strategic studies has scholarly pay-offs in broadening knowledge in the field, but as we argue in the following analysis, it also sheds important light on policy by moving beyond unit-level analysis of states' interests.

Notes

1 J. Levy and W. Thompson, 'Hegemonic Threats and Great Power Balancing in Europe, 1495–1999', *Security Studies*, 14:1 (2005), 31.
2 P. Schroeder, 'Alliances, 1815–1945: Weapons of Power and Tools of Management', in K. Knorr (ed.), *Historical Dimensions of National Security Problems* (Lawrence, KS: University of Kansas Press, 1976), 227.
3 S. Walt, 'Why Alliances Endure or Collapse', *Survival*, 39:1 (1997), 166.
4 S. Bell, 'Historical Institutionalism and New Dimensions of Agency: Bankers, Institutions and the 2008 Financial Crisis', *Political Studies*, 65:3 (2017), 735.
5 K. Waltz, *Theory of International Politics* (Long Grove, IL: Waveland Press, 1979), 166.
6 B. Frankel, 'Restating the Realist Case: An Introduction', *Security Studies*, 5:3 (1996), 9–20.
7 R. Dahl, 'The Concept of Power', *Behavioural Science*, 2:3 (1957), 202.
8 M. Barnett and R. Duvall, 'Power in International Relations', *International Organization*, 59:1 (2005), 39–75.

9 J. Pressman, *Warring Friends: Alliance Restraint in International Politics* (Ithaca, NY: Cornell University Press, 2008), 4.
10 D. Reiter, 'Learning, Realism, and Alliances: The Weight of the Shadow of the Past', *World Politics,* 46:2 (1994), 496.
11 J. Mearsheimer, 'A Realist Reply: The False Promise of International Institutions', *International Security,* 20:1 (1995), 82.
12 S. Walt, 'US Strategy After the Cold War: Can Realism Explain It? Should Realism Guide It?', *International Relations*, 32:1 (2018), 13–16.
13 For discussion on this theme, see R. Schweller and D. Priess, 'A Tale of Two Realisms: Expanding the Institutions Debate', *Mershon International Studies Review*, 41:1 (1997), 1–32.
14 C. Wallander, 'Institutional Assets and Adaptability: NATO After the Cold War', *International Organization*, 54:4 (2000), 705–735.
15 V. Lowndes, 'The Institutional Approach', in D. Marsh and G. Stoker (eds), *Theory and Methods in Political Science* (Basingstoke: Palgrave Macmillan, 2010), 60–67.
16 J. March and J. Olsen, 'Elaborating the 'New Institutionalism', in S. Binder, R. Rhodes and B. Rockman (eds), *The Oxford Handbook of Political Institutions* (Oxford: Oxford University Press, 2008), 3.
17 K. Shepsle, 'Rational Choice Institutionalism', in S. Binder, R. Rhodes and B. Rockman (eds), *The Oxford Handbook of Political Institutions* (Oxford: Oxford University Press, 2008), 23–32.
18 Lowndes, 'The Institutional Approach', 75–79.
19 Shepsle, 'Rational Choice Institutionalism', 35–36.
20 R. Keohane, *After Hegemony: Cooperation and Discord in the World Political Economy* (Princeton, NJ: Princeton University Press, 1984), 3.
21 D. Lake, 'Beyond Anarchy: The Importance of Security Institutions', *International Security*, 26:1 (2001), 137.
22 R. Keohane and L. Martin, 'The Promise of Institutionalist Theory', *International Security,* 20:1 (1995), 42.
23 J. Duffield, 'International Security Institutions', in D. Marsh and G. Stoker (eds), *Theory and Methods in Political Science* (Basingstoke: Palgrave Macmillan, 2010), 640–642.
24 Keohane and Martin, 'The Promise of Institutionalist Theory', 42.
25 Shepsle, 'Rational Choice Institutionalism', 34.
26 R. Higgott, 'International Political Institutions' in S. Binder, R. Rhodes and B. Rockman (eds), *The Oxford Handbook of Political Institutions* (Oxford: Oxford University Press, 2008), 615–616.
27 Duffield, 'International Security Institutions', 645.
28 Duffield, 'International Security Institutions', 645.
29 C. Crouch, 'Complementarity', in G. Morgan, J. Campbell, C. Crouch, O. Kaj Pedersen, and R. Whitley (eds), *The Oxford Handbook of Comparative Institutional Analysis* (Oxford: Oxford University Press, 2015), 117–134.
30 R. Jervis, 'Deterrence Theory Revisited', *World Politics*, 31:2 (1979), 289–290.

31 P. Morgan, 'The State of Deterrence in International Politics Today', *Contemporary Security Policy,* 33:1 (2012), 86.
32 F. Zagare, 'Deterrence Is Dead. Long Live Deterrence', *Conflict Management and Peace Science*, 23:2 (2006), 116.
33 J. Wirtz, 'Conclusions', in Jeffrey Knopf (ed.), *Security Assurances and Non-Proliferation* (Stanford, CA: Stanford University Press, 2012), 287.
34 D. Yost, 'Assurance and US Extended Deterrence in NATO', *International Affairs* 85:4 (2009), 764–765.
35 E. Bunn, 'Extended Deterrence and Assurance', in C. Murdock and J. Yeats (eds), *Exploring the Nuclear Posture Implications of Extended Deterrence and Assurance: Workshop Proceedings and Key Takeaways* (Washington, DC: Center for Strategic and International Studies, 2009), 90.
36 G. Snyder, *Alliance Politics* (Ithaca, NY: Cornell University Press, 1997), 180–192.
37 See, for instance, C. Layne, 'This Time It's Real: The End of Unipolarity and the Pax Americana', *International Studies Quarterly,* 56:1 (2012), 203–213.
38 M. Beckley, 'The Myth of Entangling Alliances: Reassessing the Security Risks of US Defense Pacts', *International Security,* 39:4 (2015), 17.
39 V. Cha, *Powerplay: The Origins of the American Alliance System in Asia* (Princeton, NJ and Oxford: Princeton University Press, 2016).
40 R. Keohane, 'The Big Influence of Small Allies', *Foreign Policy*, 2 (1971), 161.
41 S. Krasner, 'Structural Causes and Regime Consequences: Regimes as Intervening Variables', *International Organization,* 36:2 (1982), 185–205.
42 Lowndes, 'The Institutional Approach', 72.
43 C. Ansell, 'Network Institutionalism', in S. Binder, R. Rhodes, and B. Rockman (eds), *The Oxford Handbook of Political Institutions* (Oxford: Oxford University Press, 2008), 78.
44 Ansell, 'Network Institutionalism', 80.
45 Duffield, 'International Security Institutions', 647.
46 Higgott, 'International Political Institutions', 616.
47 March and Olsen, 'Elaborating the 'New Institutionalism', 7.
48 Duffield, 'International Security Institutions', 636–637.
49 G. Jackson, 'Actors and Institutions', in G. Morgan, J. Campbell, C. Crouch, O. Kaj Pedersen, and R. Whitley (eds), *The Oxford Handbook of Comparative Institutional Analysis* (Oxford: Oxford University Press, 2015), 64–68.
50 K. Rafferty, 'An Institutional Reinterpretation of Cold War Alliance Systems: Insights for Alliance Theory', *Canadian Journal of Political Science*, 36:2 (2003), 346.
51 J. G. Ruggie, 'Multilateralism: The Anatomy of an Institution', *International Organization,* 46:3 (1992), 561–598.
52 E. Sanders, 'Historical Institutionalism', in S. Binder, R. Rhodes, and B. Rockman (eds), *The Oxford Handbook of Political Institutions* (Oxford: Oxford University Press, 2008), 39–55.
53 M. Djelic, 'Institutional Perspectives – Working towards Coherence or Irreconcilable Diversity?' in G. Morgan, J. Campbell, C. Crouch, O. Kaj

Pedersen, and R. Whitley (eds), *The Oxford Handbook of Comparative Institutional Analysis* (Oxford: Oxford University Press, 2015), 27–28.

54 Duffield, 'International Security Institutions', 646.

55 Walt, 'Why Alliances Endure or Collapse', 156–179.

56 Jackson, 'Actors and Institutions', 77.

57 March and Olsen, 'Elaborating the 'New Institutionalism'', 12.

58 Jackson, 'Actors and Institutions', 78.

59 Djelic, 'Institutional Perspectives', 30–32.

60 A. George and A. Bennett, *Case Studies and Theory Development in the Social Sciences* (Cambridge, MA: MIT Press, 2005), 117–118.

2

Nuclear sharing and mutual dependence: Germany and NATO nuclear weapons cooperation

Among US alliances, the North Atlantic Treaty Organization (NATO) stands out in several key respects. It is the only multilateral alliance to have endured the Cold War, and is by far the most institutionalised. It has set itself global objectives in the post-Cold War era, but remains the only US alliance with a treaty clause (Article V) that commits all members to come to the defence of one another. And as far as nuclear weapons cooperation goes, no alliance comes close to rivalling NATO in terms of the breadth, depth, and endurance of commitments.

In this chapter, we analyse nuclear weapons cooperation in NATO through the prism of Germany's experience. The Second World War cast a long shadow across West Germany's attempts to reintegrate into the international community after 1945. While some NATO members remained ambivalent about West Germany's inclusion in the alliance, the US saw it as crucial to alliance burden sharing in Western Europe. West Germany's emergence as Europe's economic powerhouse, coupled with its growing political clout in Europe, elevated its status in NATO and its place in US policy considerations. After France left NATO's integrated military command structure in 1966, West Germany would come to play a central role in Cold War policy, planning, and political debates within NATO over nuclear sharing.

However, the end of the Cold War and German reunification in 1990 fundamentally changed Germany's security situation. For the first time, the country was surrounded by friendly powers. Politically, Germany remained a key member of NATO. Yet, its reluctance to make commensurate contributions to the new 'out-of-area' operations made it less central for NATO's operational integration after the Cold War than it had been when NATO had prepared to defend the alliance on the Central Front of the inner-German border.

Germany and the NATO alliance

NATO's origins lie in the Western Union established by the UK, France, and the Benelux countries under the 1948 Brussels Pact. The Western Union consolidated Britain and France's leadership of the exhausted nations of Europe, strengthened intra-European cooperation, demonstrated a new sense of European unity to the US, and created political and military institutions that foreshadowed the creation of NATO. While the US did not join the Brussels Pact, it spearheaded the formation of the new Atlantic alliance in 1949, which also included the 'stepping stone' countries of Norway, Denmark, Iceland, and Portugal. In NATO, Europeans gained access to significant economic and military US assistance, but they also had to commit to Washington to develop their national defence resources.[1]

Upon signing the Washington Treaty in 1949, the allies established a Military Committee of their defence chiefs. Five regional planning groups for each discrete NATO theatre of operations were overseen by a Standing Group of US, UK, and French senior officials.[2] The outbreak of the Korean War in 1950 gave major impetus to the development of an integrated military command structure. Dwight Eisenhower became the first Supreme Allied Commander Europe (SACEUR), and during the 1950s NATO established a host of multinational headquarters that 'required many compromises on national interests and sensitivities'.[3] Throughout the NATO command structure, many officers were 'dual-hatted' in national as well as alliance roles; this helped reduce the impact of a more cumbersome alliance decision-making process on military effectiveness.

Balancing the need for coordination with sovereign decision making of members, NATO established annual review processes for national defence planning and defence spending. Early on, it was recognised that NATO needed to ensure that political control remained paramount, which, according to Schmidt, 'called for the formation of a permanent civilian-politico-administrative unit so as to guarantee the subordination of the military units to civilian authorities'.[4] In 1952, NATO members gave the alliance a standing capacity for political-military decision making by appointing permanent representatives to the North Atlantic Council (NAC). Lord Hastings Ismay became the first Secretary General, and oversaw the civilian international staff at the new NATO Headquarters in Paris, which housed an increasing number of functional committees.[5] Close political consultation and alliance unity became values in their own right, as they enabled practical cooperation and demonstrated the sincerity of deterrence commitments.

NATO membership expanded to Turkey and Greece in 1952 (and, later, to Spain in 1982), but the most important accession during the Cold War was that of West Germany in 1955. What remained of pre-war Germany had been divided into four occupation zones in 1945. In the 1949 Occupation Statute, the UK, France, and the US had granted limited sovereignty to a newly elected government in the provisional capital of Bonn, but this did not include the right to establish military forces, armament industries, or the conduct of foreign policy. The allies continued to oversee internal security and maintained occupation forces in Germany. Although these forces came under the new NATO command structure, it was only in 1950 that the Western allies acknowledged that they might also be used to defend the (West) German population from Soviet attack.[6]

For West Germany, NATO membership promised the following: a say on the defence of its own territory against the Soviet Union; additional sovereignty and the ability to conduct its own foreign policy, including on the 'German question'; and help in anchoring liberal democracy domestically. Many existing NATO members, particularly the US, sought to make West Germany's industrial and demographic resources available for the defence of Western Europe.[7] Yet, the initial attempt to integrate West German military units into a larger European Defence Community (EDC), rather than give the country membership in NATO and sovereign military forces, foundered on the rejection of the EDC treaty by the French parliament in 1954.[8] Instead, West Germany joined NATO in 1955, and regained additional sovereignty, including over foreign policy. Within NATO, Germany was an equal member, but restrictions on the German armament industry remained in place, and it was not permitted to develop national military commands above that of an Army Corps.[9]

Germany had become a member of an alliance that, in Lord Ismay's words, existed 'to keep the Soviets out, the Americans in, and the Germans down'.[10] Bonn's influence on NATO decisions, however, grew slowly over time, and the creation of the *Bundeswehr* extended well into the 1960s.[11] Moreover, the Standing Group of British, US, and French senior military representatives in Washington, rather than the Military Committee in Paris, remained NATO's highest military decision-making forum. While other members were often consulted, they had no formal say and generally little insight into the operational planning decisions taken by the three largest allies.[12] While Germany gained NATO consensus on the principle of 'forward defence' at the inner-German border, the alliance did not have sufficient forces to reflect this in operational plans until 1963,[13] and as late as 1977 the US seems to have been less committed to forward defence than it had led the Germans to believe.[14]

By the 1960s, political tensions between France and the US, questions of nuclear strategy following the development of a Soviet second-strike capability against the North American continent, and the need to match West Germany's influence in NATO with its increasing political, economic, and military importance, posed a significant threat to the unity of the alliance. As the Cold War settled into a long-term bloc confrontation, the allies worked to increase political, economic, and technical cooperation and coordination as recommended by the 'three wise men' report of 1956.[15] Under President de Gaulle, France became increasingly opposed to the influence the US exerted through NATO on European defence, which crystallised in the debates on the new strategy of 'flexible response' proposed by the Kennedy administration.[16] At the same time, West Germany grew insistent on greater influence over NATO planning and operations, especially regarding decisions on the use of nuclear weapons. This became an important element in lengthy negotiations on a proposed Multilateral Force (MLF), consisting of nuclear ballistic missiles on surface vessels manned by crews of mixed nationality. NATO's nuclear policies became, at least in part, a matter of intra-alliance bargaining influenced by a desire to accommodate a stronger Germany. At the same time, national and international debates within the alliance sought to reconcile NATO's focus on deterrence and defence with the hopes for a political settlement between East and West in the context of détente.

In 1966–67, NATO members reached a new consensus on overall objectives and strategy that precipitated significant institutional change. Having failed to move West Germany from its strong support for the transatlantic link in NATO, France left NATO's integrated military commands and many related committees.[17] Without France, the other allies agreed to the new strategy of flexible response in 1967. In the same year, the Harmel report on the future tasks of NATO added the search for a political settlement of European relations to the alliance's basic tasks of deterrence and defence. This opened the door for NATO members to commence conventional arms control talks with the Soviet Union, recognise East Germany, create the Conference on Security and Cooperation in Europe, and consult more closely on the political implications of US–Soviet strategic arms control.[18]

The adoption of flexible response was accompanied by increased scope for the allies to influence debates on conventional and nuclear strategy and operations. NATO's Standing Group was dissolved, and its functions absorbed by the larger Military Committee. A new Nuclear Planning Group (NPG) was established, with a mix of permanent and rotating membership, which brought West Germany into the inner circle of NATO decision making on nuclear strategy.[19] Broader membership in NATO's senior decision-making committees and their co-location in the new headquarters in Belgium enabled the development of detailed political–military understandings on military strategy throughout the second half of the Cold War.[20] Thus, from the crisis of the 1960s a more cohesive NATO emerged – one that accommodated West Germany's increasing power, and balanced deterrence and détente in its relations with the Eastern bloc.[21]

In the 1970s, NATO unity was threatened by growing questions about the willingness of the US after the Vietnam War to bear the political and fiscal cost of underwriting the security of the alliance. In 1978, President Carter decided against the introduction of the enhanced radiation weapon (ERW), or 'neutron bomb', to NATO nuclear forces in Europe, although European allies had supported this modernisation in the face of significant domestic opposition. The previous year, West German Chancellor Helmut Schmidt had outlined his concerns about how much Washington might restrict US strategic nuclear forces in Strategic Arms Limitation Treaty (SALT) II negotiations with the Soviet Union, even as 'disparities of military power in Europe' persisted.[22] By 1979, however, the allies had (again) transformed this crisis of confidence into a political show of strength and unity. The dual-track decision announced in December that year committed NATO to deploy new long-range theatre nuclear forces (LRTNF) unless the Soviet Union entered into arms control negotiations on the elimination of this class of weapons.

Crucial to achieving the dual-track decision was the political-military institutional integration of the Atlantic alliance. The US decided to address European political concerns through the modernisation of NATO's LRTNF, which had already been under consideration as part of NATO's force planning process. A new High-Level Group (HLG) of senior defence officials was created to examine nuclear modernisation; on the suggestion of West Germany and the Netherlands, NATO created a 'Special Group' of equal standing to discuss arms control aspects of nuclear modernisation in 1979.[23] The same year, full membership in the NPG was finally opened to all NATO member states. West Germany accepted this change as its original aims of increased information and influence, and the deflection of domestic pressures for acquisition of nuclear weapons, had been achieved.[24]

In the 1980s, significant domestic opposition to the deployment of new Pershing II and ground-launched cruise missiles (GLCMs) in West Germany and other countries, as well as increasingly sceptical views on nuclear weapons in general, especially among the Scandinavian allies, challenged NATO unity. In 1987, the US decision to eliminate the new GLCM and Pershing II capabilities in the intermediate (range) nuclear force (INF) treaty also raised significant questions once more about alliance strategy. Even the conservative Kohl government in Germany now opposed modernising NATO's remaining short-range nuclear forces,[25] following a deep sense of betrayal over the US decision to eliminate intermediate range nuclear forces. However, the end of the Cold War stopped many of the strategic disagreements that threatened to divide NATO allies at that point. By this time, West Germany's military capability and economic strength had made it the most important non-nuclear ally of the US in NATO. In the mid-1980s, the Western allies had abolished the last restrictions on West Germany's conventional arms industry, and NATO ended the Cold War under its first German Secretary General, Manfred Wörner.

In the early 1990s, managing historical enmities in central and eastern Europe emerged as a central focus for European security. After several years of prevarication, NATO intervened in the Bosnian War. Central European countries' demands to be allowed to join NATO caused significant debate in reunified Germany, which sought to adjust to its new position in the heart of Europe. Ultimately, the Kohl government supported NATO enlargement as a means to embed institutionally US support for European stability, and recognise central Europeans' legitimate aspirations in becoming full members of the European community.[26] In order to set the political conditions for NATO enlargement, NATO allies stated that they had 'no intention, no plan and no reason' to deploy nuclear weapons on the territory of new members, and that 'in the current and foreseeable security environment', there would be no need for 'permanent stationing of substantial combat forces'.[27]

Poland, Hungary, and the Czech Republic joined NATO in 1999, followed by Romania, Bulgaria, Slovenia, Slovakia, and the three Baltic states in 2004. From 2001, the alliance's attention shifted to the Middle East as the US responded to 9/11 and dealt with the fallout of its divisive invasion of Iraq. Seeing itself surrounded by friends and reluctant to assume greater military responsibilities, Germany's security policy entered a period of drift. More often than not, Germany now found itself as a 'status quo ally' opposing adaptation of NATO not just in terms of out-of-area operations, but also US-supported proposals for missile defence, or eastern European concerns about a resurgent Russia following the latter's 2008 war with Georgia.[28]

Nevertheless, despite its preference for evolutionary over transformational change within NATO, Germany was careful to avoid risking divisions within the alliance. Notwithstanding Berlin's opposition to the US-led invasion of Iraq, German policymakers exhibited caution in challenging US leadership, were keen to preserve consensus-based outcomes in NATO, including on the role of nuclear weapons, and to preserve NATO's political role in European security.[29] From 2014, Russia's invasion of Ukraine signalled the return of collective defence to NATO's highest priority, and a role for NATO where Germany mediated debates about the balancing of different threats, as well as relations with Russia. Organisationally, in recent years, Germany has once again sought to leverage its size and geographic position to promote integration in the alliance.[30]

NATO, nuclear weapons, and Germany

Throughout the Cold War, the role of nuclear weapons in NATO strategy was largely a derivative of US nuclear strategy. The need to find agreement among allies, however, meant that NATO typically adopted major changes several years after they had been incorporated into US policy. Changes in US policy led to periods of disagreement that were ultimately resolved through political compromises reflecting European perspectives, and in formulations that left sufficient ambiguity for different interpretations. NATO nuclear strategy therefore arose from the intersection of a range of strategic debates between the allies, and reflected political as much as military considerations. As Francis Gavin has shown, despite the declaratory shift to flexible response, there were no detailed operational changes to NATO's nuclear strategy in the 1960s.[31]

During the Cold War, major issues regarding the role of tactical nuclear weapons (TNWs) remained unresolved, perhaps because they were ultimately unresolvable. These pertained to: how tactical nuclear weapons use would be 'coupled' to US strategic nuclear forces; the control of escalation following initial nuclear use; how to maintain an advantage if both sides employed nuclear weapons; the interpretation of Soviet nuclear strategy; and how to balance preparations for conventional and nuclear operations.[32]

Reflecting US strategy at the time, the alliance's first strategic concept endorsed in 1950 (DC 6/16) combined conventional defence in Germany with an immediate strategic bombing offensive against the Soviet Union.[33] Given the severe restrictions on sharing nuclear weapons information in the 1946 McMahon Act, and the insistence of the US Strategic Air Command (SAC) on primacy in nuclear operations, the US Joint Chiefs of Staff initially sought to keep nuclear strike planning for Europe outside of the new SHAPE (Supreme Headquarters Allied Powers Europe) command altogether. Only after a personal intervention by SACEUR Eisenhower with President Truman was nuclear targeting delegated to the most senior US officers in NATO's new regional commands.[34]

In 1953, President Eisenhower's New Look policy, laid down in NSC162/2, envisaged maintaining the economic viability of the Western defence effort by substituting (cheap) nuclear for (expensive) conventional forces.[35] The NAC agreed to the introduction of US tactical nuclear weapons to Europe in 1953, and to a general concept of using nuclear weapons for defending allied territory in MC48 in 1954.[36] Paul Buteux argues that 'the NATO

Council meeting of December 1954 can be taken as the marking point at which nuclear sharing emerged as a central military and political issue for the alliance';[37] although nuclear weapons became central to European NATO allies' immediate defence, they remained under US control. Thus from the mid-1950s into the 1960s, 'issues of nuclear sharing and control provided the dominant theme around which the allies patterned their alliance relationships'.[38] Nonetheless, the consequences of NATO's increased reliance on tactical nuclear weapons were not immediately apparent to all allies, including West Germany. Politically and militarily, Bonn gave little consideration to nuclear issues until the NATO exercise *Carte Blanche* in 1955, which brought to the attention of the German public and political class the enormous number of German casualties resulting from any wide-scale nuclear use by NATO.[39]

In 1957, the allies adopted a new strategic concept (MC14/2) that brought significant change to NATO's nuclear posture. With this shift, according to Legge, 'the role of NATO's limited ground forces in Europe was viewed as a means of compelling an aggressor to mobilise for an attack, holding him as far forward as possible until nuclear retaliation could take place'.[40] NATO introduced a 'stockpile' concept, through which the US would provide nuclear warheads for use by allied forces, making 1957 the year in which sharing of nuclear hardware became a key element of the alliance's strategic posture.[41] This incorporated arrangements whereby West Germany gained direct access to US nuclear weapons as part of the 'dual-key' arrangements with NATO allies; by 1958, the US had completed training the German Air Force's inaugural nuclear-capable units.[42] Yet, US operational control over these weapons was open to serious doubt. Inspecting allied forces during a visit to Europe in 1960, members of a Congressional committee 'found fighter aircraft loaded with nuclear bombs sitting on the edge of runways with [West] German pilots inside the cockpits and starter plugs inserted. The embodiment of control was an American officer somewhere in the vicinity with a revolver'.[43]

Nuclear debates in NATO after 1957 would focus on four major consequences of the decisions taken that year: new dependencies between the US and European allies that arose from nuclear sharing; European demands for additional influence that flowed from this; how to provide NATO with additional medium-range ballistic missiles (MRBMs); and how to interpret elements of flexibility and nuclear thresholds within the 1957 concept. In 1958, the US amended the McMahon Act to allow the sharing of information and warheads under strict provisions with those allies that concluded a bilateral Program of Cooperation (PoC) agreement.[44] The adoption of nuclear sharing was not universal, as NATO allies Norway and Denmark 'screened' their nuclear cooperation with the US. Nonetheless, the strategic consequences of nuclear sharing were profound for relations within NATO, as the effectiveness of Europeans' own defence forces now depended on a US decision to release nuclear warheads.

Also in 1958, the new French President Charles de Gaulle enquired about details on US nuclear weapons in France, which SACEUR Lauris Norstad – dual-hatted as the commander of US forces in Europe – was not permitted to divulge.[45] The following year, de Gaulle refused the stationing of US nuclear forces on French territory unless Paris exercised control over how these forces would be used, including a veto; this led to the US redeploying nine nuclear-strike squadrons from France to the UK and West Germany.[46] Greater desire for influence over the use of nuclear weapons was also shared by West Germany, which carefully coordinated cooperation with France and Italy to develop sovereign (European) nuclear capabilities while arguing for greater influence over nuclear use decisions in NATO. By mid-1960, NATO Secretary General Spaak informed Washington that Europeans sought major changes to nuclear arrangements in order to achieve greater involvement in nuclear planning.[47]

By the 1960s, the proposal for a sea-based MLF of nuclear ballistic missiles became central to transatlantic debates, as the US looked to a new NATO force to counter what seemed to be an increasingly close alignment between Bonn and Paris. Negotiations dragged on as Germany was determined to avoid a break with either Washington or Paris, until a demand by US President Johnson in 1964 for Europeans – in particular, London and Bonn in consultation with Paris – to agree on a joint proposal for command arrangements for the new force effectively brought the MLF to an end.[48] By this time, discussions on the British proposal for an 'Atlantic Nuclear Force' had focused increasingly on the development of ongoing consultation mechanisms for nuclear policy and planning.[49] This had also become central to discussions about NATO's nuclear strategy more broadly.

Although NATO's 1957 strategic concept placed nuclear weapons at the core of the defence of Europe, what this might mean in practice for NATO's nuclear response to Soviet attack remained subject to intense debate. MC14/2 also contained references to conventional responses to lesser contingencies, which was strongly supported by many European allies fearful of entrapment in a large US nuclear response. During the Berlin crises between 1958 and 1962, planning by the three Western Occupational Powers and NATO focused on significant conventional responses (of up to several divisions), with only selective nuclear use, foreshadowing important elements of what later would become the concept of flexible response.[50] However, the suggestion of US Secretary of State Dulles that nuclear defence (in Europe) might reduce the need for nuclear retaliation (by US strategic forces), and SACEUR Norstad's suggestion that nuclear defence could enable a 'pause' before massive retaliation, also stoked fears that Washington might not follow through with its security guarantee.[51] These fears grew when European NATO members became aware of the new Kennedy administration's strategy in 1961, which was at odds with MC14/2 in that NATO required options 'that would provide a compromise between local conventional resistance, graduated nuclear response, and massive strategic retaliation'.[52]

Reflecting on NATO's experience throughout the Cold War, Paul Schulte observes that: 'Reaching agreement on the timing and circumstances of the Alliance's response with TNWs ... inevitably focused attention on this dilemma [between fears of abandonment and entrapment], which was logically insoluble, yet had to be – and has been – politically managed, very largely by creating a common *deterrence culture* within which joint planning for nuclear contingencies could be conducted and normalized'.[53] An important step towards this common deterrence culture were the 1962 Athens guidelines that 'envisaged graduated intra-NATO crisis consultations based on the principle that the greater the risk that was taken by individual states, the more input into nuclear decisions they would be granted'.[54]

Yet, in case of a nuclear attack, the reality was that NATO planned to respond with nuclear weapons with little possibility of consultation. In case of a general conventional attack in one NATO sector, NATO would use nuclear weapons as appropriate and if necessary, with a presumption of consultation with affected members. In the case of a lesser attack threatening the integrity of a member state, consultations would be channeled through the NAC, thus giving each member a veto. As part of the implementation of the new consultation arrangements, the allies agreed to create a new Deputy SACEUR position, always staffed by a European responsible for nuclear matters; and several European allies, including West Germany, were invited to send liaison officers to the headquarters of US Strategic Command in Omaha.[55]

Formal moves to provide for greater discretion in the use of nuclear weapons in NATO strategy foundered on France's strong opposition and reservations in other countries. The basic problem facing the Kennedy administration was that it required European allies' cooperation in developing the conventional forces on which the new strategy of flexible response depended. By not expanding conventional forces, and not changing existing forces to make them less reliant on access to US nuclear warheads, West Germany could make it more difficult for the US to delay the use of nuclear weapons in a major conflict. While the introduction of Permissive Action Links reinforced US control over its shared warheads,[56] West Germany and other allies gained a US commitment as part of NATO's force structure negotiations not to reduce nuclear weapons in Europe without a consensus in the alliance.[57]

By 1964, West German opposition to amending NATO strategy weakened with the change from Chancellor Adenauer and Defence Minister Strauss to Erhard and van Hassel respectively, who were closer to the US position rather than that of the French. The West German government and public debate began to accept the need to meet different levels of aggression in different ways, but continued to reject any suggestion of an extensive conventional phase of a conflict, arguing for nuclear escalation against value targets to prevent a conflict from being confined to Europe.[58] In 1965, US Secretary of Defense Robert McNamara proposed the creation of a special ministerial committee with limited membership to discuss nuclear planning in NATO. The committee was formed later in that year, with working groups on nuclear planning, data exchange and crisis communication, and met four times throughout 1966.[59]

France's 1966 withdrawal from the integrated military structure enabled more rapid progress as the Defence Planning Committee (DPC), from which France had withdrawn, became the main forum for strategy debates. In December 1966, the DPC created a Nuclear Defence Affairs Committee that was open to all, as well as the NPG, which held its first formal meeting in 1967 and included the US, Britain, Italy, West Germany, and three rotating members.[60] The NPG became the central forum for the negotiation of deployment and employment policy for tactical nuclear weapons, as the US began to provide annual deployment reports to those countries hosting its nuclear weapons in NATO.[61]

NATO's new strategic concept, adopted as DPC/D(67)23 in 1967, was negotiated largely between the US, the UK, and West Germany as the three leading alliance members,[62] and further developed by the Military Committee (MC) in MC 14/3 and MC48/3. It was deliberately ambiguous in order to accommodate enduring disagreements, but was a clear departure from MC14/2 in defining three possible NATO reactions to major Soviet attack: deliberate defence at a similar level; deliberate escalation, including through use of nuclear weapons; and a general nuclear response.[63] These documents would remain the foundation of NATO's nuclear strategy until the end of the Cold War, as negotiations in the NPG shifted to further elaboration of consultation arrangements, political guidelines for nuclear use, and the force structure required for implementation.

Following the adoption of flexible response, the debate in NATO on nuclear strategy focused mainly on the role of tactical nuclear weapons in deliberate escalation. The first NPG meeting in 1967 assigned studies of different aspects of the challenge to a variety of countries, and in 1968 discussion of the reports revealed strong disagreement on when, how, and for what purpose NATO should initiate the use of nuclear weapons. Following agreement that the UK and Germany would provide a joint report, the 'Healey-Schröder' paper presented to NATO in 1969 favoured early but selective nuclear use and accepted that this would need to occur 'within a few days to two weeks subsequent to a massive Warsaw Pact invasion to avoid outright capitulation'.[64] Significantly, this process 'represented the first Allied attempt to work through in detail the possible implications of NATO first use of nuclear weapons at the theatre level'.[65] In the resulting 1969 'Provisional Political Guidelines for the Initial Defensive Tactical Use of Nuclear Weapons by NATO', allies agreed that initial use should have political, not military, purpose and therefore be limited to avoid triggering full-scale Soviet nuclear retaliation.[66]

In the early 1970s, the NPG considered several studies regarding follow-on use, which agreed that NATO could achieve military advantages from using tactical nuclear weapons, but only if the Soviet Union did not respond in kind. Growing interest in new technologies and questions of modernisation, however, as well as rising scepticism towards the purely political logic of nuclear use implied by the NPG at that time, meant that NATO would only agree to 'General Political Guidelines for the Employment of Nuclear Weapons in the Defense of NATO' in 1986.[67] This comprehensive document encompassed initial use, consultation arrangements, NATO communications in crises and after use, as well as sea-based weapons. Accepting the US view that military effectiveness would strengthen a political signal, it abandoned demonstration strikes, but also emphasised strikes in depth, including on the Soviet Union, as preferred by the Europeans.[68]

Despite agreement on these guidelines and the significant political unity demonstrated by the alliance in developing and implementing the 1979 double-track decision, major disagreements persisted throughout this period on the role of nuclear weapons in alliance strategy. The Europeans generally sought early, limited, and long-range use to threaten a further escalation, whereas the US placed varying emphasis on a high nuclear threshold on the one hand, and battlefield use on or close to NATO territory in direct support of NATO forces on the other.[69] These differences were not resolved by agreement to modernise long-range tactical nuclear weapons in 1979, as this happened to be a step consistent with all main schools of argument, and supported by some allies primarily to maintain political unity in the alliance.

While the accompanying arms control offer to Moscow was essential to gain internal agreement on nuclear modernisation in NATO, the elimination of intermediate nuclear forces in the 1987 INF treaty fatally undermined the alliance's ability to cover its continuing disagreements on the role of tactical nuclear weapons because it significantly curtailed the ability to threaten long-range strikes.[70] As the employment of short-range nuclear forces on German territory became the only remaining viable option for NATO first use in Europe, Bonn opposed almost all nuclear modernisation; it broke ranks with the three nuclear allies in its calls for further negotiated reductions of nuclear weapons; and it even went as far as to stall WINTEX 89 over the US refusal to vary nuclear targeting that impacted both Germanies in the exercise.[71] At the very end of the Cold War, German views on tactical nuclear weapons had returned to the initial, sceptical stance when first faced with Eisenhower's New Look policy thirty-five years earlier. However, the end of the Cold War meant that NATO never had to confront the political and strategic consequences of this widening rift.

Instead, as the Soviet threat dissipated, the NPG in its meetings between 1989 and 1991 endorsed a shift in emphasis from short-range nuclear systems towards longer-range, more flexible air-delivered nuclear capabilities.[72] This was reflected in the Presidential Nuclear Initiatives of 1991–92, through which the US withdrew all nuclear weapons stationed outside the US, with the exception of air-delivered B-61s in Europe.[73] In its 1991 Strategic Concept, NATO moved away from flexible response, stating that with the improved conventional balance the 'circumstances in which any use of nuclear weapons might have to be contemplated ... are even more remote'.[74] In 1992, NATO agreed on *Political Principles of Nuclear Planning and Consultation* for the new situation, although the decision not to target any particular country meant that SHAPE stopped developing nuclear use plans.[75]

Although Germany's ageing Tornado aircraft continued to contribute to NATO's nuclear delivery mission, elements of NATO's nuclear policies, and continued participation in nuclear sharing was repeatedly challenged, especially by parties on the centre-left. In 1998, a new coalition between Social Democrats and the Green Party assumed power in Germany and agreed to work towards a no-first-use policy and lower readiness of nuclear forces. Supported by Canada, Foreign Minister Joschka Fischer raised the possibility of a no-first-use policy at a NATO meeting in 1998. This was met with opposition from all three of NATO's nuclear powers and hence did not achieve the necessary consensus.[76] While the new 1999 Strategic Concept largely reflected the 1991 language on nuclear weapons, the allies agreed to review nuclear policies.[77] No major changes to force structure or posture followed, but NATO continued to reduce the readiness of its dual capable aircraft: from days in 1994, to a split of weeks and months in 1999, and to months for the whole force by 2003.[78]

In 2009, the liberal Free Democratic Party returned to government in coalition with the conservative Christian Democratic Union (CDU), and achieved agreement that the government would work towards removing US nuclear warheads from Germany – a demand that new Foreign Minister

Guido Westerwelle had raised as early as 2005.[79] In the wake of Obama's 2009 speech in Prague recommitting the US to nuclear disarmament, Westerwelle and his counterparts from the Benelux countries and Norway wrote to NATO's Secretary General, asking that NATO examine steps to contribute to the same objective. This prompted significant public criticism from former NATO Secretary General Robertson who argued that Germany sought to benefit from nuclear deterrence while absolving itself of responsibilities, as well as conservative politicians in Germany who highlighted the need to take into account the views of NATO's newer member states.[80] The US argued in NATO and its 2010 Nuclear Posture Review (NPR) that nuclear posture decisions should continue to be taken by consensus, and that further reductions would require some form of Russian reciprocity.[81]

In the end, Germany supported the argument that the role of NATO's non-strategic nuclear weapons should be considered in the context of US–Russian arms control,[82] but the allies dropped most of the clauses on NATO's nuclear posture in the 2010 Strategic Concept. Despite intergovernmental negotiations as well as the report of a high-profile group of external experts to advise on the new Concept, NATO's member states could not even agree on a statement about the fundamental purpose of the alliance's nuclear weapons. While some policymakers in Berlin remained sympathetic to the case for nuclear disarmament, the departure of Westerwelle as Foreign Minister in 2011 marked the beginning of a recalibration of German nuclear policy. Germany's close collaboration with France to reach compromise wording over the role of nuclear weapons in NATO was important in smoothing a pathway to the 2012 Deterrence and Defence Posture Review (DDPR) that reaffirmed NATO's commitment to nuclear sharing and extended deterrence,[83] and the 'grand coalition' government reaffirmed its commitment to German participation in NATO nuclear sharing in the 2016 Defence White Paper.[84]

Tracing nuclear weapons cooperation in the NATO alliance

Threat assessment and prioritisation

Throughout the Cold War, the US and West Germany agreed that NATO's Central Front was the highest priority sector, and considered the defence of Western Europe globally the most important (if not always the most urgent) commitment. Both countries also agreed that deterrence ultimately rested on nuclear weapons. There is thus significant support for the realist perspective that a shared threat perception underpinned close nuclear cooperation between Germany and the US.

For most of the Cold War, there was also relatively little disagreement between West Germany, the US, and the rest of NATO about the Warsaw Pact's conventional and nuclear capabilities threatening Western Europe. The important exception to this was the first half of the 1960s that also coincided with a period of significant political disagreement between Bonn and Washington over the US attempt to reduce the role of US nuclear weapons in NATO's defence against limited attack. West Germany and the US disagreed on assumptions about warning time and the availability of reinforcements, as well as on whether the main threat was from general war or from limited attack, as argued by the US and the UK.[85]

In the following years, the allies devoted significant attention to narrowing differences in their assessments through a large number of bilateral US–German studies, in trilateral discussions involving the UK, and through NATO, including the 1965 Mountbatten study in which the Military Committee asked NATO's three Supreme Commanders to assess what could be achieved with conventional forces alone in their areas of responsibility.[86] US–German study groups on atomic demolition munitions (ADMs), Warsaw Pact mobilisation and NATO warning, the role of tactical air forces, and ground combat doctrine helped clarify differences, but also led to a perception in Bonn of politicised US assessments.[87] As late as 1966, the West German chief of staff would write to his US counterpart warning against 'letting our strategic conceptions fall prey to wishful thinking out of understandable concern about the danger of escalation'.[88] However, it was through these detailed talks that Germany and the US ultimately agreed that an attack that NATO should be able to repel conventionally was only in the order of four to six Soviet divisions. This linked the number of US forces in Europe to NATO's nuclear threshold and in general paved a way towards the compromises of the flexible response concept.[89]

In general, differences over the threat to NATO during the Cold War arose more consistently from different judgements about Soviet intentions. Two broad viewpoints could be found within the domestic debates on both sides of the Atlantic: those who saw a greater likelihood of immediate Soviet intent to attack NATO and who generally sought improvements to NATO's defences in Europe and to US strategic nuclear forces, even at the cost of tensions within the alliance and with the Soviet Union; and those who considered East–West relations to be relatively stable, and focused on maintaining NATO unity as the basis of general deterrence.[90]

Following the Cold War, perceptions of threat from external actors as well as from internal disunity continued to influence NATO's debates on nuclear weapons. With the US focused on international terrorism post-9/11 and Germany seeing no significant threat to its security, Russia's conflict with Georgia in 2008 led some of NATO's eastern European members to request publicly changes in NATO's military planning and deployments to address what they saw as an increased threat from Russia, and raise the importance of NATO's nuclear posture as a commitment to collective defence.[91] Although initially somewhat dismissive of newer NATO members pushing for the reassertion of NATO nuclear posture, US missile defence deployments, as well as tripwire conventional force deployments in the Baltic states and Poland, Germany became much more receptive to these proposals following the annexation of Crimea in 2014. However, this took place as the avoidance of an enduring rift in the alliance also became a more important factor in internal NATO force posture and strategy debates.[92]

Policy objectives regarding cooperation on nuclear weapons

Material cost and the relative benefit from cooperation were significant elements in the policy objectives of NATO allies regarding cooperation on nuclear weapons during the Cold War. West Germany feared that it might be isolated politically from its allies over major questions concerning its own security or the status of Germany as a divided country. It therefore sought to avoid situations in which it could be singled out on any major policy issue. In 1963, for example, Bonn refused NATO Secretary General Stikker's request to station 300 MRBMs in West Germany, only accepting a part of the force if it was distributed across the alliance in order to share the risk of nuclear attack.[93] In the 1970s, Chancellor Schmidt insisted that at least one other country besides West Germany should deploy the ERW.[94] As NATO negotiated the modernisation of its long-range tactical nuclear weapons in the late 1970s, Germany also insisted that it should not be the only country to host such systems. This came as a surprise to the US and many other allies, and was only overcome when Belgium, Italy, the Netherlands, and the UK agreed to become host nations.[95]

The US often looked to nuclear weapons as a more economical alternative than conventional forces to extend deterrence to its allies and, in the 1950s, to provide for NATO defensive power in general. In contrast, West Germany saw allied investment in its security as a proxy for political commitment, and viewed with suspicion both the shift towards nuclear rather than conventional armament of US forces in the 1950s and reversal of this in the 1960s. Although Bonn attempted on strategic grounds to delay the implementation of both shifts, with regard to the force posture of the *Bundeswehr*, this was counterbalanced by the political objective of achieving equality with the allies. West Germany's political status was also a major argument of Defence Minister Strauss in favour of jointly acquiring nuclear weapons with France and Italy.[96]

In the early 1960s, the US sought to acknowledge Germany's increasing military and economic importance by enabling greater influence for Bonn over NATO nuclear policy, with a view to avoiding a split in the alliance as well as stemming further nuclear proliferation. The US tried to use the MLF as a way of ceding to allies a greater say over part of NATO's posture, counterbalancing French influence in Bonn.[97]

Despite its focus on national control of nuclear use embodied in McNamara's thinking on flexible response, there was thus strong support within the Kennedy administration for developing NATO through additional institutionalisation and defence programmes – and greater institutionalisation was an objective that Germany sought to progress as well, particularly as a means to manage conflicting interests. The 1961 Berlin crisis and general views of the new Kennedy administration increased West German doubts about the reliability of the US, leading Bonn to attempt to institutionalise where possible allied support in case of attack.[98] Following the agreement on the Athens guidelines in 1962, however, West Germany did not push questions of political participation on nuclear release within NATO, as seeking to pursue a German veto on nuclear release came with political advantages, but with military disadvantages if other governments sought similar influence as well. Instead, West Germany focused questions of political participation on the separate MLF discussions.[99]

In that context, Bonn accepted the US veto on nuclear use but did not want, for reasons of military credibility, to accept vetoes by European member states. It proposed voting weights that meant West Germany and one additional European state would have been enough to achieve European consent to release the weapons, but all other European countries had to agree to overcome German opposition to release.[100] West Germany insisted, however, on NATO forward defence along the inner-German border, rather than a posture of defence in depth that would trade (German) space for time and tactically advantageous positions along the Weser, Lech, and Rhine rivers. Given the lack of forces, forward defence was complicated by West Germany's rejection of any fortification of the border, which would have been in conflict with its principle of rejecting Germany's division into two states. NATO depended on early use of short-range nuclear forces, however, and it is in this context that West Germany's objectives – limiting territorial losses while reducing damage to Germany also from NATO operations – were most directly in conflict.[101] Hence, during the 1960s, Germany edged towards a greater appreciation of national veto over nuclear weapons use, and by 1966 it sought to develop further the Athens guidelines so that consultation became an instrument for participation on decisions on the use or non-use of nuclear weapons.[102]

Even after the failure of the MLF, demonstrating the US commitment to NATO remained a significant policy objective of direct relevance for deployment of tactical nuclear weapons. As US Secretary of Defense James Schlesinger noted in a 1975 report for Congress: 'US theater nuclear forces deployed in Europe have been for years a major symbol of the earnest US commitment to the common defense of the Alliance. Consequently, possible changes in the theater nuclear force posture must be carefully evaluated from both the military perspective and with an eye to the message these changes convey to Allies and adversaries.'[103] While this objective generally acted as a brake against reductions of tactical nuclear weapons stockpiles in Europe from the 1960s onwards, it most clearly found expression in the US decision in 1979 to address European concerns about Washington's attention to their strategic anxieties through the modernisation of NATO's long-range tactical nuclear forces.

An unexpected feature of nuclear weapons cooperation in NATO after 1991 was that these more symbolic, endogenous objectives that reflected the aims and values of the alliance overall endured. In general, after the Cold War NATO chose to avoid public debate about the relevance of its nuclear weapons by framing changes to its posture as modernisation or adaptation decided behind closed doors, rather than as part of broader political initiatives as it had done in 1979 and in the debate on short-range forces in the late 1980s.[104] On the other hand, NATO communiqués and strategic concepts from 1991 emphasised the transatlantic symbolism of US nuclear weapons in Europe, and by 2010 it began to refer to itself as a 'nuclear alliance' to underscore nuclear burden sharing. Even as her centre-left coalition partners in 2009 called for the removal of US nuclear weapons from Germany, Chancellor Angela Merkel appeared to give greater credence to the argument that influence on nuclear decisions derived from participation in nuclear sharing.[105] Although the 2009 coalition agreement conceded that Germany would 'engage within the Alliance, as well as across the table with the American Allies, such that the remaining nuclear weapons in Germany are removed',[106] their symbolic importance for NATO was a major factor in the German debate on the initiative.[107] It is significant that Berlin did not try to overturn the convention that nuclear posture decisions required consensus in the alliance.

Nuclear strategy

Ivo Daalder argues that NATO's nuclear debates during the Cold War revolved around four basic strategies. 'Pure deterrence' was most influential in the 1950s and rejected the notion of graduated nuclear use of any kind, threatening instant and massive retaliation against any form of attack.

'Conventional deterrence' sought to limit escalation by maintaining a 'firebreak' between conventional defence and nuclear retaliation, and saw only a limited role for tactical nuclear weapons as a symbol of the risk of escalation. 'Escalation deterrence' sought early but limited long-range strikes to impose and demonstrate costs of escalation early in a conflict, whereas 'war-fighting deterrence' focused on the use of short-range, tactical nuclear weapons as militarily necessary in order to defend NATO territory successfully.[108] In general, German and US preferences regarding nuclear strategy matched the realist expectation that they would reflect the relative cost and benefit that arose from these strategies for the allies. In terms of outcomes, however, none of these map easily onto either US or NATO strategy, as they were more or less coherent compromises, rather than clear choices between these different views. They functioned more as ideational frameworks that allowed allies to negotiate and interpret, often in different ways, the political meaning of specific force structure and posture decisions.

Cold War West German policymakers strongly believed that their country's security rested on deterrence based on the US strategic arsenal, and generally sought early nuclear use that would minimise the damage to Germany itself. Hence, they had an enduring preference for long-range nuclear strikes as part of a concept more akin to 'pure deterrence' in the 1950s, and 'escalation deterrence' in the 1970s and 1980s. Until the 1980s, they gave little support to a strong conventional defence capability as a replacement for early nuclear escalation. Still, at the operational level, Germany preferred the ability to mount mobile, armoured defence operations over more static, nuclear operations, and did not engage much in early thinking on escalation before the reduction of US forces in Germany in 1956.[109] The same year also saw the appointment of the pro-nuclear Minister for Defence Franz Joseph Strauss, who would later famously deride the notion of any nuclear threshold (along with all US strategic concepts) as 'conceptual aids for the precalculation of the inconceivable and the incalculable nature of the specific'.[110]

West German support for massive use of tactical nuclear weapons to hasten inevitable escalation lessened as the political and strategic need for more nuanced response options acquired currency in the early 1960s. The concept of flexible response, however, remained open to widely different interpretation; this was reflected in the many years of negotiation on NATO's political guidelines for tactical nuclear weapons use. Whereas the Nixon administration sought the ability for NATO to defend conventionally for ninety days, Europeans only saw a need for a conventional phase to be long enough to negotiate initial nuclear use.[111] NATO's strong reliance on tactical nuclear weapons was more a consequence of their being the only area where the alliance had a numerical advantage over the Warsaw Pact than because NATO had a coherent concept for their use during the 1970s. At a meeting of the US National Security Council (NSC) in 1970, Chairman of the Joint Chiefs of Staff Admiral Thomas Moorer concluded that NATO allies were 'living in a dream world about our nuclear support. They believe there will be an immediate shift to nuclear weapons in any war and that conventional forces are unnecessary'.[112]

Insofar as flexible response and suggestions of war-fighting deterrence were premised on the assumption that nuclear escalation could be controlled, both raised fears among Europeans that a conflict might be contained to their continent; this led to a preference for long-range systems that in effect blended in with US strategic forces while allowing political control as favoured by the US. Therefore US commentators often mistook German opposition to the ERW in the 1970s as broader ambivalence in Bonn about nuclear deterrence.[113] Whereas the West German 1975–76 White Paper confirmed NATO's guidance that 'initial use of nuclear weapons is not intended so much to bring about a military decision as to achieve political effect', it also reinforced the notion of 'gapless deterrence', which emphasised that the shadow of nuclear weapons should hang over every phase of conflict so that the main threshold would be between war and peace.[114] Although US governments expressly dismissed the notion of 'demonstrative use' of nuclear weapons, NATO never agreed to do so, and West German Chair of the Military Committee, General Altenburg, referred to it as late as 1987 at a time when US support for a 'war-fighting' posture of integrated nuclear and conventional forces was at its strongest since the 1950s.[115] The elimination of NATO's LRTNF under the INF treaty, however, removed the scope for ambiguity that had concealed these different interpretations of Alliance strategy, as well as removing the option of deliberate, but limited long-range escalation as part of NATO follow-on attacks, thus creating one of the most severe – and ultimately unresolved – disagreements on strategy in the alliance.[116]

With the end of the Cold War, operational considerations lost almost all of their relevance for NATO nuclear strategy, beyond the general recognition of the value of longer-range weapons and flexibility encapsulated in the NPG decisions of 1989–91. In the words of the 2001 NATO *Handbook*, '[alliance] strategy remains one of war prevention, but it is no longer dominated by the possibility of nuclear escalation'.[117] Martin Smith has aptly characterised the resulting posture as one of 'existentialism plus', consisting of a small arsenal whose size and properties had little connection to specific scenarios, but that maintained a politically motivated element of geographic distribution in order to demonstrate US commitment to Europe and the alliance.[118] Hence, a number of senior US officers during the 2000s seemed to believe that there was no military rationale for the continued presence of US nuclear weapons in Europe. In the words of the 2008 US Defense Secretary's Task Force on Nuclear Weapons Management, however, the strategic rationale for their presence continued to rest on 'the political value our friends and allies place on these weapons, the political costs of withdrawal, and the psychological impact of their visible presence as well as the security linkages they provide'.[119]

Domestic factors

Throughout the Cold War, national public debate on nuclear policy became an increasingly important context for the allies' ability to achieve and maintain consensus on major decisions regarding nuclear weapons. From the 1970s, it led to a moderation of extreme positions in the alliance debates.[120] Allied governments' policy preferences reflected the competing arguments that animated these debates, especially about the balance between deterrence and détente, but there are few instances in which domestic considerations per se can be said to have clearly shaped decisions on NATO nuclear posture or structure. In the late 1950s, the Dutch and Belgian governments declined to host nuclear MRBM as a result of domestic opposition.[121] President Carter's decision to defer indefinitely the production of the neutron bomb was because of his personal rather than domestic concerns[122] and did not extend to the modernisation of NATO's LRTNF.

The most sustained and clear challenge to NATO from domestic policy arose from Denmark in the 1980s. The government in Copenhagen did not command a majority on foreign and defence policy issues in parliament, where the centre-left opposition imposed its views through parliamentary resolutions. Through the 'Footnote Policy', Denmark noted its non-support of a number of policies in NATO.[123] When Denmark refused to pay its required share of the NATO-funded infrastructure for the deployment of GLCM and Pershing II, other countries picked up Denmark's share of the cost, while Copenhagen agreed to fund an equivalent amount of non-nuclear infrastructure expenses.[124]

Despite this ability to contain the practical impact of Danish domestic policy through institutional adaptation, allies took very seriously the possibility of more severe damage to the alliance's posture. Announcing the end of the ANZUS alliance with New Zealand over that country's refusal to accept US nuclear-armed vessels into its ports, US Secretary of State George Shultz openly acknowledged the intention to set an example, stating that 'I'd hate to see the New Zealand policy spread'.[125] When the Folketing (Danish Parliament) demanded that Denmark follow New Zealand's policy on ship visits in 1987, the government resigned rather than risk the same fate.[126]

In West Germany, there was significant public debate in 1958 about the conservative government's agreement to arm the *Bundeswehr* with US nuclear warheads. Although the agreement went ahead, public opinion as well as the Social Democratic Party were largely opposed, and the debate in the Bundestag 'proved to be one of the most emotional and controversial debates in the history of the FRG'.[127]

By the 1960s, support for West German rearmament and NATO membership had become key elements in the German Social Democratic Party's pitch for electoral respectability. Its accession to government in the 'grand coalition' of 1966 brought with it some policy adjustment. Germany dropped its notional pursuit of the MLF, as well as becoming less ambivalent about the Nuclear Non-Proliferation Treaty (NPT) in response to US pressure.[128] Under the Social Democratic Defence Minister Richard Schröder, Bonn also began to give greater emphasis to political consultation over military effectiveness when considering nuclear use arrangements.[129] But in a pattern that has persisted throughout the chancellorships of Schmidt in the 1970s, Gerhard Schröder at the turn of the century, and Angela Merkel's 'grand coalition' of the 2010s, Social Democrat politicians in government have consistently been more supportive of the role of nuclear weapons in NATO than has the parliamentary party. Ironically, the most significant challenge to NATO's nuclear policies that was motivated by domestic policy considerations came in the form of conservative Chancellor Kohl's call for arms control over modernisation of short-range nuclear forces in 1989.[130]

Importance of Germany for US security

The immediate importance of West Germany for US security during the Cold War rested on the size and combat potential of the German armed forces. However, the development of this potential after West Germany's accession to NATO in 1955 took time, and correlates well with the growing influence of Germany on NATO and US national policies. While German rearmament began in 1955, it was not until 1973 that the *Bundeswehr* achieved its planned size and structure.[131] West Germany was almost completely dependent on US military supplies in the 1950s, and had yet to gain permission to re-establish its own armament industry. Bonn was conscious of the importance of its military contribution for political influence (for example it increased the length of conscription in 1961 to enable an increase in the size of its armed forces in the context of the Berlin Crisis),[132] but it only played a relatively minor role in the strategic debates that led to the 1957 Strategic Concept.

By the 1960s, the importance of the country was growing as West Germany was courted by Paris on the one hand, and London and Washington on the other with competing visions for transatlantic order. Increasing German demands for institutional influence in NATO raised the spectre of West Germany seeking a measure of strategic independence once more, and the US believed, as President Johnson put it in a letter to UK Prime Minister Wilson in December 1965, that 'what is essential is a stable and healthy Germany that can play a constructive role on the side of the West'.[133] Following French criticism of the December 1962 Nassau agreement on US–UK nuclear cooperation, and the January 1963 Élysée treaty establishing close cooperation between West Germany and France, the Kennedy administration had used the MLF proposal as a way to give Germany greater institutional influence while cementing the transatlantic element of the NATO alliance.[134] From Washington's perspective, West Germany's post-MLF shift to support for the nascent NPT was also regarded as important in building a broader allied coalition in favour of non-proliferation.

The reforms to NATO institutions and strategy in the late 1960s reduced the danger that West Germany might distance itself from political–military integration in the transatlantic alliance. France's withdrawal from military integration, British economic decline, and US preoccupation with the Vietnam War and Watergate meant that West Germany became the most important US ally economically as well as militarily, especially under the leadership of Chancellor Helmut Schmidt who had a formidable reputation as a leading European thinker on defence policy.[135] From an alliance perspective, Schmidt was pivotal largely because of his moderate leadership of West Germany's largest centre-left party, his broader influence in European capitals, and his consistent support for the US alliance and NATO.

Material factors are, however, less able to explain the persistence of the NATO alliance and close institutional integration, including on nuclear weapons, that developed since the 1970s, much less its persistence into the post-Cold War era. As European economic strength (and commitment to non-proliferation norms) increased, it can be argued that the importance of NATO for the security of the North American continent diminished, even before the threat that animated its existence in the first place disappeared in 1989–91. In that sense, the question of what sources exist of allied influence on the US become another version of the question of why NATO has endured after the Cold War despite realist predictions that it should have dissolved,[136] and the strong path dependency that arises from the value of institutionalisation in the face of new strategic challenges.[137]

Access to information

Throughout the first two decade of the Cold War, the US significantly restricted information about US deployments of nuclear weapons to

Europe, as well as plans for their use in NATO. As West Germany's institutional integration in NATO commands and the role of its Army and Air Force in delivering nuclear weapons increased in the 1960s, however, so too did its ability to understand the plans and approaches of its main ally. Beginning with the 1962 Athens summit, the US began to use increased access to information as a means of finding and shaping consensus. This shift was formalised by the creation of the NPG, which aimed to create trust in US commitments and alliance consensus through transparency on nuclear policy issues.

Tuschhoff writes that 'German participation in NATO planning, policy-making, and information exchange were the most important instruments allowing the Federal Republic to catch up with its allies',[138] but it took some years for West Germany's political leadership to understand the implications of nuclear employment plans in sufficient detail to influence the balance between Germany's competing policy objectives of early use while limiting damage to its own population. While West German officers gained access to parts of the NATO atomic strike plan once German Air Force wings were allocated nuclear targets, West Germany only acquired access to other nations' targeting allocations once German officers gained senior positions within allied commands in the late 1960s.[139] SACEUR was often willing to divulge additional information to address Germany's concerns in an informal manner. In 1959, German Defence Minister Strauss asked for information about NATO nuclear targeting in order to ascertain its impact on the West German population. SACEUR responded that the atomic strike plan was the prerogative of NATO commands and would not be shared with national ministries, but nevertheless agreed to provide a briefing to a senior German officer who could verbally report to the minister.[140] The briefing reinforced German concerns, especially about repeated strikes, which West Germany subsequently managed to convince SHAPE to reduce. In addition, Bonn argued for changes to NATO exercises to restrict wider knowledge of the extent of NATO nuclear targeting within Germany.[141]

Access to information on the US nuclear systems available to NATO were a key element of European concerns about US reliability as an ally in the 1960s. President de Gaulle's unsuccessful request in 1958 for information about US nuclear weapons in France had been couched in terms of national sovereignty, and had been rebuffed by the US. Similarly, West Germany demanded confirmation from the new Kennedy administration in 1961 that the US still maintained sufficient warheads in Europe for the provision of allied forces given NATO stockpile arrangements.[142] At the 1962 meeting of defence ministers in Athens, the US tried to address allied concerns by divulging additional detail on US capabilities. US Secretary McNamara provided information on US strategic forces, nuclear targeting plans that had not previously been made available to US allies, and information on the number and type of US warheads in Europe.[143] McNamara also promised 'to provide information about our nuclear forces and consult about basic plans and arrangements for their use on a continuing basis'.[144] As part of the negotiations and study of the MRBM plan, questions of access to information and decisions on nuclear use gained increasing prominence in West German policy in the early 1960s; in return for participating in the MLF and accepting a US veto over the employment of the planned force, Germany sought to achieve greater consultation with the US on nuclear policy within NATO.[145] By the late 1960s, the US sought to use actively the inclusion of Germany's defence leadership in the development of nuclear concepts as a means of gaining consensus on a shift in NATO strategy.

The manner in which information was divulged by the US thus conveyed intentions as much as the information itself. In the late 1970s, the US again used increased access to information as a means of addressing allied concerns, which at that point focused on the US approach to bilateral SALT talks with the Soviet Union, rather than NATO plans as such. Before 1977, there had been minimal consultation on SALT. At the May 1977 NATO summit, and later that year at an NPG meeting, West German officials expressed concern over the US approach to cruise missiles in the SALT talks.[146] This led to 'hodgepodge' briefings by US Department of State and Defence officials on cruise missiles to the NAC – rather than by Defence officials alone to the NPG – which reinforced European suspicions about US intentions.[147]

Once the US decided to address European concerns as part of the modernisation of NATO's long-range tactical nuclear forces, it again deliberately adapted the way it shared information to bring about consensus in the alliance.[148] Despite extensive discussions of the modernisation programme in the NPG at staff and ambassadorial level, ministers in home capitals were not always closely engaged in the discussions. NATO therefore established a new HLG of senior defence officials, which had broader representation than the NPG. In addition, since the question of nuclear modernisation could not be separated from national US decisions on the development and deployment of the new capabilities, the HLG was chaired by the US representative rather than the NATO International Staff, and it was customary for Pentagon officials to prepare the background papers for HLG meetings.[149] Whereas at the beginning of the Cold War the US used its role in NATO to restrict the access of member states to information about US national capabilities even if they were assigned to the alliance, by the late 1970s Washington was using NATO to create new arrangements to enable even more direct allied consultation on US nuclear posture and policy.

Both the NPG and HLG continued to fulfil their roles after the Cold War, even as the frequency of ministerial NPG meetings was reduced to one per year in the early 2000s.[150] All new NATO allies that have joined since 1999 have become members of both the NPG and HLG. However, as NATO's concerns shifted once more towards managing the escalation of conflict with Russia, it became clear that the understanding of nuclear strategy in national capitals and national delegations had waned over time. Hence, the alliance's nuclear planning directorate used the meetings of the HLG, NPG, and its regular work with the nuclear staff group in the NATO Headquarters to once more, over time, 'raise the nuclear IQ' in the alliance through the staff training, exercises, and engagement of senior national officials. For countries as small as Estonia or as large as Poland, the ability to rotate defence policy staff through the nuclear staff group in Brussels was a particularly important way of building capacity in national bureaucracies to engage in questions of nuclear policy.[151]

Conclusion

As the most significant military actor in NATO throughout the Cold War, a continuing US commitment to collective defence was seen by its European allies as critical. The fact that NATO nuclear strategy broadly followed US national strategy, albeit with some delays, and that it did so even after European objections, reflects the material importance and leadership of the US in the alliance. However, the US also made significant compromises regarding NATO strategy during negotiations of new strategic concepts. Short of giving up its presidential veto over the release of US nuclear weapons, the US also made significant concessions in terms of real allied influence on the deployment and employment of US nuclear warheads. At the beginning of the Cold War, allies had very little information on what nuclear weapons the US stored even on their own territory, and nuclear targeting remained the sole purview of senior US officers. Yet, over time, officers from all allies participated in planning for nuclear operations in the command structure; the US agreed to negotiate increasingly detailed guidelines for nuclear employment as well as to detailed consultation arrangements in case of the use of nuclear weapons.

In these developments, West Germany was central to almost every debate. German influence in NATO increased with the realisation of its economic and military potential in the 1960s and 1970s. The most significant attempts by Washington to develop new arrangements to accommodate German concerns and give West Germany particular influence above that of other allies were during the MLF negotiations. The commitment of the US to working with allies on the modernisation of long-range theatre nuclear weapons was also largely a reaction to the concerns brought forward by

Chancellor Schmidt in his 1977 London speech and the backlash against Washington's unilateral decision making over the ERW issue.

The extent to which the US involved its NATO allies in decisions from the development to deployment and planning for nuclear weapons use during the Cold War points to the practical importance of the institutional context of the Alliance. In particular, NATO was (and remains) a political, not just military, alliance that places a premium on unity and consensus, as well as the political acceptance of close military integration. The Athens guidelines and the very process of their negotiation helped to build trust precisely because this grounded expectations in a better understanding of respective priorities. And while the strategic concept of 1967 remained a compromise, subject to many different interpretations until the end of the Cold War, the way it was achieved also owed much to the broader institutional context, for instance, in the work on force structure guidance in MC100/1 that underscored the underlying strategic assumptions and policy judgements of the allies.[152]

However, institutional integration in NATO did not just facilitate compromise on nuclear cooperation: it also created new dependencies that constrained the US ability to leverage its overall dominance in hard power terms. The introduction of nuclear sharing from 1957 meant that the independent operational capability of European allies' forces was significantly reduced as they now depended on the US release of nuclear warheads. But at the same time, the US ability to change the tactical nuclear weapons posture in Europe without undercutting NATO's military credibility also depended on European allies' active cooperation. This mutual dependence both characterised and reinforced the nuclear relationship between the US and its NATO allies during the Cold War; it was this interdependence that made it impossible for Washington to impose the original vision of 'flexible response' on its allies in the way it had done when the alliance agreed to the introduction of the nuclear stockpile in 1957. In that sense, the success of 'software' integration through the NPG built on, rather than being an alternative to, the 'hardware' focus of the 1950s and 1960s. For crucial non-nuclear allies such as West Germany, this mutual dependence provided a degree of influence that widened options to achieve national policy objectives. As we shall see in the next chapter, this dynamic was relevant even in the case of smaller, less influential NATO allies.

Notes

1 L. Kaplan, *The Long Entanglement: NATO's First 50 Years* (Westport, CT: Praeger, 1999), 7–22.

2 T. A. Sayle, *Enduring Alliance: A History of NATO and the Postwar Global Order* (Ithaca, NY: Cornell University Press, 2019), 18.
3 D. Kruger, 'Institutionalizing NATO's Military Bureaucracy: The Making of an Integrated Chain of Command', in S. Mayer (ed.), *NATO's Post-Cold War Politics: The Changing Provision of Security* (Houndmills: Palgrave Macmillan, 2014), 55–56.
4 G. Schmidt, 'From London to Brussels: Emergence and Development of a Politico-Administrative System', in S. Mayer (ed.), *NATO's Post-Cold War Politics: The Changing Provision of Security* (Houndmills: Palgrave Macmillan, 2014), 41.
5 S. Mayer, 'Introduction: NATO as an Organization and Bureaucracy', in S. Mayer (ed.), *NATO's Post-Cold War Politics: The Changing Provision of Security* (Houndmills: Palgrave Macmillan, 2014), 17.
6 M. Trachtenberg, *The Cold War and After: History, Theory, and the Logic of International Politics* (Princeton, NJ: Princeton University Press, 2012), 128–129.
7 S. Weber, 'Shaping the Postwar Balance of Power: Multilateralism in NATO', *International Organization*, 46:3 (1992), 652.
8 In a conversation with their US counterparts, French officials noted that they wanted 'an assurance there would be no independent *Wehrmacht*'. See Department of State, 'Memorandum of Conversation: US Embassy France Telegram 1135 to Department of State, 16 September 1954', RG 59, Central Decimal Files 1950–1954, 740.5/9–1654.
9 D. Bark and D. Gress, *A History of West Germany: From Shadow to Substance, 1945–1963*, 2nd edition (Cambridge, MA: Blackwell, 1993), 324–334.
10 Quoted in 'NATO Leaders: Lord Ismay', www.nato.int/cps/en/natohq/declassified_137930.htm
11 L. Daugherty, '"Tip of the Spear": The Formation and Expansion of the Bundeswehr, 1949–1963', *Journal of Slavic Military Studies*, 24:1 (2011), 147–177.
12 Schmidt, 'From London to Brussels', 41.
13 C. Tuschhoff, *Deutschland, Kernwaffen und die NATO 1949–1967* (Baden-Baden: Nomos, 2002), 32–35.
14 In 1977, a leak of a presidential memorandum (PRM-10) suggested that the US planned for NATO to fall back on the Weser-Lech line, but not to acknowledge this change. See D. Schwartz, *NATO's Nuclear Dilemmas* (Washington, DC: Brookings Institution, 1983), 213–214.
15 Sayle, *Enduring Alliance*, 31.
16 See W. Kohl, *French Nuclear Diplomacy* (Princeton, NJ: Princeton University Press, 1971), chapter 2.
17 P. Gordon, *France, Germany and the Western Alliance* (Boulder, CO: Westview Press, 1995), 14–15.
18 J. Shea, 'How the Harmel Report Helped Build the Transatlantic Security Framework', *The New Atlanticist*, 29 January 2018, www.

atlanticcouncil.org/blogs/new-atlanticist/how-the-harmel-report-helped-build-the-transatlantic-security-framework/

19 P. Buteux, *The Politics of Nuclear Consultation in NATO: 1965–1980* (Cambridge: Cambridge University Press, 1983), chapter 2.

20 Schmidt, 'From London to Brussels', 43–46.

21 C. Tuschhoff, 'Alliance Cohesion and Peaceful Change in NATO', in H. Haftendorn, R. Keohane and C. Wallander (eds), *Imperfect Unions: Security Institutions Over Time and Space* (Oxford: Oxford University Press: 1999), 140.

22 H. Schmidt, 'The 1977 Alastair Buchan Memorial Lecture', *Survival*, 20:1 (1978), 3–4.

23 Henry Gaffney, 'Euromissiles as the Ultimate Evolution of Theater Missile Forces in Europe', *Journal of Cold War Studies*, 16:1 (2014), 191–197.

24 Buteux, *The Politics of Nuclear Consultation in NATO*, 200–202.

25 P. Schulte, 'Tactical Nuclear Weapons in NATO and Beyond: A Historical and Thematic Examination', in T. Nichols, D. Stuart and J. D. McCausland (eds), *Tactical Nuclear Weapons and NATO* (Carlisle: USAWC SSI, 2012), 57–59.

26 For discussion, see G. Mattox, 'NATO Enlargement and the United States: A Deliberate and Necessary Decision?', in C. David and J. Lévesque (eds), *The Future of NATO: Enlargement, Russia, and European Security* (Montreal: McGill-Queen's University Press, 1999), 79–94.

27 'Founding Act on Mutual Relations, Cooperation and Security between NATO and the Russian Federation, Signed in Paris, 27 May 1997', www.nato.int/cps/en/natohq/official_texts_25468.htm?

28 P. Keller, 'Germany in NATO: The Status Quo Ally', *Survival*, 54:3 (2012), 95–110.

29 S. Rynning, 'The Divide: France, Germany and Political NATO', *International Affairs,* 93:2 (2017), 267–289.

30 H. Lunde Saxi, 'British and German Initiatives for Defence Cooperation: The Joint Expeditionary Force and the Framework Nations Concept', *Defence Studies*, 17:2 (2017), 171–197; C. M. Scaparotti and C. B. Bell, *Moving Out: A Comprehensive Assessment of European Military Mobility* (Washington, DC: Atlantic Council, 2020), 12, 43.

31 F. Gavin, 'The Myth of Flexible Response: United States Strategy in Europe During the 1960s', *The International History Review*, 23:4 (2001), 847–875.

32 See D. Yost, 'The History of NATO Theater Nuclear Force Policy: Key Findings from the Sandia Conference', *Journal of Strategic Studies,* 15:2 (1992), 248–257.

33 For the development of NATO strategy, see G. Pedlow, 'The Evolution of NATO Strategy, 1949–1969', in G. Pedlow (ed.), *NATO Strategy Documents, 1949–1969* (Brussels: NATO, 1997), xi–xxv.

34 P. Roman, 'Curtis LeMay and the Origins of NATO Atomic Targeting', *Journal of Strategic Studies,* 16:1 (1993), 59–60.

35 J. Gaddis, *Strategies of Containment: A Critical Appraisal of Postwar American National Security Policy* (Oxford: Oxford University Press, 1982), chapter 5.

36 M. Wheeler, 'NATO Nuclear Strategy, 1949–1990', in G. Schmidt (ed.), *A History of NATO*, Vol 3: *The First Fifty Years* (Houndmills: Palgrave Macmillan, 2001), 126–127.
37 Buteux, *The Politics of Nuclear Consultation in NATO*, 1
38 Buteux, *The Politics of Nuclear Consultation in NATO*, 4.
39 A. Messemer, 'Konrad Adenauer: Defence Diplomat on the Backstage', in J. Gaddis, P. Gordon, E. May, and J. Rosenberg (eds), *Cold War Statesmen Confront the Bomb: Nuclear Diplomacy Since 1945* (Oxford: Oxford University Press, 1999), 242.
40 J. M. Legge, 'Theater Nuclear Weapons and the NATO Strategy of Flexible Response', *RAND Corporation Paper*, R-2964-FF, March 1983, 5.
41 Schwartz, *NATO's Nuclear Dilemmas*, 75–76.
42 J. Schofield, *Strategic Nuclear Sharing* (Houndmills: Palgrave Macmillan, 2014), 68.
43 J. Steinbruner, *The Cybernetic Theory of Decision: New Dimensions of Political Analysis* (Princeton, NJ: Princeton University Press, 1974), 182. This was a major factor in the Kennedy administration's subsequent decision to install Permissive Action Links (PALs) in US nuclear weapons deployed overseas.
44 Steinbruner, *The Cybernetic Theory of Decision*, 180–181.
45 Schulte, 'Tactical Nuclear Weapons in NATO and Beyond', 46–47.
46 Department of State, 'National Security Council Report: Statement of US Policy on France, November 4, 1959', in *Foreign Relations of the United States, 1958–1960, Western Europe,* Vol. 7, Part 2, https://history.state.gov/historicaldocuments/frus1958–60v07p2/d145
47 F. Chernoff, *After Bipolarity: The Vanishing Threat, Theories of Cooperation, and the Future of the Atlantic Alliance* (Ann Arbor, MI: University of Michigan Press, 1995), 68.
48 C. McArdle Kelleher, *Germany and the Politics of Nuclear Weapons* (New York: Columbia University Press, 1975), 253–254.
49 T. Macintyre, *Anglo-German Relations During the Labour Governments, 1964–1970* (Manchester: Manchester University Press, 2007), 64.
50 Pedlow, 'The Evolution of NATO Strategy, 1949–1969', xxi–xxii.
51 Schwartz, *NATO's Nuclear Dilemmas*, 51–59.
52 Legge, 'Theater Nuclear Weapons and the NATO Strategy of Flexible Response', 8.
53 Schulte, 'Tactical Nuclear Weapons in NATO and Beyond', 25. Emphasis in original.
54 M. Smith, 'To Neither Use Them Nor Lose Them: NATO and Nuclear Weapons Since the Cold War', *Contemporary Security Policy*, 25:3 (2004), 525.
55 Yost, 'The History of NATO Theater Nuclear Force Policy', 247.
56 D. Caldwell, 'Permissive Action Links: A Description and Proposal', *Survival*, 29:3 (1987), 224–225.
57 G. Gerzhoy, 'Alliance Coercion and Nuclear Restraint: How the United States Thwarted West Germany's Nuclear Ambitions', *International Security*, 39:4 (2015), 111.

58 R. Kugler, 'The Great Strategy Debate: NATO's Evolution in the 1960s', *RAND Note*, N-3252-FF/RC, 1991, 70–71.
59 Schwartz, *NATO's Nuclear Dilemmas*, 183–185.
60 Kruger, 'Institutionalizing NATO's Bureaucracy', 61–62.
61 Schulte, 'Tactical Nuclear Weapons in NATO and Beyond', 40–41.
62 Kugler, 'The Great Strategy Debate', 96–97.
63 Pedlow, 'The Evolution of NATO Strategy', xxiv–xxv.
64 T. Terriff, *The Nixon Administration and the Making of US Nuclear Strategy* (Ithaca, NY: Cornell University Press, 1995), 36.
65 Legge, 'Theater Nuclear Weapons and the NATO Strategy of Flexible Response', 19–20.
66 B. Heuser and K. Stoddart, 'Difficult Europeans: NATO and Tactical/Non-strategic Nuclear Weapons in the Cold War', *Diplomacy and Statecraft*, 28:3 (2017), 461–462.
67 Heuser and Stoddart, 'Difficult Europeans', 462.
68 I. Daalder, *The Nature and Practice of Flexible Response: NATO Strategy and Theater Nuclear Forces Since 1967* (New York: Columbia University Press, 1991), 87–92.
69 Freedman L. and J. Michaels, *The Evolution of Nuclear Strategy*, 4th edition (Houndmills: Palgrave Macmillan, 2019), 291–300.
70 Sayle, *Enduring Alliance*, 212.
71 Daalder, *The Nature and Practice of Flexible Response*, 92–93; and M. Healy, 'NATO Cancels War Games to Shift Scenarios', *Los Angeles Times*, 20 May 1990, www.latimes.com/archives/la-xpm-1990–05–20-mn-179-story.html
72 D. Yost, 'The US Debate on NATO Nuclear Deterrence', *International Affairs*, 87:6 (2011), 1407.
73 J. Larsen, *The Future of US Non-strategic Nuclear Weapons and Implications for NATO Drifting Toward the Foreseeable Future: A Report Prepared in Accordance with the Requirements of the 2005–06 Manfred Worner Fellowship for NATO Public Diplomacy Division* (Brussels: NATO, 31 October 2006), 30–33.
74 'The Alliance's New Strategic Concept Agreed by the Heads of State and Government Participating in the Meeting of the North Atlantic Council, 7–8 November 1991', www.nato.int/cps/en/natohq/official_texts_23847.htm
75 Larsen, *The Future of US Non-strategic Nuclear Weapons*, 37.
76 'Germany Raises No-first-use Issue at NATO Meeting', *Arms Control Association* (November 1998), www.armscontrol.org/act/1998–11/press-releases/germany-raises-first-use-issue-nato-meeting
77 'NATO's Nuclear Weapons: The Rationale for No-first-use', *Arms Control Association* (July 1999), www.armscontrol.org/act/1999–07/features/natos-nuclear-weapons-rationale-first-use
78 Larsen, *The Future of US Non-strategic Nuclear Weapons*, 30.
79 'Amerikanische Atomwaffen aus Deutschland abziehen', *Frankfurter Allgemeine,* 25 April 2005, www.faz.net/aktuell/politik/atomwaffen-amerikanische-atomwaffen-aus-deutschland-abziehen-1232522.html

80 R. Neukirch, 'Westerwelle legt sich mit Clinton an', *Der Spiegel*, 25 February 2010, www.spiegel.de/politik/deutschland/streit-ueber-atomwaffen-abruestung-westerwelle-legt-sich-mit-clinton-an-a-680122.html
81 H. Muller, 'Flexible Responses: NATO Reactions to the US Nuclear Posture Review', *The Nonproliferation Review*, 18:1 (2011), 120.
82 Yost, 'The US Debate on NATO Nuclear Deterrence', 1416–1417. 'Successful arms reduction talks' are also identified as a 'precondition' for the withdrawal of remaining nuclear weapons from Germany in the 2018 coalition agreement between the SPD and CDU. See *Koalitionsvertrag 19. Legislaturperiode* (signed Berlin, 12 March 2018), www.bundesregierung.de/resource/blob/975226/847984/5b8bc23590d4cb2892b31c987ad672b7/2018–03–14-koalitionsvertrag-data.pdf?download=1
83 'France and Germany Agree on Truce over Nuclear Arms Control Committee as NATO Works on Deterrence and Defense Posture Review', *Arms Control Now*, 3 October 2011, www.armscontrol.org/blog/2011–10–03/france-germany-agree-truce-over-nuclear-arms-control-committee-nato-works-deterrence; and 'NATO Deterrence and Defence Posture Review, 20 May 2012', www.nato.int/cps/en/natohq/official_texts_87597.htm
84 Die Bundesregierung, *Weissbuch zur Sicherheitspolitik und zur Zukunft der Bundeswehr: 2016*, www.bmvg.de/resource/blob/13708/015be272f8c0098f1537a491676bfc31/weissbuch2016-barrierefrei-data.pdf
85 H. Haftendorn, *NATO and the Nuclear Revolution: A Crisis of Credibility, 1966–67* (Oxford: Oxford University Press, 1996). 45.
86 Haftendorn, *NATO and the Nuclear Revolution*, 46–59.
87 Tuschhoff, *Deutschland, Kernwaffen und die NATO*, 157.
88 Quoted in Haftendorn, *NATO and the Nuclear Revolution*, 49.
89 Tuschhoff, *Deutschland, Kernwaffen und die NATO*, 239–240.
90 Daalder, *The Nature and Practice of Flexible Response*, 63–66.
91 M. Ruhle, 'NATO and Extended Deterrence in a Multinuclear World', *Comparative Strategy*, 28:1 (2009), 14.
92 Interview with German Ministry of Foreign Affairs official, Berlin, 20 July 2015.
93 Department of State, 'Memorandum of Conversation: Problems of the NATO Alliance, Washington DC, October 16, 1963', in *Foreign Relations of the United States, 1961–1963, Western Europe and Canada*, Vol. 13, https://history.state.gov/historicaldocuments/frus1961–63v13/d215
94 K. Spohr Readman, 'Germany and the Politics of the Neutron Bomb', *Diplomacy and Statecraft*, 21:2 (2010), 277.
95 Spohr Readman, 'Conflict and Cooperation in Intra-Alliance Nuclear Politics', 74–86.
96 P. Ahonen, 'Franz Joseph Strauss and the German Nuclear Question, 1956–1962', *Journal of Strategic Studies*, 18:2 (1995), 32–33.
97 M. Hampton, 'NATO at the Creation: US Foreign Policy, West Germany and the Wilsonian Impulse', *Security Studies*, 4:3 (1995), 627–651.
98 Tuschhoff, *Deutschland, Kernwaffen und die NATO*, 178–188.
99 Steinbruner, *The Cybernetic Theory of Decision*, 301–304.

100 Tuschhoff, *Deutschland, Kernwaffen und die NATO*, 299–307.
101 Freedman and Michaels, *The Evolution of Nuclear Strategy*, 292.
102 Gerzhoy, 'Alliance Coercion and Nuclear Restraint', 113.
103 Secretary of Defense J. Schlesinger, *The Theater Nuclear Force Posture in Europe: A Report to the United States Congress in Compliance with Public Law* 93–365 (1 April 1975), 3.
104 Larsen, *The Future of US Non-strategic Nuclear Weapons*, 21–22.
105 D. Yost, 'Assurance and US Extended Deterrence in NATO', *International Affairs*, 85:4 (2009), 773.
106 Yost, 'The US Debate on NATO and Nuclear Deterrence', 1416.
107 See H. Bacia, 'Atomwaffenfrei', *Frankfurter Allgemeine*, 6 May 2010, www.faz.net/aktuell/politik/abruestung-atomwaffenfrei-1979108.html
108 Daalder, *The Nature and Practice of Flexible Response*, chapter 2.
109 B. Heuser, 'The Development of NATO's Nuclear Strategy', *Contemporary European History*, 4:1 (1994), 43–44.
110 Quoted in McArdle Kelleher, *Germany and the Politics of Nuclear Weapons*, 282.
111 Department of State, 'Paper Prepared by the National Security Staff, no date', in *Foreign Relations of the United States, 1969–1976*, Vol. 41: *Western Europe; NATO, 1969–1972*, https://history.state.gov/historicaldocuments/frus1969–76v41/d52
112 Department of State, 'Minutes of a National Security Council Meeting, Washington DC, October 14, 1970', in *Foreign Relations of the United States, 1969–1976*, Vol. 41: *Western Europe; NATO, 1969–1972*, https://history.state.gov/historicaldocuments/frus1969–76v41/d49
113 On US–German tensions over the ERW decision, see Spohr Readman, 'Germany and the Politics of the Neutron Bomb', 272–276.
114 Quoted in Daalder, *The Nature and Practice of Flexible Response*, 20.
115 Daalder, *The Nature and Practice of Flexible Response*, 87.
116 Heuser and Stoddart, 'Difficult Europeans', 468–469.
117 'NATO's Nuclear Forces in the New Security Environment', *NATO/OTAN Handbook* (Brussels: NATO Office of Information and Press, Brussels, 2001), 29.
118 Smith, 'To Neither Use Them Nor Lose Them', 536.
119 Quoted in Muller, 'Flexible Responses', 111.
120 Heuser, 'The Development of NATO's Nuclear Strategy', 65.
121 Schwartz, *NATO's Nuclear Dilemmas*, 71–75.
122 R. Burt, 'Neutron Bomb Controversy Strained Alliance and Caused Splits in the Administration', *New York Times*, 9 April 1978, https://www.nytimes.com/1978/04/09/archives/neutron-bomb-controversy-strained-alliance-and-caused-splits-in-the.html.
123 See N. Petersen, 'Footnoting' as a Political Instrument: Denmark's NATO Policy in the 1980s', *Cold War History*, 12:2 (2012), 295–317.
124 R. Bell, 'The Challenges of NATO Nuclear Policy', Working Paper 105 (Helsinki: Finnish Institute of International Affairs, 2018), 8.

125 B. Gwertzman, 'Shultz Ends US Vow to Defend New Zealand', *New York Times*, 28 June 1986, https://www.nytimes.com/1986/06/28/world/shultz-ends-us-vow-to-defend-new-zealand.html.
126 M. Petersson and H. Lunde Saxi, 'Shifted Roles: Explaining Danish and Norwegian Alliance Strategies', *Journal of Strategic Studies*, 36:6 (2013), 767–768.
127 S. Schrafstetter, 'The Long Shadow of the Past: History, Memory and Debate Over West Germany's Nuclear Status, 1954–69', *History and Memory*, 16:1 (2004), 122.
128 A. Lutsch, 'Merely 'Docile Self-Deception'? German Experiences with Nuclear Consultation in NATO', *Journal of Strategic Studies*, 39:4 (2016), 542.
129 Legge, 'Theater Nuclear Weapons and the NATO Strategy of Flexible Response', 24–25.
130 S. Schmemann, 'Kohl Sets Stage for NATO Fight by Laying Out New Arms Policy', *New York Times*, 28 April 1989.
131 Tuschhoff, *Deutschland, Kernwaffen und die NATO*, 75–77.
132 Tuschhoff, *Deutschland, Kernwaffen und die NATO*, 191.
133 Department of State, 'Letter from Johnson to Wilson, 23 December 1965', in *Foreign Relations of the United States, 1964–1968*, Vol. 13: *Western Europe Region*, https://history.state.gov/historicaldocuments/frus1964–68v13/d121
134 Sayle, *Enduring Alliance*, 110.
135 Spohr, K. *The Global Chancellor: Helmut Schmidt and the Reshaping of the International Order* (Oxford: Oxford University Press, 2016), 34–36.
136 R. McCalla, 'NATO's Persistence After the Cold War', *International Organization,* 50:3 (1996), 445–475.
137 S. Walt, 'Why Alliances Endure or Collapse', *Survival*, 39:1 (1997), 156–179.
138 Tuschhoff, 'Alliance Cohesion and Peaceful Change in NATO', 153.
139 Tuschhoff, *Deutschland, Kernwaffen und die NATO*, 162–163.
140 Tuschhoff, *Deutschland, Kernwaffen und die NATO,* 158–159.
141 Tuschhoff, *Deutschland, Kernwaffen und die NATO,* 160–161.
142 R. Dietl, 'In Defence of the West: General Lauris Norstad, NATO Nuclear Forces and Transatlantic Relations: 1956–1963', *Diplomacy and Statecraft*, 17:2 (2006), 369–370.
143 Department of State, 'Circular Telegram from the Department of State to Certain Missions, Washington DC, 9 May 1962', in *Foreign Relations of the United States, 1961–1963*, Vol. 13: *Western Europe and Canada*, https://history.state.gov/historicaldocuments/frus1961–63v13/d137
144 R. McNamara, 'Speech to NATO Council, Athens, 5 May 1962', in P. Bobbit, L. Freedman, and G. Treverton (eds), *US Nuclear Strategy: A Reader* (Houndmills: Macmillan Press, 1989), 220.
145 See McArdle Kelleher, *Germany and the Politics of Nuclear Weapons*, chapter 9.
146 B. Weinraub, 'NATO Voices Concern Over Plans to Limit Cruise Missile Range', *New York Times*, 13 October 1977, www.nytimes.com/1977/10/13/archives/nato-voices-concern-over-plans-to-limit-cruise-missile-range.html
147 Schwartz, *NATO's Nuclear Dilemmas*, 211–212.

148 Z. Brzezinski, *Power and Principle: Memoirs of the National Security Adviser, 1977–1981* (London: George Weidenfeld and Nicholson, 1983), 307–310.
149 Daalder, *The Nature and Practice of Flexible Response*, 176.
150 Larsen, *The Future of US Non-strategic Nuclear Weapons*, 29.
151 Interviews, Brussels, 23–25 September 2019.
152 Pedlow, 'The Evolution of NATO Strategy', xxiii.

3

Local accommodation: Norway and nuclear weapons cooperation in NATO

Norway was a founding member of NATO and has hosted a number of key US intelligence facilities that contribute directly to the US global nuclear intelligence network. During the Cold War, Oslo also agreed to stationing several facilities on Norwegian territory that could support US nuclear operations in the event of war. Yet, Norwegian decision makers have consistently imposed key conditions on nuclear cooperation with the US and NATO. As Norway's 2017 foreign and security policy White Paper noted: 'As a NATO member, Norway is part of the Alliance's nuclear weapons policy. However, Norway has made it clear that nuclear weapons are not to be stationed on Norwegian territory in peacetime. This policy has helped to reduce conflict and ease tensions.'[1] These conditions have existed in large part because of domestic sensitivities, and a desire to maintain a regional geopolitical balance in Scandinavia with the Soviet Union. In this chapter, we trace nuclear weapons cooperation in the US–Norwegian relationship in the context of the broader NATO alliance. As Lindgren and Graeger note, 'having a close bilateral relationship with the United States was widely recognised in Norway as providing extra reassurance of the guarantee under NATO's Article 5'.[2] The chapter shows that, despite its close institutional integration in NATO overall, Norway has generally been successful in realising its policy preferences with respect to the local particularities that Oslo sought for nuclear cooperation on Norwegian territory and its waters.

Norway, the US, and NATO

Despite obvious differences of size, the journeys of Norway and the US to the NATO alliance have many parallels. In both countries, support for isolationism was deeply embedded in society. At the same time, the US and Norway considered themselves part of the North Atlantic community, with Norway's merchant navy being one of the country's main strategic assets in both world wars. War was forced on both countries by unprovoked surprise attacks by Axis powers, which led them to work in a close coalition with the UK. After 1945, a new generation of Norwegian political leaders assumed responsibility for the country, many of whom had been members of the resistance and interned in Nazi concentration camps. Through signing the Washington Treaty to establish NATO, these political leaders attempted to define a new basis for Norwegian security that accounted for the country's wartime experience of vulnerability to aggression, its values, its experience of the Atlantic wartime coalition, and its investment in a system of international law with the UN as the basis for global security.[3] Norway has been a staunch supporter of NATO's Atlantic orientation on a foundation of democratic values, and of US political and strategic leadership in NATO.

In the words of leading defence analyst and government minister Johan Jørgen Holst, Norway joined the NATO alliance to obtain 'drawing rights on countervailing military power to the regional preponderance of the Soviet Union'.[4] In the 'small détente' between Stalin's death in 1953 and the Hungarian uprising in 1956, Norway remained more focused on the Soviet military build-up than other Nordic countries, and Oslo was more sceptical of the argument that a fundamental change was occurring in East–West confrontation.[5] In the 1980s, Norway's foreign policy aligned with those of social democratic parties in Europe in debates about the Reagan administration's Strategic Defense Initiative (SDI), nuclear weapons modernisation, and the proposal for a Nordic nuclear-weapons-free zone. Nonetheless, its focus on the external threat from the Soviet Union meant that Norway was perceived as a 'loyal ally', especially in comparison with Denmark's more unpredictable stance in NATO.[6] However, support for US leadership did not equate with unconditional Norwegian support for US policies. As an unnamed Norwegian politician told the US ambassador to Oslo in 1960: 'We desperately want American leadership, we do not want to be told what to do, but we want the United States to follow policies we can support.'[7] In particular, Norway placed consistently greater emphasis on détente before this became central to US policy, and sought to lessen NATO's reliance on nuclear weapons well before the US turned to flexible response in the 1960s.

Yet, Norway was also keenly alert to how its NATO membership would be perceived in Moscow. Oslo saw its own security as part of a broader Nordic area that included fellow NATO members Iceland and Denmark, neutral (but West-leaning) Sweden, as well as Finland, which was bound to the Soviet Union through the 1948 Agreement on Friendship, Cooperation and Mutual Assistance.[8] Norway, however, chose to turn down Sweden's 1948 proposal for a formal Scandinavian alliance in favour of signing the Washington Treaty.[9] Oslo had to perform a delicate balancing act between its participation in NATO's common defence, while avoiding moves that might lead to Soviet pressures on Sweden and Finland. Commonly described in terms of 'deterrence and reassurance', or 'integration and screening', this meant that Oslo often sought to impose caveats on NATO policies and defence preparations in relation to Norwegian participation, even if it supported them for NATO as a whole.[10]

Central to this screening was the so-called 'no-bases' policy, which arose from an exchange of notes with Moscow in the lead-up to the signature of the North Atlantic Treaty. In these notes, Oslo stated that 'the Norwegian government will not enter in any agreement with other States involving obligations to open bases for the military forces of foreign powers on Norwegian territory as long as Norway is not attacked or exposed to threats of attack'.[11] At the time, Norway assessed that the Soviet Union may well have reacted to the establishment of allied bases by forcing its own bases on Finland, which would have significantly complicated Sweden's defence.[12]

Throughout the Cold War, the Soviet Union used the no-bases policy to exert political pressure on Norway by interpreting it as a binding guarantee at odds with whatever further integration into NATO that Norway was contemplating at the time.[13] Political fine-tuning of the allied presence on Norwegian territory became a constant theme of Norway's membership in NATO. For example, Norway would not permit NATO forces to exercise in Finnmark, its northernmost territory, and restricted allied vessels and aircraft operating from its territory, airspace, and territorial waters if they were east of 24 degrees of longitude east.[14] Norway's inclusion in the US Air Force Co-located Operating Bases Program, and the pre-positioning of US and NATO equipment and supplies, required Norwegian policymakers to weigh operational and political considerations in light of the no-bases policy.[15]

The policy did not mean a wholesale rejection of any allied presence. Norway permitted the pre-positioning of allied equipment; the preparation of facilities, in particular airbases, to receive allied reinforcements; and the presence of NATO Headquarters with permanent international staff. In addition, Oslo encouraged allied participation in exercises on Norwegian territory as 'a symbolic expression of the allied commitment to the northern flank',[16] as well as for the benefits of inter-operability and deterrence. The US–Norwegian Mutual Defense Assistance Program also had the effect of promoting closer links between the two countries' armed forces.[17]

Although Norway's own defence effort could seek to delay a Soviet invasion, defence of the country (and ultimately deterrence of attack) rested on reinforcement by allied forces. Gaining political commitment from NATO allies for reinforcement, translating these commitments into force allocations, and giving credence to these allocations through regular exercises and pre-positioning of equipment, would be enduring Norwegian concerns throughout the Cold War.[18] In the early 1950s, Norway first sought to ensure US and UK membership in the Northern European Regional Planning Group to bind these two countries to the defence of NATO's northern flank. It achieved this objective when a UK Admiral became commander of the new Allied Forces Northern Europe (AFNORTH) command in Kolsås near Oslo in 1952, with air operations under the command of a US flag officer.[19]

While NATO allies recognised the importance of Norway as an anchor of the northern flank of the alliance, it was, nonetheless, ultimately a flank of lesser priority for resources than NATO's Central Front. The willingness of allies to commit to reinforcements, the decisions on when and where they would be sent, and with what objectives, remained governed first and foremost by the views of Norway's allies on its relative importance to the Central Front. Seen in this context, allied interest in southern Norway, northern Norway and the Norwegian Sea were influenced by different considerations.

Finnmark was one of the theatres where NATO always had to contemplate 'limited' conflict and what might be a feasible response for an alliance whose priority was the prospect of general war on the Central Front. In a general war, the Soviet Union might try to occupy Finnmark as part of its defence of the Kola 'bastion'. For Norway and NATO, however, the significance of Finnmark was not primarily of a military nature, and as a consequence the area received little attention from AFNORTH until the early 1960s.[20] In 1961, NATO created the Allied Mobile Force (AMF) as a quick-reaction capability to manage crises on NATO's flank areas, including northern Norway. As a 'politico-military symbol of alliance solidarity',[21] rather than a force sufficient to provide credible defence, the AMF was nonetheless one of the first meaningful preparations by NATO for crises outside the Central Front area. The formal adoption of NATO's new strategic concept of flexible response in 1967 coincided with a significant increase in attention on the flank areas, which manifested itself in the creation of the Standing Naval Forces Atlantic in 1968 under the command of NATO's second strategic commander, Supreme Allied Commander Atlantic (SACLANT).[22]

While Norway's territory and coastal waters fell under the responsibility of SACEUR, the North Atlantic (through which any reinforcements would have had to flow) and all naval, naval air, and amphibious forces that could support the defence of northern Norway, were commanded by SACLANT. Although this division created some operational complications,[23] it meant that Norway had in SACLANT a strategic commander who was more focused on the High North than SACEUR, and who also had command of powerful carrier forces that could provide significant direct support. From a SACLANT perspective, NATO control of northern Norway mattered insofar as it provided access to air and naval bases that could support allied maritime operations in the Norwegian and Barents Sea. Early interest in such operations was related to the use of carriers as nuclear strike platforms during the 1950s. In the late 1960s, the build-up of Soviet naval forces, including subsurface ballistic nuclear (SSBN) submarines and air and naval forces that could threaten NATO supply lines over the North Atlantic, led to an increasing focus on NATO's maritime strategy in the Atlantic.[24] By the late 1970s, operations against the 'Kola bastion' had become central to the US debates on its naval strategy and force structure, which Norway influenced through the 'US–Norwegian Study Group' on strategic, operational, and technical aspects of operations in the High North.[25] US interest in the High North culminated with the adoption of the US Maritime Strategy under the Reagan administration, which included aggressive forward operations by US attack submarines and carrier battlegroups.[26]

The end of the Cold War witnessed the beginning of a gradual transition in Norway's strategic policy. The demise of the Soviet Union led to a reassessment of the country's threat environment, with Oslo looking to develop closer relations with Moscow and former Warsaw Pact states during the 1990s. At the same time, Oslo was keen to hedge against the resurgence of a Russian threat. As Petersson and Saxi note, 'the Kola Peninsula was still highly militarized, Russian democracy was seen as unstable, and Norway still had territorial disputes with its eastern neighbor'.[27] As a consequence, Norway was keen to maintain allied interest in the High North. Hence, it continued to support pre-positioning of US military equipment on its territory, and established NATO's Joint Warfare Centre in Stavanger despite major cuts to defence military spending in the 1990s and early 2000s.[28]

Norway's concern over Russia accelerated following the latter's invasion of Georgia in 2008, which was accompanied by a major spike in Russian bomber patrols near Norway's borders. This, in conjunction with cyber attacks against Estonia, crystallised a view within the Norwegian Ministry of Defence that 'Russia was back'.[29] Oslo's response was to deepen its military cooperation with the US, lobby other NATO members (with mixed success) to reference Arctic security in the alliance's summit documents,[30] and increase the prominence of collective defence in the 2010 Strategic Concept. Norway had accelerated the transition of its military organisation away from exclusive homeland defence towards a greater capacity to undertake out-of-area NATO expeditionary operations after 9/11.[31] At the same time, however, it continued to work with the US on constructing new-generation surveillance and intelligence facilities in Norway's Arctic region to monitor Russian submarine traffic in the Barents Sea and ballistic missile developments on the Kola Peninsula.[32] Following Russia's invasion of Ukraine in 2014, Washington and Oslo agreed in 2016 to establish a rotational deployment of US marines in Norway: a clear sign of the continued centrality of the US to Norway's security, and a step that went beyond the traditional interpretations of the no-bases policy of the Cold War.[33]

Norway and nuclear weapons in the alliance

Norway developed a substantial capability in nuclear technology in the early atomic age, leveraging its status as an internationally significant producer of heavy water. A large investment of military funds was made in order to develop a Norwegian reactor in the 1940s, even though it was recognised at the time that a bomb programme would be beyond the country's means. Moreover, the argument that a Norwegian bomb might, in fact, increase the risk of attack, and that seeking an alliance with the US would be a wiser choice, was aired in reports by the defence research establishment to the country's Defence Commission as early as 1946. Throughout the 1950s, Norway's own nuclear programme waned as it struggled to find a commercially viable path forward.[34]

By signing the North Atlantic Treaty, Norway firmly based its security on the general deterrent of US conventional and nuclear forces. However, the relevance of nuclear weapons for the direct defence of Norway only emerged over time. In the late 1940s, nuclear weapons had little relevance for the defence of NATO territory, and even by 1954, SHAPE did not expect the Soviet Union to allocate nuclear weapons to an attack on Norway before mid-1957.[35] Simply because of its position astride the geostrategically significant 'great circles' from North America to the Soviet Union, however, Norway assumed an early direct relevance for US strategic nuclear forces.

In the late 1940s and early 1950s, the US Air Force explored the potential for both offensive operations and intelligence gathering, as well as early warning, that Norway's location offered in relation to critical targets in the Soviet Union.[36] At the time, Soviet bases and infrastructure in the Arctic were of particular concern for the US, which saw them as key launch areas for attacks against the North American continent.[37]

The first formal arrangement for receiving allied forces in Norway dates to 1952, when two Norwegian airbases were made available to the SAC in case of war.[38] Two years later, Norway agreed to host US Globecom communication facilities, including one in Bodø that provided a US presence in northern Norway and which also housed a key airbase for intelligence operations (including U2 flights) against the Soviet Union.[39]

With the advent of longer-range aircraft, the importance of Norwegian bases for extending the range of US strategic bombers declined, though they remained relevant for post-strike operations, emergency recoveries, and reconnaissance.[40] However, Norway's broader role and relevance for US strategic nuclear capabilities endured. In 1954, Norway and the US signed the NORUSA Pact that established a detailed and wide-ranging signals intelligence relationship, providing a critical window for US intelligence agencies into the Soviet Union.[41] Norway was close to the Soviet nuclear and missile test area at Novaya Zemlya, and also to the Soviet SSBN bases of the Northern Fleet. Both became the targets of intelligence cooperation between Norway, the US, and the UK in monitoring Soviet nuclear and missile tests, as well as the activity of Soviet strategic nuclear forces.[42] A rapidly improvised surveillance effort of the large Soviet nuclear test series in 1961 led to an agreement on longer-term cooperation in this field. At the same time, Norway and the US began emplacing hydrophone cables to detect Soviet SSBNs on their way from northern bases to the North Atlantic.[43] Although all these activities were of limited immediate value to the defence of Norway, they did make a contribution to the US strategic nuclear deterrent and increased the importance of Norway's northern territories to the US – a value demonstrated by the fact that Washington covered the cost of all materiel and roughly half of Norway's staffing costs for these intelligence installations.[44]

With the decision to introduce tactical nuclear forces into NATO in 1954, Norway had to formulate a national position on the role of nuclear weapons in its own immediate defence, and in NATO strategy more broadly. On the one hand, the introduction of tactical nuclear weapons, and the admission of West Germany to NATO, made the defence of south Norway far more feasible than it had been before.[45] From 1955, large parts of the Norwegian military establishment acknowledged that Soviet nuclear capabilities were expanding faster than expected, and military authorities were in favour of nuclear arms for Norway's defence.[46] On the other hand, there was also growing public ambivalence regarding nuclear weapons, fuelled by political support for neutrality, and moral and existential concerns about the effects of nuclear weapons.[47] In the second half of the 1950s, Norwegian territory began to be significantly affected by fallout from Soviet atmospheric nuclear weapons tests,[48] and Norway became an active proponent of nuclear test limitations and non-proliferation.

Once confronted with the question of whether to allow nuclear weapons on Norwegian territory, Oslo developed a policy based on its rejection of the permanent allied presence that would have accompanied such warheads. In 1957, Prime Minister Gerhardsen communicated to the Soviet Union that the stationing of US troops on Norwegian soil to supervise nuclear ammunition would not be permitted under the no-bases principle.[49] Norway had thus formulated a principle on nuclear weapons that was in line with the no-bases policy, but at odds with the proposals for nuclear sharing that were agreed at the 1957 NATO summit. Yet, at the same time, Oslo had not rejected the use or deployment of nuclear weapons outright. Norway's security depended on allied reinforcements, and insofar as these forces would rely on, and be equipped with, nuclear weapons, this was accepted. Moreover, the government did not reject the option that Norwegian forces might use nuclear charges provided by NATO in a conflict, not least because it feared that rejection would lead to a loss of political influence in NATO. What was not accepted was the peacetime pre-positioning of nuclear weapons (and their allied guards) on Norwegian territory.[50]

For Norway, the North Atlantic Council (NAC) was an important forum to make the case for its nuclear policy to the Alliance as a whole. Allied political opposition towards Norway's nuclear policy peaked with the Alliance's Ministerial Meeting in December 1959.[51] Norway mounted a major political effort to make its case, centred on a broadly based strategy paper on its nuclear policy. Delivered to the NAC in April 1960, it emphasised the assessments underlying the Norwegian base policy, Norway's status as a country bordering the Soviet Union, and consideration of national political character, including broad neutralist sentiments.[52]

Until NATO embraced flexible response in 1967, Norway's conditional position on nuclear weapons integration remained under challenge from a range of quarters. Both Finland and Sweden proposed plans for nuclear-weapon-free zones, which were incompatible with Norway receiving nuclear support from allied forces in wartime.[53] At the same time, although Norway's position was generally met with understanding at the highest political levels in Washington and London, Norwegian policy was also challenged by other elements of the US government and by some senior NATO officials.[54] The US embassy in Norway, through confidential briefings, and the commanders of NATO's AFNORTH, tried to convince Norway to change its nuclear policy by stressing NATO's inability to defend northern Norway.[55] The multi-year force requirements set down by NATO in MC70 in 1958 became a focal point for these discussions, as they were based on the assumption of nuclear weapons integration into all of NATO's 'shield' forces. It called for Norwegian forces to be equipped with nuclear warheads for its air defence, including Nike missiles, Honest John short-range missiles, and one fighter-bomber squadron. In addition, NATO proposed to store atomic ammunition in Norway in peacetime.[56]

In principle, Oslo continued to maintain the option of introducing nuclear weapons to the Norwegian armed forces,[57] suggesting in classified settings that it 'had accepted these weapons with their eyes open and that they would take the nuclear hurdle when they came to it, but till then silence was golden!'[58] Oslo agreed in 1959–61 to the construction of NATO-funded, nuclear-capable ammunitions facilities at several air and missile bases across the country. Built for peacetime use and thus not systematically linked to wartime plans, the construction of nuclear storage facilities was nonetheless supported by Norway to give more credibility to the option of receiving allied nuclear-armed reinforcements and for the significant NATO investment in Norway's base infrastructure they provided.[59]

Oslo also agreed to regular NATO exercises in Norway that included planning and practice for the use of nuclear weapons in and from Norway.[60] SNOWCAT (support of nuclear operations with conventional attacks) missions from Norway against targets ranging from East Germany to the Russian Arctic were a major focus for the Norwegian Air Force in the 1950s and 1960s. Governments in Norway were concerned about the impact these operations would have on Norway's ability to defend its own airspace, but never objected to such preparations.[61] From 1970, however, AFNORTH began to prioritise the defence of Norwegian territory in its air tasks, and Norway acquired aircraft that reflected the new emphasis on defensive counter-air missions.[62]

By that time, the prospect of introducing nuclear weapons into Norway's armed forces in crisis and war, although never formally ruled out, had become infeasible from a practical point of view. Aside from storage, Norway had rejected any practical preparation of its Nike missiles and aircraft, including training of personnel, to handle nuclear weapons. It also never concluded a PoC agreement with the US.[63] Given the lack of trained personnel in Norway, insufficient allied personnel to assist at short notice, and the lack of a legal agreement, SACEUR concluded in 1963 that plans for the transfer of nuclear warheads to Norwegian forces could not be developed.[64]

Although the military consequences of Norway's no-nuclear and no-bases policies had therefore largely been settled by the late 1960s, nuclear weapons remained an important factor in political and foreign policy debates. Opposition to NATO's 1979 double-track decision by centre-left parties throughout Europe was mirrored in Norway. While the government supported the double-track decision, there was also rising interest in the idea of a Nordic nuclear-free zone.[65] In the end, however, the collapse of the Soviet Union came earlier than any fundamental change in Norway's Cold War nuclear weapons policy that might have occurred.

During the 1990s, Norway welcomed the reduction of the role of nuclear weapons in NATO strategy, while reaffirming its long-established 'screening' policy.[66] Over time, underlying support in Norway for nuclear disarmament, which had been kept in check by Norwegian policymakers during the Cold War, began to be reflected in policy. This reached a high point between 2005 and 2013 when Norway was governed by a centre-left coalition that underscored the country's active support for nuclear disarmament and devoted growing diplomatic resources to that effort.[67] In 2008, the Norwegian government co-sponsored a conference in Oslo on nuclear disarmament that was followed by a series of speeches by government ministers canvassing the idea of banning nuclear weapons.[68] At the 2010 NATO Summit, Norway (along with the Benelux states) supported Germany's campaign to insert in NATO's Strategic Concept a commitment 'to create the conditions for a world without nuclear weapons'.[69] Invoking the spirit of President Obama's 2009 Prague speech, these same states had earlier called for the removal of all US nuclear weapons from Europe.[70] The US, supported by France, the UK, Turkey, as well as newer NATO members in eastern and central Europe, successfully insisted on the inclusion of a statement in the summit communiqué that NATO was a 'nuclear alliance'.[71]

There is some evidence that Norway's proactive approach to nuclear disarmament caused friction with the Washington under the Obama administration. As calls for a global nuclear ban treaty gathered pace in 2015, Norway's centre-left government strongly associated itself with the initiative, which resulted in a formal démarche from Washington and reportedly drew a blunt warning from the US embassy in Oslo that advocacy of a ban 'conflicted with Norway's membership in NATO'.[72] However, these tensions largely evaporated with the demise of the centre-left government in 2015 and increasing anxiety among Norwegian policymakers about Russian aggression in the wake of the annexation of Crimea the previous year. Moscow's decision to issue thinly veiled nuclear threats against Norway in 2016 and 2018 in response to an agreement with Washington to station (and subsequently double) a contingent of US marines on Norwegian territory underscored the importance of the nuclear umbrella in the wider NATO context.[73] Significantly, it also led to a decline in Norwegian enthusiasm for a global nuclear ban treaty, and in late 2019 Norway announced that it would not sign or ratify the Treaty on the Prohibition of Nuclear Weapons.[74]

Tracing nuclear weapons cooperation

Threat assessment and prioritisation

Throughout the Cold War, Norwegian and US assessments of Soviet capabilities that could threaten Norway broadly coincided, not least because both countries maintained close cooperation in intelligence assessments of Soviet forces in the High North. US interest was driven mainly by the strategic air and naval forces that could threaten the continental US and Atlantic sea lines. Whereas US attention waxed and waned over the Cold War in alignment with global and regional strategic concerns, Norway's concern with Soviet forces in its neighbourhood was more enduring.

Norway was thus focused on the particular challenge of limited war far earlier than NATO as a whole, and hence more concerned about relying on the strategy of massive retaliation in the 1950s. For the US, the challenge of limited war in the 1950s and 1960s was mainly one of strategy and force structure in local areas of superpower confrontation, such as Berlin and Quemoy and Matsu, or in peripheral theatres such as Vietnam. For Norway, limited war presented foremost a political challenge of alliance unity, in case of an attack on a NATO member below the threshold of global war. In this context, Johan Jørgen Holst has argued that a defence posture predicated on forward-based, shared nuclear weapons in Norway would have raised the risks of escalation of a limited conflict in the north that may have devalued the credibility of allied guarantees to the country.[75]

Moreover, Norway was also focused more than the US on consequences for its security from threats to the 'Nordic balance' short of major war. Norway was conscious throughout the Cold War that it had never been at war with Russia, and that successful cooperation with Moscow continue on economic and environmental issues in its common border areas, including the sensitive Svalbard archipelago.[76] Overall, Norwegian concerns about the Soviet Union arose mainly from strategic pressures in the wider area of Scandinavia. In this context, Norway was conscious that its own defence benefited greatly from Sweden's continued ability to defend itself, which in turn benefited from the absence of Soviet bases in Finland.[77]

Although NATO officials acknowledged the logic of Norway's arguments, they did not always share Norway's conclusions. The British commander of AFNORTH, for example, informed US officials in the 1950s that he had advised the Norwegians that their need for nuclear munitions outweighed the risk of the Soviet Union establishing bases in Finland.[78] At the political level, however, Washington acknowledged the particular regional context of Scandinavia, and was mostly concerned that Norway's reassurance policy towards Russia did not undermine the unity of the alliance as a whole. In April 1960, for example, the US NSC endorsed a 'Statement of U.S. Policy Toward Scandinavia' that concluded the US should 'stress the danger to Scandinavian and Free World security of unilaterally neutralizing or demilitarizing Scandinavia', while at the same time 'encourage cooperation among the Scandinavian and Nordic countries ... particularly in assisting Finland to oppose Soviet pressure and maintain its Western ties'.[79] Despite public rebukes in the 1950s and early 1960s, Washington did not press its objections to Nordic reassurance policies towards the USSR. In the words of Dov Zakheim, while the US was 'not thrilled with the limitations that Nordic reassurance policies placed upon NATO flexibility in the North ... it did not dwell upon them, not only because of the degree of covert cooperation that was taking place, but also because of the benefits flowing from the keenness of the NATO Nordic allies to preserve the delicate *status quo*'.[80]

After the Cold War, notwithstanding its increasingly outspoken views on nuclear disarmament, Norway remained strongly committed to NATO and the bilateral security relationship with the US. As was the case with previous Norwegian governments, centre-left governments believed they could simultaneously pursue a lower profile for nuclear weapons globally and within NATO while retaining NATO as a strong hedge against Russian aggression. Although the US expressed its displeasure with Norway's growing sympathy for a global ban treaty and Oslo's indication of support for removing US nuclear weapons from Europe, Washington's assessment of the threat environment in northern Europe converged with Norway's most of the time, and this convergence strengthened significantly following Russia's annexation of Crimea in 2014.

Policy objectives regarding nuclear weapons cooperation

Norway never showed serious interest in acquiring nuclear weapons of its own, so non-proliferation was not a significant factor in US nuclear policy towards its ally.[81] To the contrary; in line with Norway's preference for US leadership in the Atlantic alliance, Oslo preferred that Washington remain central to any decision on nuclear weapons use by NATO. Oslo began to argue against the proliferation of nuclear weapons within NATO from mid-1956, highlighting the importance of political control of nuclear use by the alliance, and the ultimate responsibility of the US President.[82] In 1962, in the midst of the NATO deliberations on the MLF, Norway declared it had no intention to acquire nationally controlled warheads.[83] Indeed, Norway saw no plausible military rationale for the MLF, with Prime Minister Gerhardsen stating publicly that 'no nuclear forces belonging to NATO or allied powers [will] get bases in Norway or in other ways be allowed to establish themselves in Norwegian territorial waters'.[84]

During the 1950s, however, the difference between the Norwegian local and the more NATO-wide US perspective led to disagreements between both allies on the role and value of nuclear weapons in the defence of Norway. In December 1959, the US Chairman of the Joint Chiefs of Staff stated the following at a NATO Military Committee meeting:

> Some NATO nations appear to feel that they are doing the United States a favour in making ... arrangements [to restrict adoption of atomic munitions].

> They desire security which can be provided only through atomic capable forces, but they want none of the responsibility for accommodating weapons, and in some cases strike forces, on their own soil. From a military viewpoint, our collective defences are obviously weakened by such governmental attitudes.[85]

In the end, the US did not press the issue to a point at which it might have caused a rift in relations. Although the US NSC identified Denmark's and Norway's base and nuclear weapons policy as a problem of 'special significance' in 1960, the main concern was that it would 'tend to limit modernization of Danish and Norwegian forces'.[86]

While Norway largely avoided entanglement of its own forces in NATO's nuclear posture, allied forces may well have used nuclear weapons in its defence, especially during the 1950s. By virtue of AFNORTH's location in Kolsås, Norwegian policymakers had direct access to senior US and UK alliance military commanders who they could engage on defence issues and who Oslo believed would become advocates for reinforcing Norway in wartime.[87] This included the use of nuclear weapons on Norwegian territory, which Norway's Ministry of Defence had raised as early as 1953. In particular, Oslo wanted a right of veto to be included in SACEUR's central defence plan for Europe,[88] and probably achieved an informal consultation arrangement with Commander-in-Chief Northern Europe (CINCNORTH). Norway continued to bring up its request for veto rights, leading to a Standing Group decision in 1960 that if nuclear weapons were to be used on Norwegian territory, SACEUR would communicate directly with CINCNORTH, who would communicate with Norwegian authorities 'to the maximum practicable extent' and 'as fully as practical'.[89] This effectively confirmed the earlier informal arrangements, and Norway seems not to have pressed the issue any further. Although West German authorities believed in 1961 that Norway had achieved a special direct agreement with SACEUR, there is no evidence of the existence of such an arrangement.[90] However, Norway deliberately curtailed international officers from serving in peacetime in Defence Commands North and South Norway, which remained national commands despite their commanders being dual-hatted as NATO principal subordinate commanders. In the latter role, they could have requested the release of nuclear weapons in support of the defence of Norway itself, and developed the force requirements that were the basis of NATO's defence planning process.[91]

Hence, while Norway did seek institutional mechanisms in NATO's nuclear planning to influence the use of nuclear weapons on Norwegian territory, it could focus its attempts to do so on NATO's military commands in AFNORTH, rather than the more distant senior military and political forums in Washington and Paris. By the early 1960s, however, its need to use NATO institutions to defend its particular posture in the alliance diminished. US Secretary of Defense McNamara saw no need for Norway to operate nuclear warheads under his preferred interpretation of flexible response.[92] As NATO adopted the new concept and consultation guidelines, the spectre of nuclear weapons use in Norway over its objections receded. Notably, Norway was not keen to press for membership of the NPG until it was opened to all allies in 1979[93], and behind closed doors Norway (like Denmark) remained one of the least enthusiastic proponents of NATO's LRTNF deployment decision the same year.[94]

Nuclear strategy

Consistent with the way it framed its strategic objectives and prioritised integration across NATO, the US never formulated a nuclear strategy specific to the defence of Norway. Instead, US, NATO, and Norwegian military authorities approached the role of nuclear weapons in the defence of Norway as part of the broader NATO strategy for nuclear use. This NATO strategy, however, was always developed with the Central Front as the foremost consideration. Given Norway's aversion to nuclear forward basing and nuclear sharing, this meant that disagreements about nuclear strategy and the benefits of nuclear use by NATO were most prevalent in the late 1950s and early 1960s, when alliance policy on nuclear weapons was dominated by massive retaliation and the diffusion of nuclear weapons throughout NATO's 'shield' forces.

Norway never articulated a particular approach for the use of nuclear weapons in its own defence, but its preferences regarding NATO strategy exhibited similarities with the concept of flexible response. Both Norway and Denmark unsuccessfully argued for softening the strategy of massive retaliation in the early 1950s.[95] This was supported by Norway's senior military authorities who felt that NATO's strategy did not sufficiently address contingencies short of an all-out war.[96] In terms of Norway's immediate defence, receiving allied reinforcements was generally more important than the types of weapons systems these forces would employ. This was particularly so in the case of limited war in the High North, which would have tested the alliance in a political, as well as military, sense. Oslo thus supported the reduced reliance on nuclear weapons and stronger conventional defence proposed in NATO strategy debates throughout the late 1950s and 1960s, including the new strategic concept (MC14/3) of 1967.[97]

In that sense, the different preferences between Norway and the US about NATO nuclear strategy in the 1950s and 1960s coincided with their perception of the relative material consequences of both strategies; however, these consequences were as much a result of the allied focus on major war that was implied in preparations for large-scale nuclear use, than the use of such weapons itself. Hence, they diminished with the increased alliance focus on limited contingencies, conventional operations, and the Alliance's flanks under 'flexible response'.

If there was a particular Norwegian nuclear 'strategy', it related to the way Oslo could use the conditional nature of its no-bases policy to influence Soviet attempts to shift the Nordic balance in its favour. It relied on the idea that its 'screening' of NATO integration preserved latitude for Norwegian national policy that acceptance of US bases would arguably have denied.[98] The prime example of this was the Finnish Note Crisis of 1961 that followed the Soviet Union's request for consultations with Finland under the Treaty of Friendship, Cooperation, and Mutual Assistance. Moscow claimed that West Germany sought to re-establish German domination of Nordic Europe.[99] While the Finnish government sought to stall the talks, Norway warned the Soviet Union that continued pressure on Finland would cause it to review its prohibition on foreign bases and nuclear weapons. In a speech, Defence Minister Gudmund Harlem claimed that it was Stalin and Molotov who had 'scared' Norway into NATO, and that attempts 'to scare us out' would 'frighten us even further into NATO'. Harlem then made reference to Norway's nuclear policy, leaving the impression that this policy could be overturned.[100] Soon afterwards, Khrushchev met with the Finnish President and agreed to defuse the situation.[101] Norway's threat to re-examine its no-bases policy was seen as the primary reason for Khrushchev's change of heart, and Norwegian governments would point to this experience as evidence of the contribution that Norwegian restraint made to NATO's security.[102]

Domestic factors

There is no doubt that Norwegian policymakers were confronted with a domestic population more sceptical about the security value of nuclear weapons than many other NATO allies. Moreover, the question of NATO nuclear weapons became a focal point for those who continued to be sympathetic towards Norway's traditional neutralist policies. Domestic factors were therefore a major influence on Norway's nuclear policy, even as constraints on Norwegian policy from domestic opinion, and the preferences of the main policymakers at the time, were not always clearly different. Certainly, Norwegian politicians had an interest in emphasising the former; in 1952, then UN Secretary General and former Norwegian Foreign Minister Trygve Lie suggested to the US and British ambassadors that the Norwegian leadership 'understood clearly the need for foreign troops' but feared a split in the Labour Party and loss of political control over the issue.[103]

As early as 1949, when Norway joined the NATO alliance, the issue of nuclear weapons was a sensitive one for the government in Oslo, which sought to play down their role with the Norwegian public.[104] Norway and Denmark argued that strategic bombing should not be directly mentioned in NATO's 1949 Strategic Concept, as they feared domestic political opposition if the document became publicly available. As a result, the alliance agreed on semantic changes that did not alter the substance of the text.[105]

The US announcement in 1957 that it would supply NATO allies with short-range missiles, including with nuclear warheads, triggered significant domestic debate about the scope of Norway's alliance commitment and contribution. Prime Minister Gerhardsen, Security Policy Advisor Andreas Andersen, and Chairman of the Foreign Affairs Committee Finn Moe, were particularly critical of Norwegian nuclear armament and, to some extent, of NATO membership in general.[106] The Labour Party Convention decided in 1957 as part of its four-year programme that 'nuclear weapons should not be placed on Norwegian soil', which confirmed Norway's position well in advance of the NATO Summit in Paris in December the same year.[107] Following the summit, there were calls for a Norwegian veto in NATO against the stationing of nuclear weapons in West Germany. This was, however, rejected by the political leadership of the Labour Party. Norway's ambiguous stance regarding nuclear weapons remained under pressure and was the subject of a well-organised domestic nuclear disarmament campaign in the 1960s that accentuated major political divisions in the Labour Party.[108]

In later decades, nuclear weapons remained the foreign policy issue with the greatest potential to mobilise public opinion, and Norway's refusal to host nuclear weapons continued to attract strong support. In a 1979 survey by Norges Markedsdata, for example, 80 per cent of respondents stated that Norway should maintain its policy on nuclear weapons, and only 10 per cent thought it should allow the forward basing of nuclear weapons on Norwegian territory.[109] When Norway agreed to NATO's dual-track decision in 1979, more of the Norwegian public was opposed than in favour of the decision.[110]

Although such views did not create a crisis for the government in Oslo similar to that in Denmark at the time, the domestic debate on nuclear weapons nevertheless became far more challenging in Norway when the Conservative Party led a coalition government with the Labour Party. In the early 1980s, the idea of a Nordic nuclear-weapons-free zone enjoyed robust support within the left wing of the Labour Party. The government's support for the LRTNF decision was thus contentious, and the coalition had to agree to compromise language on the nuclear weapon free zone proposal.[111] However, the Labour Party leadership's support for such a radical step was always lukewarm and couched in relation to a broader European framework, which helped to defuse, if not entirely resolve, intra-party tensions by the mid-1980s.[112] While Norwegian government elites pointed to domestic opposition to nuclear weapons in support of the opt-outs the country claimed for itself under the no-bases policy, they did support the role of nuclear weapons in NATO overall, even in the face of domestic opposition.

Norwegian public opinion on defence issues showed little substantive change over time, and ultimately even the debates on nuclear weapon free zones and the NATO double-track decision of 1979 did not undermine public support for Norway's defence policy as a whole.[113] Domestic politics and public opinion in Norway have clearly reflected more sceptical views regarding nuclear weapons in terms of morality and strategic value than were evident in NATO policy as a whole. This was certainly apparent with the Norwegian government's enthusiastic endorsement between 2005 and 2013 of more ambitious nuclear disarmament measures, including support for a global ban treaty in the face of US opposition. Nonetheless, although a broad national consensus has held that nuclear weapons are a necessary evil from which Norway should disassociate itself where possible, a view has ultimately prevailed that this should not come at the expense of undermining the essential security benefits that Norway derives from NATO membership.[114]

The importance of Norway for US security

In a hard-power sense, Norway's military has never substantially contributed to NATO force structure as a whole. Defence expenditure between 2.5 and 3 per cent of GDP during the Cold War was insufficient to equip all of Norway's forces with modernised equipment.[115] Norway remained dependent on NATO reinforcements to defend northern Norway, while the country's own modest defence capability did not divert significant Soviet forces from commitments elsewhere. Most important for the US, however, was Norway's geographic position; loss of Norway as an ally would have had significant consequences for US security. The desirability of bases in Norway for US bombers was identified in US planning as early as 1945 and would be a recurring theme in US strategic air planning in subsequent years.[116] The US Joint War Plans Committee completed a 'strategic study of Western and Northern Europe' in 1947, which emphasised that 'Soviet ships using the sea route from Murmansk (or Archangel) passing through the Arctic Ocean to the Atlantic Ocean would ... be extremely vulnerable to an attack from Allied bases in the Scandinavian countries, particularly in Northern Norway'.[117] In 1948, a joint report by the US Air Force

Directorate of Intelligence and the Office of Naval Intelligence referred to Norway as being 'the key to the entire northern Europe and may be termed a gigantic Gibraltar'.[118]

Norway was conscious of its own strategic importance. In 1948, Norwegian Defence Minister Hauge asked US Naval and Air Force attachés in Oslo what place Norway might have in American air strategy, what aid might be expected in the early stages of war, and whether, where, and at what stages in such a scenario the US would want to establish air, sea, and land bases in Norway.[119] In the negotiations between the original Brussels Treaty member states and Canada and the US in 1948, Norway was considered one of the 'stepping stone' states alongside Iceland, Denmark, Portugal, and Ireland. Norway's membership was considered vital, given its geographic location astride the transatlantic sea lines of communication.[120] Reinforced by the increasingly broad intelligence collection relationship that developed during the Cold War, Norway's importance for the US therefore lay in where it was, rather than what it did: a fact that has not changed, as demonstrated by Donald Trump's comment in 2018 that Norway is 'NATO's eyes and ears' on its northern flank,[121] and continued US interest in additional intelligence facilities in northern Norway, such as the Globus III radar emplaced in Finnmark in 2020.[122]

Norway also proved valuable for Washington from a political and institutional point of view, especially in the 1950s when disagreements on nuclear posture were most acute. The US saw Norway as an implicit benchmark for Denmark and Iceland on questions of NATO policy. Both countries provided vital basing facilities to the US, and for both of them Norway's membership had been an important factor in their initial decision to join NATO, and US officials thus thought that a Norwegian disassociation from NATO would lead to similar policies in Denmark and Iceland.[123] Indeed, Iceland had taken the unusual step of requesting Norwegian authorities to provide military advice during its negotiations of the US basing agreement in 1951; when Iceland's parliament called for a withdrawal of US forces in 1956, Washington actively sought Norway's advice and support in general, and that of Foreign Minister Lange in particular, to maintain existing basing arrangements on the island.[124]

Access to information

By virtue of its NATO membership, Norway had substantial access to information about alliance thinking regarding the strategic balance, policies, and strategy in the High North. Throughout the Cold War, access to US national thinking and debates also improved, not least because of personal links between the US and Norwegian defence establishments that led to the creation of the 'US–Norwegian Study Group' in the late 1970s.[125] Over the years, the study groups were convened on a range of strategic, operational, and technical issues relating to the strategic situation and operations in the Arctic, and the forum remains in use to this day.[126] But while Norway was (and is) keenly aware of the importance of institutional links for influence and awareness of debates in the Pentagon, it has not sought the same with regard to NATO nuclear policy and planning.

Norway's defence establishment paid little attention to nuclear strategy before 1955, as defensive considerations dominated before the NATO decisions of 1957,[127] and the first exercise involving NATO use of nuclear weapons in Norway only occurred in 1955.[128] Through the institutional integration of defence planning, command, and training within NATO, Norway had considerably more access to information about nuclear warfare than would otherwise have been the case. Without a PoC agreement, Norwegian personnel were restricted from accessing US information about nuclear weapons covered by the Atomic Energy Act. But some Norwegian personnel may have received instruction in nuclear procedures and manuals for weapon systems operated by Norway. Selected Norwegian pilots received training in bombing techniques that were particularly suitable for the delivery of nuclear weapons.[129] As Norway clarified its policy on nuclear sharing, however, it rejected US offers to educate Norwegian personnel on the nuclear use of its Starfighter aircraft in 1963.[130] Although Norway has had access to high-level NATO nuclear planning information as a member of the NPG since 1979, as a country that was not prepared to deliver nuclear weapons, it remained excluded from some of the NPG's deliberations during the Cold War; its representatives had to leave the room when discussions turned to specific target sets.[131] Yet, ultimately, this lack of information about the practical aspects of nuclear weapons use was a consequence, rather than a cause of, or concern regarding, Norway's nuclear policy decisions.

Only in regard to operational plans concerning the use of nuclear weapons on Norwegian territory was Norway confronted with similar issues of access to such plans as confronted West Germany and other allies that were not part of NATO's Standing Group. In 1955, the Norwegian Joint Chiefs of Staff sought access to CINCNORTH's atomic strike plan and requested the right to approve the plan before it was passed on to SACEUR. According to Bjerga and Skogrand, AFNORTH accepted this during the 1950s, and Norway was able to obtain copies of the nuclear plans and to suggest alterations.[132] In 1960, however, AFNORTH cited security reasons for leaving the strike plan out of the regional defence plan provided to Norway's Joint Chiefs of Staff. Despite strong protests, Norway's Joint Chiefs of Staff Committee was only able to obtain the plans informally through Norwegian officers posted to NATO commands.[133]

Conclusion

Like all NATO members, Norway has sought to develop a close security relationship with the US in parallel with its multilateral alliance commitments. Always conscious of the Soviet threat – Norway was the only founding NATO member to share a border with the USSR – and aware of the country's strategic vulnerability to invasion, successive governments in Oslo remained highly supportive of US leadership of NATO throughout the Cold War. Despite its historic posture of non-alignment and desire to maintain national autonomy in relation to the broader European project after the Second World War, Norway's commitment to NATO stemmed from its shift to an Atlantic-focused foreign policy following Nazi occupation and a view that the best means of defending its territorial sovereignty and democratic values lay in joining the Western alliance.

At the same time, Oslo sought to reassure Moscow that it would not base NATO forces on Norwegian territory as a potential staging area for an attack on the Soviet Union. It also aimed to forestall Soviet pressure on Finland and Sweden that would have led to a deterioration of the Nordic balance. Yet, Norway was careful not to frame its policy in a way that would undermine NATO's functioning as a viable security alliance, which ultimately underpinned its own security; the credibility of Norwegian nuclear restraint rested on the fact that NATO did demonstrate nuclear integration elsewhere. Therefore, when it could not get support for its national preferences within NATO, Norway in the end supported majority decisions on NATO strategy.

In the area of nuclear cooperation during the Cold War, the US–Norway relationship operated within the institutional framework of NATO. Norway's refusal to station nuclear weapons on its territory meant that it was not included in many of the formal nuclear policy coordination discussions within the alliance. At the same time, Norway was keen to acquire strategic reassurance from the US in the form of the nuclear umbrella. Indeed, notwithstanding deep-seated domestic ambivalence over Norway's involvement in the nuclear arms race, Oslo approved the construction of a number of facilities that were capable of supporting US nuclear operations against the Soviet Union, as well as intelligence facilities that contributed to the US global nuclear command and control network.

Bilateral US–Norwegian interaction on nuclear matters was firmly situated in the context of NATO as a highly institutionalised alliance. From the late 1970s in particular, Norway also had a significant direct link and influence on US defence thinking in regard to the High North; this was a result of Oslo's recognised expertise on regional matters and was facilitated through the US–Norwegian Study Group. Regarding practical cooperation with the US, however, Norway tended to view NATO as a politically more convenient avenue than direct bilateral arrangements. For example, Norway preferred to embed the SAC basing agreement into a broader NATO framework on strategic bases, which was accepted by the US and the rest of the alliance.[134] Facilities for US aircraft in Norway were embedded in NATO through SACLANT, although their overwhelmingly utility was for US strategic operations, as distinct from those under NATO.[135] As such, the political 'cover' of NATO helped to mitigate domestic Norwegian sensitivities about direct defence cooperation with the US, especially with respect to nuclear weapons.

Despite considerable differences between Washington and Oslo regarding the role of nuclear weapons, these did not lead to a public break or significant tensions between Norway and the US. The US was not willing to risk retaining broader Norwegian cooperation, in a bilateral or NATO setting, in pursuit of deeper nuclear integration. In general, the US was concerned not to rekindle what it saw as 'neutralist' sentiment in Norway, while also showing increasing understanding during the 1950s of the local context of Norway's decisions.[136] Washington may not have liked Norway's restrictions, but in the end their impact on US plans and forces was limited, because it was locally confined and Norway did not seek to extend these restrictions beyond its own particular strategic context.

Notes

1 Ministry of Foreign Affairs, *Setting the Course for Norwegian Foreign and Security Policy*, Meld. St. 36 (2016–2017), report to the Storting (White Paper), www.regjeringen.no/contentassets/0688496c2b764f02995 5cc6e2f27799c/en-gb/pdfs/stm201620170036000engpdfs.pdf

2 W. Yennie Lindgren and N. Graeger, 'The Challenges and Dynamics of Alliance Policies: Norway, NATO and the High North', in M. Wesley (ed.), *Global Allies: Comparing US Allies in the 21st Century* (Canberra: ANU Press, 2017), 94.

3 For background, see W. Cole, *Norway and the United States 1905–1955* (Ames: Iowa State University Press, 1989).

4 J. Holst, 'The Nordic Region: Changing Perspectives in International Relations', *Annals of the American Academy of Political and Social Science*, 512 (1990), 10.

5 J. Aunesluoma, M. Petersson, and C. Silva, 'Deterrence or Reassurance? Nordic Responses to the First Détente, 1953–1956', *Scandinavian Journal of History*, 32:2 (2007), 183–208.

6 M. Petersson and H. Lunde Saxi, 'Shifted Roles: Explaining Danish and Norwegian Alliance Strategy 1949–2009', *Journal of Strategic Studies*, 36:6 (2013), 761–788.
7 Department of State, 'Despatch from the Embassy in Norway to the Department of State, 29 July 1960, Subject: Norway and U.S. Leadership', in *Foreign Relations of the United States, 1958–60, Western Europe*, Vol. 7, Part 2, https://history.state.gov/historicaldocuments/frus1958–60v07p2/d301
8 J. Holst, 'The Pattern of Nordic Security', *Daedalus*, 113:2 (1984), 195–225.
9 Yennie Lindgren and Graeger, 'The Challenges and Dynamics of Alliance Policies', 94.
10 G. Lundestad, 'The Evolution of Norwegian Security Policy: Alliance with the West and Reassurance in the East', *Scandinavian Journal of History*, 17:2–3 (1992), 227–256
11 J. Lund, *Don't Rock the Boat: Reinforcing Norway in Crisis and War* (Santa Monica: RAND Corporation, 1989), 13.
12 R. German, 'Norway and the Bear: Soviet Coercive Diplomacy and Norwegian Security Policy', *International Security*, 7:2 (1982), 59.
13 German, 'Norway and the Bear'.
14 R. Bitzinger, *Denmark, Norway, and NATO: Constraints and Challenges* (Santa Monica: RAND Corporation, 1989), 16; and O. Knudsen, 'Norway: Domestically Driven Foreign Policy', *Annals of the American Academy*, 512 (1990), 111.
15 R. Tamnes, 'The High North: A Call for a Competitive Strategy', in J. Andreas Olsen (ed.), *Security in Northern Europe: Deterrence, Defence and Dialogue* (London: Routledge, 2018), 10.
16 K. Bjerga and K. Skogrand, 'Securing Small State Interests: Norway in NATO', in V. Mastny, S. Holtsmark, and A. Wenger (eds), *War Plans and Alliances in the Cold War: Threat Perceptions in the East and West* (London: Routledge, 2006), 230.
17 H. Danielson, 'Military Assistance, Foreign Policy, and National Security: The Objectives of US Military Assistance to Norway, 1950–1965', *Scandinavian Journal of History*, 45:1 (2020), 71–94.
18 Bitzinger, *Denmark, Norway, and NATO*, 13.
19 G. Pedlow, 'The Evolution of NATO's Command Structure: 1951–2009', https://shape.nato.int/resources/21/Evolution%20of%20NATO%20Cmd%20Structure%201951–2009.pdf
20 Holst, 'The Pattern of Nordic Security', 204.
21 M. Zapfe, 'NATO's Spearhead Force', *CSS Analyses in Security Policy*, 174 (2015), https://css.ethz.ch/content/dam/ethz/special-interest/gess/cis/center-for-securities-studies/pdfs/CSSAnalyse174-EN.pdf
22 G. Dyndal, 'How the High North Became Central to NATO Strategy: Revelations from the NATO Archives, *Journal of Strategic Studies*, 34:4 (2011), 557–585.
23 J. Borresen, 'Alliance Naval Strategies and Norway in the Final Years of the Cold War', *Naval War College Review*, 64:7 (2004), 1–20.
24 Dyndal, 'How the High North Became Central to NATO Strategy'.

25 R. Tamnes, *The United States and the Cold War in the High North* (Aldershot: Dartmouth, 1991), 245–248.
26 See J. Mearsheimer, 'A Strategic Misstep: The Maritime Strategy and Deterrence in Europe', *International Security*, 11:2 (1986), 3–57.
27 Petersson and Saxi, 'Shifted Roles', 777.
28 Yennie Lindgren and Graeger, 'The Challenges and Dynamics of Alliance Politics', 102.
29 Interview with Norwegian defence official, Oslo, 28 July 2015.
30 H. Haftendorn, 'NATO and the Arctic: Is the Atlantic Alliance a Cold War Relic in a Peaceful Region Now Faced with Non-military Challenges?', *European Security*, 20:3 (2011), 342.
31 For analysis, see O. Bogen and M. Hakenstad, 'Reluctant Reformers: The Economic Roots of Military Change in Norway, 1990–2015', *Defence Studies*, 17:1 (2017), 23–37.
32 A. Higgins, 'On a Tiny Norwegian Island, America Keeps an Eye on Russia', *New York Times*, 13 June 2017, www.nytimes.com/2017/06/13/world/europe/arctic-norway-russia-radar.html
33 S. Neubauer, 'The Plan to Deploy US Troops to Norway: How Oslo and Moscow Could Respond', *Foreign Affairs*, 9 November 2016, www.foreignaffairs.com/articles/norway/2016–11–09/plan-deploy-us-troops-norway
34 A. Forland, 'Norway's Nuclear Odyssey: From Optimistic Proponent to Nonproliferator', *Nonproliferation Review*, 4:2 (1997), 1–16.
35 K. Skogrand and R. Tamnes, *Fryktens likevekt: Atombomben, Norge og verden 1945–1970* (Oslo: Tiden Norsk Forlag, 2001), 102–103.
36 M. Berdal, *The United States, Norway and the Cold War, 1954–60* (Basingstoke: Macmillan Press, 1997), 16, 23.
37 Tamnes, *The United States and the Cold War in the High North*, 99–100.
38 Tamnes, *The United States and the Cold War in the High North*, 73–74.
39 O. Riste, *The Norwegian Intelligence Service: 1945–1970* (London: Frank Cass, 1999), 69–70.
40 Tamnes, *The United States and the Cold War in the High North*, 102.
41 A. Jacobsen, 'Scandinavia, SIGINT and the Cold War', *Intelligence and National Security*, 16:1 (2001), 227.
42 J. Richelson, *Spying on the Bomb: American Nuclear Intelligence from Nazi Germany to Iran to North Korea* (New York: W. W. Norton and Company, 2006), 120–121.
43 O. Cote Jnr. 'The Third Battle: Innovation in the US Navy's Silent Cold War Struggle with Soviet Submarines', *Federation of American Scientists*, March 2000, https://fas.org/man/dod-101/sys/ship/docs/cold-war-asw.htm
44 O. Njolstad, 'Atomic Intelligence in Norway During the Cold War', *Journal of Strategic Studies*, 29:4 (2006), 666.
45 Tamnes, *The United States and the Cold War in the High North*, 146.
46 Skogrand and Tamnes, *Fryktens likevekt*, 109.
47 Skogrand and Tamnes, *Fryktens likevekt*, 105.
48 Njolstad, 'Atomic Intelligence in Norway During the Cold War', 659–660.

49 Tamnes, *The United States and the Cold War in the High North*, 164.
50 Skogrand and Tamnes, *Fryktens likevekt*, 120–123.
51 Skogrand and Tamnes, *Fryktens likevekt,* 139.
52 Skogrand and Tamnes, *Fryktens likevekt,* 140–143.
53 S. Lodgaard, 'A Nuclear Weapon Free Zone in the North? A Reappraisal', *Bulletin of Peace Proposals*, 11:1 (1980), 33–39.
54 Skogrand and Tamnes, *Fryktens likevekt*, 170–171.
55 Skogrand and Tamnes, *Fryktens likevekt,* 128–129.
56 Tamnes, *The United States and the Cold War in the High North*, 161.
57 Skogrand and Tamnes, *Fryktens likevekt*, 128.
58 Quoted in Tamnes, *The United States and the Cold War in the High North*, 161.
59 Skogrand and Tamnes, *Fryktens likevekt*, 254–269. According to Skogrand and Tamnes, there are indications that non-nuclear components for nuclear bombs were stored at Flesland, the war base for AFNORTH's strike force. However, it is not known whether Norway was informed about this, which would technically not have been contrary to Norway's rejection of stationing nuclear weapons in peacetime. See Skogrand and Tamnes, *Fryktens likevekt*, 213, 215–216.
60 Skogrand and Tamnes, *Fryktens likevekt*, 220–221.
61 Bjerga and Skogrand, 'Securing Small State Interests', 228–229.
62 H. Ole Sandnes, *The 1970–1974 Combat Aircraft Analysis* (Trondheim: Tapir Academic Press, 2010), 25–27; and Skogrand and Tamnes, *Fryktens likevekt*, 197–199.
63 Skogrand and Tamnes, *Fryktens likevekt*, 236–240, 244–248, 277–279.
64 Skogrand and Tamnes, *Fryktens likevekt,* 282–284.
65 L. Van Dassen and A. Wetter, 'Nordic Nuclear Non Proliferation Policies: Different Traditions and Common Objectives', in G. Herolf, A. Bailes, and B. Sundelius (eds), *The Nordic Countries and the European Defence Policy* (Oxford: Oxford University Press and SIPRI, 2006). Notably, however, a nuclear weapon free zone could also be conceived of more as a development of longstanding Norwegian interests in the security of Scandinavia and the risks of escalation in the region, than as a break with NATO's nuclear policy. See J. Holst, 'A Nuclear Weapon-free Zone in the Nordic Area: Conditions and Options – A Norwegian View', *Bulletin of Peace Proposals*, 14:4 (1983), 227–238.
66 S. Lodgaard, 'Norway and NATO at 50', *Perceptions: Journal of International Affairs*, 41:1 (1999), http://sam.gov.tr/pdf/perceptions/Volume-IV/march-may-1999/SVERRE-LODGAARD.pdf
67 See K. Egeland, 'Oslo's New Track: Norwegian Nuclear Disarmament Diplomacy, 2005–2013', *Journal for Peace and Nuclear Disarmament*, 2:2 (2019), 468–490.
68 Egeland, 'Oslo's 'New Track', 470.
69 O. Meier, 'NATO Revises Nuclear Policy', *Arms Control Association*, December 2010, www.armscontrol.org/act/2010–12/nato-revises-nuclear-policy

70 J. Borger, 'Five NATO States to Urge Removal of US Nuclear Arms in Europe', *Guardian*, 23 February 2010, https://www.theguardian.com/world/2010/feb/22/nato-states-us-nuclear-arms-europe.
71 M. Landler, 'US Resists Push by Allies for Tactical Nuclear Cuts', *New York Times*, 22 April 2010, https://www.nytimes.com/2010/04/23/world/europe/23diplo.html.
72 K. Egeland, 'Spreading the Burden: How NATO Became a "Nuclear' Alliance"', *Diplomacy and Statecraft*, 31:1 (2020), 160.
73 J. Wither, 'Svalbard: NATO's Arctic "Achilles' Heel"', *RUSI Journal*, 163:5 (2018), 36.
74 United Nations, 'First Committee: Nuclear Cluster, Statement by Norway to the United Nations, 21 October 2019', www.un.org/disarmament/wp-content/uploads/2019/10/statement-by-norway-nw-oct-21–19.pdf
75 Holst, 'The Pattern of Nordic Security', 210–211.
76 For background, see A. Jorgensen-Dahl, 'The Soviet–Norwegian Maritime Disputes in the Arctic: Law and Politics', *Ocean Development and International Law*, 21:4 (1990), 412–413.
77 On the related issue of Nordic defence cooperation and its relationship to Russia, see J. E. Moller, 'Trilateral Defence Cooperation in the North: An Assessment of Interoperability between Norway, Sweden and Finland', *Defence Studies*, 19:3 (2019), 235–256.
78 Tamnes, *The United States and the Cold War in the High North*, 164.
79 Department of State, 'National Security Council Report: Statement of US Policy Toward Scandinavia, 6 April 1960, Subject: General Considerations', in *Foreign Relations of the United States, 1958–60, Western Europe,* Vol. 7, Part 2, https://history.state.gov/historicaldocuments/frus1958–60v07p2/d301
80 D. Zakheim, 'The United States and the Nordic Countries During the Cold War', *Cooperation and Conflict*, 33:2 (1998), 122 (emphasis in original).
81 A. Lanoszka, *Atomic Assurance: The Alliance Politics of Nuclear Proliferation* (Ithaca, NY: Cornell University Press, 2018), 140–142.
82 Skogrand and Tamnes, *Fryktens likevekt*, 106–113.
83 Forland, 'Norway's Nuclear Odyssey', 13.
84 Quoted in N. Orvik, 'Scandinavia, NATO, and Northern Security', *International Organization*, 20:3 (1966), 387–388.
85 Quoted in Tamnes, *The United States and the Cold War in the High North*, 164.
86 Department of State, 'National Security Council Report: Statement of US Policy Toward Scandinavia'.
87 Bjerga and Skogrand, 'Securing Small State Interests', 224.
88 Skogrand and Tamnes, *Fryktens likevekt*, 206–207.
89 Bjerga and Skogrand, 'Securing Small State Interests', 227.
90 Skogrand and Tamnes, *Fryktens likevekt*, 207–209.
91 Borresen, 'Alliance Naval Strategies and Norway in the Final Years of the Cold War', 114; and Bjerga and Skogrand, 'Securing Small State Interests', 221.
92 Dyndal, 'How the High North Became Central in NATO Strategy', 565.

93 P. Buteux, *The Politics of Nuclear Consultation in NATO: 1965–1980* (Cambridge: Cambridge University Press, 1983), 58.
94 R. Garthoff, 'The NATO Decision on Theater Nuclear Forces', *Political Science Quarterly*, 98:2 (1983), 206–207.
95 K. Honkanen, *The Influence of Small States on NATO Decision-making* (Stockholm: FOI, 2002), 50.
96 Ole Sandnes, *The 1970–1974 Combat Aircraft Analysis*, 25–27.
97 Dyndal, 'How the High North Became Central in NATO Strategy', 581.
98 Holst, 'The Pattern of Nordic Security', 201.
99 For background, see R. Allison, *Finland's Relations with the Soviet Union: 1944–1984* (London: Macmillan, London, 1986), 46–47.
100 German, 'Norway and the Bear', 69.
101 Allison, *Finland's Relations with the Soviet Union*, 49.
102 Lund, *Don't Rock the Boat*, 18.
103 Quoted in Berdal, *The United States, Norway and the Cold War*, 168.
104 Lundestad, 'The Evolution of Norwegian Security Policy', 235.
105 Tamnes, *The United States and the Cold War in the High North*, 71.
106 Skogrand and Tamnes, *Fryktens likevekt*, 105.
107 Forland, 'Norway's Nuclear Odyssey', 13.
108 S. Lodgaard and N. Petter Gleditsch, 'Norway – the Not So Reluctant Ally', *Cooperation and Conflict*, 12:4 (1977), 211.
109 R. Waldahl, 'Norwegian Attitudes Toward Defense and Foreign Policy Issues', in G. Flynn and H. Rattinger (eds), *The Public and Atlantic Defense* (New York: Rowman and Littlefield, 1985), 299.
110 J. Holst, 'Norwegian Security Policy for the 1980s', *Cooperation and Conflict*, 17:4 (1982), 226.
111 N. Petersen, 'The Security Policies of Small NATO Countries: Factors of Change', *Cooperation and Conflict*, 13 (1988), 153.
112 Lundestad, 'The Evolution of Norwegian Security Policy', 250–251.
113 Waldahl, 'Norwegian Attitudes Toward Defense and Foreign Policy Issues', 287. See also the survey data in Holst, 'Norwegian Security Policy for the 1980s', 215–217.
114 A poll taken in 2019 showed that 78 per cent of Norwegian respondents believed their government should sign and ratify the Treaty on the Prohibition of Nuclear Weapons. See ICAN [International Campaign to Abolish Nuclear Weapons], 'Norway', www.icanw.org/norway.
115 A. Urnes Johnson, K. Hove and T. Lillekvelland, 'Country Survey: Military Expenditure and Defence Policy in Norway 1970–2013', *Defence and Peace Economics*, 28:6 (2017), 669–675.
116 Skogrand and Tamnes, *Fryktens likevekt*, 77.
117 Quoted in Berdal, *The United States, Norway and the Cold War*, 14.
118 Berdal, *The United States, Norway and the Cold War*, 14.
119 Berdal, *The United States, Norway and the Cold War*, 15.
120 M. Smith, *NATO Enlargement During the Cold War* (Houndmills: Palgrave, 2000), 26–28.

121 P. Stewart and A. Doyle, 'Norway Renews NATO Spending Pledge and Trump's Defense Chief Visits', *Reuters*, 15 July 2018, www.reuters.com/article/us-norway-usa-mattis/norway-renews-nato-spending-pledge-as-trumps-defense-chief-visits-idUSKBN1K40LJ
122 GlobalSecurity.org, 'Globus III', www.globalsecurity.org/space/systems/globus-iii.htm
123 Aunesluoma, Petersson and Silva, 'Deterrence or Reassurance?', 183–208, 193.
124 Berdal, *The United States, Norway and the Cold War,* 142–147; and Aunesluoma, Petersson, and Silva, 'Deterrence or Reassurance?', 183–208, 193.
125 Tamnes, *The United States and the Cold War in the High North*, 245–248.
126 Interviews, Washington, DC, December 2017.
127 Skogrand and Tamnes, *Fryktens likevekt*, 230–232.
128 Skogrand and Tamnes, *Fryktens likevekt,* 288–290.
129 Skogrand and Tamnes, *Fryktens likevekt,* 290–295.
130 Skogrand and Tamnes, *Fryktens likevekt,* 271–277.
131 Tamnes, *The United States and the Cold War in the High North,* 219.
132 Bjerga and Skogrand, 'Securing Small State Interests', 226.
133 Bjerga and Skogrand, 'Securing Small State Interests', 226.
134 Tamnes, *The United States and the Cold War in the High North,* 72, 87; and Berdal, *The United States, Norway and the Cold War*, 177.
135 Berdal, *The United States, Norway and the Cold War*, 45, 177–178.
136 Berdal, *The United States, Norway and the Cold War*, 162–169.

4

Security at arm's length: US–Japan nuclear weapons cooperation

As the only country to have been subjected to a nuclear attack, Japan's relationship with nuclear weapons is complicated. The anti-nuclear norm is deeply embedded in Japanese society, but Japan's alliance with the US is characterised by consistent cooperation on nuclear weapons. The main focus of this cooperation today is extended nuclear deterrence, but for many decades after the Second World War, Tokyo collaborated with Washington on basing and transiting nuclear weapons in Northeast Asia. Japan's alliance with the world's biggest nuclear weapons state – the very state that subjected it to nuclear attack – has been at odds with the anti-nuclear norm permeating Japanese society. The pragmatism of Japanese elites in searching for security guarantees that obviate the need for Tokyo to take drastic strategic measures, including acquiring nuclear weapons of its own, has been a hallmark of the US–Japan alliance for the past seventy years.

This chapter examines nuclear weapons cooperation in the US–Japan alliance and outlines the factors that have shaped that cooperation since the 1950s. Japan has been content with maintaining an arm's length approach and has not sought operational intimacy with US nuclear forces. Largely because of the intensity and resilience of anti-nuclear sentiment in Japan, successive governments in Tokyo have been acutely conscious of maintaining distance from Washington publicly on nuclear weapons in the context of the alliance. Because of Japan's status as the most important US ally outside NATO and the country's critical role in supporting US nuclear forces, successive US administrations have avoided placing pressure on Tokyo to take on additional commitments when it comes to nuclear weapons cooperation.

The US–Japan Alliance

Japan's alliance with the US has been central to its post-war development. As a psychologically broken country, following its unconditional surrender in 1945, Japan's grand strategy hinged upon strong economic recovery underwritten by a comprehensive alliance with its chief wartime foe. Named after the country's first post-war Prime Minister, Yoshida Shigeru, the so-called 'Yoshida Doctrine' comprised three elements:[1] in return for a security guarantee from the US, Japan would host the deployment of US forces on Japanese soil; there would be no deployment of Japanese forces away from the home islands; and Japan would focus on economic development domestically and internationally. The overall vision of the Yoshida Doctrine was that Japan would become a pacifist nation, protected by the world's strongest military, and with an export-driven industrial economy as the foundation for achieving rapid levels of growth. For Japan, commercial aims would be paramount. While the US successfully insisted on the creation of the Self-Defense Force (SDF) in 1954 and encouraged the expansion of Japan's arms industry, Yoshida and his supporters managed to ensure that civilian exports remained central to driving Japan's manufacturing sector.[2]

The 1951 US–Japan Mutual Security Treaty (MST) was a corollary of the San Francisco Peace Treaty of the same year, which required Japan to conclude a bilateral security agreement with the US.[3] The MST granted the US unrestricted access to maintaining bases in Japan and effective control over the island of Okinawa 'until "peace and security" were achieved in the Far East'.[4] In the context of US security alliances in the post-1945 era, the MST was unique in that it granted the US control over significant parts of a sovereign state, and did not provide for a reciprocal commitment on the part of Japan to defend US interests in the region. Moreover, the treaty included a provision that permitted the US to intervene domestically in Japan, and did not require Washington to consult with Tokyo before moving US forces in and out of the country.

The Japanese government pushed hard for renegotiating the treaty to ensure a more equal status, and in 1960 the Eisenhower administration agreed to a new Treaty of Mutual Cooperation and Security that increased consultative arrangements, eliminated any scope for US intervention domestically in Japan, and sharpened the US commitment to defend Japan against external attack.[5] Of particular note was the creation of the Security Consultative Committee (SCC) in 1960 that spawned a host of subcommittees and groups to coordinate the alliance, including the Status of Forces Agreement, as well as general security matters of concern to both sides.[6]

Yet the US–Japan relationship was much broader than the security alliance; the economic and political dimensions of the relationship were equally if not more important from Washington's perspective. In the decade after the 1951 Peace Treaty, two-way trade between the US and Japan increased approximately sevenfold, and Japan's integration into international organisations and the Asian region was due in no small measure to consistent and active US support for this with countries across the region.[7] In contrast to the alliance with NATO, and even with South Korea, successive US administrations before the 1970s were unconcerned with burden sharing on the part of Japan.

Indeed, in many important respects, the relationship between Washington and Tokyo was removed from the rough and tumble of typical alliance politics. As Chalmers Johnson has noted, until the mid-1970s, the US role was more that of a benefactor than an alliance partner, with successive Republican and Democratic administrations 'treating Japan as a beloved ward, indulging its every economic need and proudly patronising it as a star capitalist pupil'.[8] The notion of Japan as a US protectorate in the security sphere seemed appropriate in a context in which Japanese governments were content to renounce collective defence constitutionally, and where the defined role of the SDF meant that in practice it played no meaningful part in alliance activities or operations. As Richard Samuels points out, 'the SDF were seen as little more than a National Guard, an adjunct to the real military who wore the stars and stripes'.[9] Operationally, the alliance was driven by the US, which focused on using Japanese bases and ports for air and naval operations, with the tempo growing rapidly as combat operations in Southeast Asia escalated in the second half of the 1960s.

Until the early 1970s Japanese governments were not seriously concerned with defence policy from a national perspective. The almost exclusive economic focus of decision makers relegated security and defence to a low level of priority in policy debates, which was reflected and reinforced by the second-rank bureaucratic status of the SDF and Japanese Defence Agency (JDA), neither of which had representation in the Japanese Cabinet.[10] Preoccupied with powering economic development and constrained by a pervasive 'anti-militarisation' norm internationally and domestically, postwar Japanese governments essentially contracted out their defence policy to Washington. This meant there was little appetite to frame an independent defence posture informed by national interest considerations, as distinct from alliance obligations.

By the early 1970s, however, at least three factors proved important in changing this approach. The first was a view, which solidified following President Nixon's 1969 Guam Doctrine and Washington's opening to China in 1971, that the US was reassessing the depth of its commitment to allies in Asia. Of course, Japanese policymakers were not unique in forming this perspective; South Korean and Australian elites shared a similar view. Yet, free-riding on the assumption that US extended deterrence circumvented the need for an independent Japanese defence strategy was no longer seen as viable by the late 1960s. The second factor was the strategic assessment that Japan's security situation was deteriorating. China's acquisition of nuclear weapons, looming US defeat in Vietnam, and the Nixon administration's unilateral announcement in 1970 that it intended scaling back the presence of US forces in South Korea converged to increase anxiety levels in Tokyo and stoke fears of abandonment.[11] This was exacerbated by growing US economic nationalism that pointed to the large trade imbalance with Japan and prescribed import tariffs and a revaluation of the US dollar.[12] The third factor was the rise of Yasuhiro Nakasone as Director General of the JDA in 1970. Hailing from the nationalist right of the governing Liberal Democratic Party, Nakasone was committed to a more 'autonomous' defence strategy for Japan, and drew an explicit distinction between Japan's defence effort and the alliance with the US. Starting with Nakasone, the JDA and SDF would become serious players in the development of Japanese strategic policy.[13]

The result was a flurry of internal studies analysing Japan's current and future defence options that considered nuclear as well as conventional options. These studies were initiated against the background of a highly classified Cabinet Research Office cost–benefit analysis that assessed a potential Japanese nuclear weapons programme. Yielding a two-part report entitled 'A Basic Study of Japan's Nuclear Policy', completed in 1968 and 1970, the Cabinet Research Office assessment reportedly explored scenarios of a Japanese bomb programme, but concluded that the likely costs incurred by the resultant international isolation, disruption to the US alliance, and adverse domestic opposition would outweigh any feasible strategic advantages.[14]

Concerned by what he regarded as Washington's declining resolve to uphold extended deterrence commitments as the US situation in Vietnam worsened, in 1970 JDA Director-General Nakasone also commissioned a group of experts to provide an assessment of Japan's capacity to support a nuclear weapons force as well as a more robust conventional military.[15] The JDA study group assessed that 'a nuclear weapon programme would take five years at maximum and an investment of around 40% of the entire FY 1970 defence budget'; notably, the report also concluded that a large-scale conventional military build-up by Japan was 'unrealistic'.[16] Japan's inaugural Defense White Paper released in 1970 endorsed strengthening the capabilities of the SDF, but repudiated the nuclear option while affirming the

US alliance as the country's means of defending itself against major external threats.[17]

The 1970 White Paper was a watershed not just in terms of the deeper thinking it evinced among Japanese policymakers about defence strategy, but also because it signalled a growing willingness by Tokyo to engage in detailed operational discussions with the US. This was undoubtedly motivated by a desire to bind the US closer to the alliance as doubts emerged over US engagement in Asia, but the Nixon and Ford administrations were actively encouraging Japanese policymakers in this direction. In accordance with its broader strategy of pushing allies to do more to bolster their own defence capabilities, Washington endorsed higher levels of Japanese defence spending as well as more focused joint operational planning and coordination between US and Japanese military forces.[18] Reiterating many of the prominent themes of the 1970 White Paper, the 1976 National Defense Program Outline (NDPO) noted that Japan relied on the US nuclear umbrella for protection from nuclear threats, but also underscored the need for Japan to 'possess an adequate defense capability of its own ... a defense posture capable of dealing with any aggression should be constructed, through maintaining the credibility of the Japan–US security arrangement and ensuring the smooth functioning of that system'.[19]

Also in 1976, in the absence of a joint military command, Washington and Tokyo created an additional subcommittee of the bilateral SCC tasked with formulating an integrated framework for joint cooperation in military operations, logistics, and intelligence.[20] This resulted in the landmark 1978 US–Japan Defense Guidelines that endorsed detailed arrangements for joint operations, intelligence collection and exchange, and command and control. Under the heading 'Posture for Deterring Aggression', the US commitment to maintaining 'a nuclear deterrent capability' was stated alongside 'the forward deployments of combat ready forces and other forces capable of reinforcing them'.[21] The Defense Guidelines were a milestone in the US–Japan alliance because they endorsed specific SDF missions and 'normalised' joint military exercises between the US and Japanese militaries, which was itself a major step forward for Japanese policymakers given the depth of public opposition to 'remilitarisation'. Although the 1978 Guidelines did not lead to the creation of a joint military command like the US–ROK Combined Forces Command (also created in 1978), they were the first public endorsement of joint planning and exercises between US and Japanese armed forces.[22]

Yet, as military cooperation grew between Japan and the US, so too did US concerns about burden sharing. Conscious of Japan's increasing economic might and an unfavourable two-way trade balance for the US, the Carter administration placed pressure on Tokyo to increase its defence spending, which had been capped at 1 per cent of GDP in 1976.[23] While Japanese policymakers remained circumspect in response to this pressure, the large-scale reinforcement of the Soviet Union's ground force presence in the disputed northern territories, coupled with the USSR's deployment of new-generation strategic bombers and missile systems, triggered 'a significant shift in Japan on defense issues, a change that allowed Japanese politicians to raise many issues that had previously been taboo'.[24] This altered atmosphere paved the way for the rise of former JDA Director-General Nakasone to the prime ministership in 1982. Although his immediate predecessors had overseen a period during which Japan had moved to integrate operationally to a far greater extent than previously with the US, Nakasone's vivid characterisation of Japan as 'an unsinkable aircraft carrier' captured the spirit of his commitment to the alliance.[25] For its part, the Reagan administration sought to engage Japan as a more equal alliance partner.

The most prominent feature of closer US–Japan military cooperation was joint naval operations to protect critical sea lines of communication in a context in which containing Soviet military power worldwide was the priority of US global strategy. Enhanced operational coordination between the US Navy and the Maritime Self Defense Force had been a major theme of the 1978 Defense Guidelines, and the Reagan administration was keen to expand Japan's support function in countering Soviet naval and air power in Northeast Asia as part of its maritime strategy.[26]

As the second Cold War intensified, Japan's strategic importance for US global strategy was becoming even clearer. Concurrent with endorsing an ambitious five-year defence plan, which included a commitment to boosting defence expenditure, the Nakasone government authorised the export of defence-related technology to the US in a bid to become part of the Reagan administration's Strategic Defense Initiative.[27] At the operational level, the SDF intensified joint operations with US forces, focusing on defending sea lines of communication (SLOCs) and command post exercises.[28] By the late 1980s, US–Japan relations had assumed most of the key characteristics of a traditional alliance, including joint operations, military technology transfer, and public affirmations of binding commitments under the security treaty.[29] Although Japan's capacity and willingness to assume a more operational role in the alliance remained constrained by constitutional restrictions on collective defence, as the Cold War wound down in the late 1980s, the depth of strategic cooperation in the US–Japan alliance was radically different to the client state bilateral relationship of the 1950s and 1960s.

Following Washington's critical reaction to Japan's refusal to send forces to support US-led combat operations in the 1991 Gulf War, and against a background of Japanese concern regarding long-term US commitment to Asia after the Cold War, the Murayama government in 1995 approved the first revision to Japan's National Defence Program Guidelines (NDPG) since 1976. The guidance endorsed a more globally oriented strategic posture, which was reinforced by the 2004 NDPG released in the wake of Japan's support for US operations in the 'Global War on Terror' after the 9/11 attacks.[30] In response to Chinese military modernisation and North Korea's acquisition of nuclear weapons, the 2010 and 2014 NDPG elaborated on the concept of a 'dynamic defence force' with enhanced readiness and mobility. This included closer coordination with the US in the deterrence, intelligence, and cyber domains, with special reference to responding to threats in so-called 'grey zones'.[31]

More directly pertinent to the US–Japan alliance were the changes to the US–Japan Defense Guidelines agreed to in 1997 and 2015. Following the 1991 Gulf War experience, the 1993–94 Korean Peninsula crisis, and the Taiwan Strait crisis in 1995–96, the 1997 Guidelines expanded the remit of joint operations beyond merely responding to an armed attack on Japan, to 'situations in areas surrounding Japan'. Noteworthy was that, in addition to the maintenance of US bases on its territory, Japan committed to provide 'rear area' support for American forces operating 'on the high seas and international airspace around Japan'.[32] While not as path breaking as the 1997 changes, the 2015 revised Guidelines strengthened expectations with respect to potential Japanese contributions outside East Asia, and formally established an Alliance Coordination Mechanism (ACM) to manage bilateral responses to specific operational contingencies.[33] An addition to the established institutional architecture of the alliance, the ACM constitutes 'a whole-of-government standing arrangement' that draws on a wide range of agencies in both governments and 'is part of an effort to compensate for the absence of an integrated command structure for the alliance'.[34] Complementing these changes was a formal reinterpretation of Japan's constitution by the Abe government, which opened the door to collective self defence in security legislation passed by the Diet in 2015 that allowed the SDF 'to operate alongside US forces in defence of the United States and other "close" countries subject to aggression'.[35] In addition, US–Japanese security cooperation began to extend to relations to third countries, as so-called 'minilateral' security cooperation with like-minded states across the Indo-Pacific increased the importance of Tokyo to US regional strategy.[36]

Although the Abe government was more successful than many other allied governments in forging a close working relationship with the Trump administration, the latter had a mixed impact on the US–Japan alliance. On the one hand, the President was inclined to treat Japan less harshly than NATO allies or South Korea on the vexing issue of alliance cost sharing, and Tokyo's position on China remained more aligned than any other US ally with the hardline posture in Washington.[37] Indeed, Japan remained the most enthusiastic backer of the 'Free and Open Indo-Pacific' vision, endorsing the initiative at the 2019 ('2 + 2') Security Consultative Meeting.[38] Many substantive polices of the Trump administration, however, such as the US withdrawal from the Trans-Pacific Partnership, were notably at odds with Tokyo's policies, and Trump's erratic and unpredictable conduct of foreign policy remained a strategic concern for Japanese elites.[39]

Japan and nuclear weapons in the alliance

Nuclear weapons have been an important factor in the US–Japan alliance since its inception. Despite the resilience of the anti-nuclear norm in Japanese social and political life, a consistent thread running through Japanese strategic behaviour has been a desire for nuclear reassurance from the US in the form of extended deterrence commitments. In an attempt to bolster this commitment, successive governments in Tokyo have played a critical role in enabling the US to maintain its nuclear weapons presence in Northeast Asia. Contrary to popular perceptions, since the 1950s, Japan has been intimately involved in embedding nuclear weapons in its alliance with the US. Notwithstanding occasional differences of opinion regarding mechanisms for consultation, nuclear weapons have been seen by Washington and Tokyo as integral to the bilateral alliance. Although both sides have attempted to impose a low profile on nuclear weapons cooperation, primarily in an effort to assuage Japanese domestic sensitivities, the depth of this cooperation has been significant.

Paradoxically, in light of this cooperation and the country's disavowal of maintaining major armed forces or using military force internationally, consideration by Tokyo of the possibility of acquiring nuclear weapons has been a long-standing element of its defence thinking. Beginning with Prime Minister Nobusuke Kishi in 1957, successive Japanese leaders publicly observed that a 'defensive' national nuclear force would not be incompatible with Article 9 of the country's constitution,[40] although a landmark nuclear cooperation agreement that was concluded with the US in the following year expressly prohibited Japan from using US-supplied nuclear materials or equipment for weapons-related research and development.[41] Following in Kishi's footsteps, consecutive Japanese policymakers have been unwilling to publicly rule out that Japan might acquire its own nuclear arsenal should strategic circumstances radically alter. The nuclear weapons issue became a recurring theme in Japan's internal strategic discourse from the 1960s onwards and has persisted in varying forms ever since. However, with the possible exception of the early 1970s, there are few grounds to conclude this was the result of serious doubts about the credibility of the

US nuclear deterrent. Although formal reference in US strategic planning documents to the applicability of extended nuclear deterrence to Japan did not appear until the early 1970s, from 1967 in its public documents the JDA began referring to the nuclear umbrella covering Japan.[42] As distinct from their South Korean counterparts, there was little evidence of anxiety among Japanese policymakers during the Cold War regarding the credibility of the US nuclear umbrella.

The country's approach to developing an indigenous capability can best be described as 'nuclear hedging', whereby policymakers maintain the requisite breakthrough technologies to develop nuclear weapons, while at the same time observing international non-proliferation commitments.[43] This posture is in keeping with guidance provided in a 1969 policy paper produced by the Foreign Ministry, which among other things stated that 'Japan will take a policy not to possess nuclear weapons for a while, but maintain an economic and technical potential for nuclear weapon production and pay attention to not being restricted from doing so by others'.[44]

The massive expansion of the country's civilian nuclear programme, which was underwritten by the 1955 Atomic Energy Act, provided Japan with a high degree of credibility when it came to its potential to acquire a threshold nuclear weapons capability. Even at the height of Japan's anti-nuclear commitment in the late 1960s, Tokyo was focused on analysing in detail the costs and benefits of an indigenous weapons programme, and as mentioned above, consideration of a domestic nuclear option was a prominent part of the internal policy debate leading to the 1970 White Paper. The creation of a highly ambitious space launch programme in the 1960s and a successful satellite launch in 1970 enabled no less than a dozen successful rocket launches between 1970 and 1980 that rendered plausible a Japanese long-range missile delivery capability.[45]

Yet, as Hymans points out, in spite of the massive injection of resources into civilian nuclear development in Japan, industry and key government agencies (most notably MITI and the Atomic Energy Commission) acted as 'veto players' to promote a situation where 'Japanese prime ministers were much more institutionally constrained from deciding to acquire the bomb than their counterparts in almost any other state'.[46] By the mid-1970s, when Japan ratified the NPT, most of the US intelligence community doubted that Japan would acquire the bomb, despite it possessing the requisite industrial, financial, and scientific resources to go nuclear within two-to-twenty-four months.[47] The six-year interregnum between Tokyo's signature (in 1970) and its ratification of the NPT (in 1976) can be seen as indicating that Japanese governments at the time were concerned that the treaty would constrain the country's scope to acquire nuclear weapons in future, but it seems more likely that concerns over the intrusive nature of international safeguards, the threat of espionage, and the deleterious commercial impact on Japan's nuclear industry loomed largest.[48] Significantly, the US has displayed few concerns over Japan's nuclear hedging. As part of a bilateral nuclear agreement with the US signed in 1988, Washington accepted that Japan would undertake nuclear enrichment and reprocessing – activities that are acknowledged as carrying inherent proliferation risks.[49]

By contrast, ensuring the secret transit of US nuclear weapons throughout Japanese sovereign territory was undoubtedly the major challenge in alliance nuclear cooperation. When the short-lived Hatoyama government briefly contested the US movement of nuclear systems on ships to Japan in the mid-1950s, Secretary of State John Dulles bluntly informed his counterpart 'that Japan could raise a renegotiation of the terms of the alliance when it could pay for its own military, defend itself, and help the United States abroad'.[50] Washington had made it clear early in the alliance that smooth nuclear transit arrangements were a key plank in American nuclear strategy globally, not just in Northeast Asia. Being able to move US nuclear weapons freely and the platforms that carried them was crucial in executing targeting plans in the US Single Integrated Operational Plan (SIOP) and promoting the survivability of US forces in the event of global conflict.

From the very beginning of the formal alliance, Japan played a major role in supporting US nuclear strategy by dint of its status as a US protectorate. During the Korean War, the Truman administration established a command and control post in Tokyo to coordinate the deployment of several nuclear assets to Guam.[51] Retained as US sovereign territory (until 1972) under the 1951 Peace Treaty, Okinawa was the hub of the American nuclear force presence in the Asia-Pacific, alongside Guam. High-yield strategic weapons for B-52s, tactical systems for battlefield deployment, and nuclear air-to-air and ground-to-air weapons were all stationed on Okinawa until its reversion to Japan in 1972.[52] The US also stationed nuclear weapons in smaller islands that it occupied (Chichi Jima and Iwo Jima), as well as fully and partially assembled nuclear weapons at a series of airbases on the Japanese mainland. In an arrangement kept highly secret until the late 1990s, Chichi Jima and Iwo Jima were configured to serve as key back-up bases should US nuclear infrastructure in the rest of Japan (including Okinawa) be destroyed in wartime; the islands were designed 'as secret "recovery and reload" bases for submarines and bombers, which after withdrawing to the islands, would go on to wage a new offensive'.[53]

Documents reveal that as early as 1957, around a dozen individual locations in Japan 'had nuclear weapons or components, or were earmarked to receive nuclear weapons in times of crisis or war'.[54] Under the SIOP, US nuclear weapons stored at the Kadena airbase were assigned to strike missions against major targets in the Soviet Union and China.[55] One former

US nuclear war planner noted that tanker aircraft based in Okinawa were tasked with delivering nuclear weapons to airbases during a crisis and that special arrangements were put in place at the Iwakuni airbase for landing ships 'to be anchored offshore with nuclear weapons aboard, loaded onto amphibious tractors, just for the small group of planes on this base'.[56]

For all intents and purposes, Japanese officials were generally aware of US nuclear deployment activities. While not conceding publicly that US nuclear weapons were deployed in large numbers on occupied territory and transiting regularly through the home islands, Japanese governments were careful to assert that the presence of 'defensive nuclear weapons' on Japanese soil was legally permissible.[57] The 1960 negotiations on the Treaty of Mutual Cooperation and Security also resulted in a secret understanding between Washington and Tokyo that permitted the US to transit nuclear weapons through Japanese territory (including Honshu), in addition to the declared stationing of American nuclear weapons in Okinawa.[58] The US and Japan agreed that Washington would not be required to consult with Tokyo before authorising nuclear-armed vessels and aircraft to transit through Japanese ports and airbases; the US frequently made use of this agreement, as nuclear-capable vessels docked in ports including Yokosuka and Sasebo.[59] This was distinguished from 'the introduction into Japan of nuclear weapons', in which case consultation would be required under the agreement.[60]

This covert arrangement remained in place even as there was growing domestic pressure in Japan for the government in Tokyo to take a more proactive anti-nuclear stance in its approach to the US alliance.[61] This reached its height in the mid-1960s under Prime Minister Eisaku Sato. Sato's explicit request for a US extended nuclear deterrent commitment was received positively by the Johnson administration in 1965, and was a key factor that underpinned Sato's confidence in promulgating the three non-nuclear principles in 1967: non-possession, non-manufacture, and non-transit of nuclear weapons through Japanese territory.[62]

In practice, 'prior consultation' was thus discussed in flexible terms by US and Japanese policymakers. Masakatsu Ota observes that in a conversation between Sato and US Defense Secretary Robert McNamara in 1965:

> Sato warned McNamara about the subtle differences between nuclear deployment on Japanese land and stationing nuclear weapons on US naval vessels navigating Japanese territorial or neighbouring waters. The former option was automatically subjected to bilateral prior consultation regulated by the US–Japan mutual security treaty. However, the latter option was not covered by the prior consultation clause of the treaty; therefore, the US Navy could launch a nuclear attack through its nuclear-equipped carriers, attack submarines, and surface ships, without any formal discussion with the Japanese.[63]

Although much of the focus in the public domain with respect to nuclear transit was on ensuring Japanese prior consultation, the comments by Sato illustrate Tokyo's desire that freedom of US nuclear operations not be inhibited by the 1960 agreement. From Japan's perspective, this was crucial to extended deterrence and in promoting confidence in Washington that Tokyo would not seek to challenge the operational flexibility required to uphold the credibility of nuclear reassurances within the alliance.

Negotiations over the reversion of Okinawa to Japan crystallised many of the pointed debates within the US and Japanese governments regarding nuclear weapons basing and transit rights in the alliance. The importance of Okinawa for US nuclear strategy was underscored by the Joint Chiefs of Staff in a memorandum to US Defense Secretary McNamara in 1965, when they noted that '[l]ess than full US administrative control of Okinawa would inhibit the flexibility of US military forces based there and might directly affect our nuclear capabilities in the Far East'.[64]

While the Sato government's preference was to remain non-committal over whether US nuclear weapons would continue to be deployed on Okinawa after reversion, the strength of Japanese public opinion left it with little choice politically but to foreshadow the removal of nuclear forces by 1968.[65] This public commitment concerned the SDF, with senior levels expressing the view that any withdrawal of US nuclear weapons would dilute the extended nuclear deterrence commitment under the alliance.[66] For its part, the US Joint Chiefs of Staff strongly urged the Nixon administration to insist on written guarantees from Japan that it would permit the 'emergency re-entry' of nuclear weapons if requested by US officials.[67] This formed part of the US negotiating position and was eventually included in the final reversion agreement.[68] Despite telling the Japanese public that no US nuclear weapons would be (re)introduced to Okinawa after reversion, the Sato government secretly committed in a memorandum of understanding that Japan had 'no disagreement with the US on matters of substance' in relation to US nuclear weapons re-entering the island.[69] Not only were US authorities and the Japanese SDF intent on retaining a nuclear redeployment option for Okinawa, South Korea also reportedly expressed concern over the potentially adverse implications for US extended deterrence of the nuclear withdrawal.[70]

As late as 1976, the Director of the US Policy Planning Staff, Winston Lord, commented that of all the issues in the US–Japan relations, nuclear transit remained 'potentially the most disruptive'.[71] Increased operational cooperation between the US and Japanese armed forces in the 1980s did, however, also include some greater direct Japanese support for US nuclear operations, as the SDF supported the operation of US EC-135 aircraft in exercises practicing the transfer of nuclear launch orders to US strategic nuclear submarines and aircraft carriers operating in the waters around Japan.[72] However, Japan's willingness to play a direct role itself in strengthening US regional capabilities had limits. When the Reagan administration proposed that Japan host US nuclear weapons during the INF negotiations to balance the USSR's deployment of the SS-20 and Backfire bomber in its Far Eastern military region, Tokyo rejected this proposal.[73]

The withdrawal of nuclear weapons from all US surface vessels in 1992 removed the need for a continued political balancing act on the part of Japanese and US administrations. The fact that US surface ships traversing Japanese waters and docked in ports would no longer by definition be armed with nuclear weapons rendered redundant long-standing public criticism of the alliance in relation to nuclear transit and its associated risks.[74] For Japan, however, the end of the Cold War provided only a brief respite from nuclear challenges. The first North Korean nuclear crisis in 1993–94 saw the US edge towards pre-emptive military strikes, while North Korea's flight test of the *Taepodong* missile over Japanese territory in 1998 constituted a major strategic shock for Japan. This ultimately led to a formal decision by the Japanese Cabinet in 2003 to partner with the US in deploying missile defence systems on Japanese soil as well as *Aegis* ship-based systems.[75] Like the *Taepodong* test eight years previously, North Korea's first nuclear test in 2006 triggered consternation among Japanese policymakers. This led to a demand for a formal statement of reassurance from Washington of the US extended nuclear deterrence commitment and coincided with a leaked study that reviewed the opportunities and challenges confronting Japan if it decided to acquire a nuclear weapons capability of its own; it is likely that this study was leaked by the Japanese government to increase Tokyo's leverage with a view to extracting a robust statement of reassurance from Washington regarding the nuclear umbrella.[76]

Notwithstanding specific extended nuclear deterrence reassurances by the Bush administration in 2006 and the Obama administration following North Korea's second nuclear test in 2009, Japanese officials were increasingly anxious about the credibility of the nuclear umbrella. These concerns were stoked by growing belligerence from Pyongyang, increasing Chinese assertiveness supported by large-scale military modernisation, and nagging doubts about Washington's long-term commitment to the nuclear umbrella after President Obama's 2009 Prague speech.[77] The US decision to decommission the remaining Tomahawk land attack missile – nuclear (TLAM – N)[78] provoked further unease in Tokyo. Japanese officials lobbied their US counterparts intensively in an effort to dissuade the Obama administration from embracing a nuclear no-first-use commitment in the 2010 NPR, and argued strongly against the US accepting the principle of mutual vulnerability in its strategic nuclear relationship with China.[79] Following the 2010 NPR, the Obama administration agreed to establish a US–Japan Extended Deterrence Dialogue (EDD) to address Japan's concerns through periodic consultations on the operational direction of US nuclear strategy, and greater transparency on the development of the hardware assets underpinning the US arsenal.[80]

The Trump administration's renewed emphasis on the role of nuclear weapons in US global strategy, including in its more assertive rivalry with China, appears to have diluted earlier concerns in Tokyo about US extended deterrence resolve. Like the Obama administration in 2010, the Trump administration consulted widely with allies in preparing the 2018 NPR. However, from Japan's perspective, the 2018 consultations were not coloured by concern that Washington lacked commitment to the nuclear dimension of extended deterrence, and the 2018 NPR was seen much more positively by Tokyo than the review of 2010.[81]

Tracing nuclear weapons cooperation

Threat assessment and prioritisation

During and after the Cold War, the influence of external threats on Japanese policy aligns strongly with realist views on the reassurance and abandonment fears arising from shared or divergent threat perceptions in the alliance. Japanese policymakers were vocal about the threat emanating from China's acquisition of nuclear weapons in 1964, although there is little evidence that Tokyo was directly threatened by Beijing, other than political attacks on the Sato government.[82] In an operational sense, Japanese defence policy was focused primarily on the military threat from the Soviet Union for most of the Cold War, which was also the main US concern. The rapid expansion of the USSR's ability to project conventional military power in the North Pacific during the 1970s was reinforced by a substantially improved Soviet nuclear first-strike capability against targets in Asia. For Japan, as noted earlier, major ground force deployments by the USSR in the northern territories and the stationing of new-generation strategic nuclear bombers in eastern Siberia underscored the direct military threat posed by the Soviet Union. Conscious that the Soviet Union would target US military installations and air and naval assets based in Japan in the early stages of any global conflict, Japanese policymakers sought deeper operational cooperation with Washington in deterring the USSR.

While there was no fundamental disagreement between US and Japanese policymakers about the significance of China's military modernisation and its growing strategic assertiveness in Asia between 2000 and 2020, for historical and geographical reasons, Tokyo's assessment tended to be harder-edged than Washington's. Territorial disputes in the East China Sea with Beijing magnified Tokyo's concerns, and there has been a view among some Japanese observers that the credibility of US extended deterrence could be attenuated in the event of a US strategic accommodation of China.[83] Indeed, as the US–China economic relationship took off in the 2000s, policymakers in Japan were conscious of any sign the US might be tempted to carve out a closer relationship with China that traded off security assurances for regional allies, including Japan.[84]

In a similar vein, Japanese elites have displayed a high level of concern regarding North Korea's destabilising behaviour and related anxiety that Washington may overlook Japan's security concerns in bargaining with Pyongyang. In the midst of negotiations over the 1994 Agreed Framework, Japanese officials expressed misgivings over proposed US security assurances for Pyongyang that Tokyo regarded as weakening the potential for a US nuclear response to a conventional strike from North Korea.[85] One feature of Tokyo's concerns is the decoupling of Japan's security from US extended nuclear deterrence that might arise from a North Korean capability to carry out nuclear retaliation against the continental US.[86] Japanese policymakers have therefore evinced some unease about hints from the Trump administration that it might be willing to negotiate a cap on North Korea's nuclear-armed intercontinental (range) ballistic missile (ICBM) capability without addressing shorter-range systems that can strike targets in Asia.[87]

Japanese policymakers have thus remained preoccupied since the 2000s with the nuclear dimension of American security guarantees. In practice, this has been evident in behind-the-scenes lobbying for more structured consultation with Washington on extended nuclear deterrence. Converging threat assessments between Washington and Tokyo in relation to China and North Korea have made this process easier, but the constant vigilance of Japanese policymakers regarding any discernible shift in the tone or substance of American extended nuclear deterrence renders this no easy feat. As Toshi Yoshihara and James Holmes have pointed out, 'even barely perceptible signs of weakness in the US nuclear posture' have the capacity 'to trigger alarms and overreactions in Japan'.[88]

Policy objectives regarding nuclear weapons cooperation

Like all US allies, Japan has differed with the US on a range of issues. On issues pertaining to nuclear weapons cooperation, however, there have been very few differences separating Washington and Tokyo. Throughout the Cold War in particular, US and Japanese policy objectives were closely aligned, and focused on reducing the political cost while maximising the strategic benefit of nuclear weapons cooperation.

For the US, the objective was preserving relative freedom (operationally and politically) to make use of Japan for nuclear operations in Northeast Asia. Japanese territory was a major operational hub not only for America's conventional military strategy in Asia, but also for the stationing of nuclear weapons at key island locations, and the ability to transit nuclear-armed platforms through Japan's territorial waters was a significant force multiplier for US nuclear strategy worldwide. For this reason, US policymakers remained concerned during the 1980s that Japan could potentially emulate New Zealand's decision to refuse entry to US nuclear-capable platforms unless Washington declared they were not carrying nuclear weapons.[89]

For Japan, the overriding aim was to preserve the ability of the US to exercise relative freedom operationally and politically as the basis of extended deterrence. As the US embassy in Tokyo noted in a cable to Washington in 1968, 'the security relationship with the US is primarily valued for the "nuclear umbrella" it gives Japan and the role of US forces in the security of South Korea and Taiwan'.[90] In order to support this, Japanese governments sought to avoid any revelation publicly that Tokyo was complicit in promoting nuclear transit through Japanese territory. As one author noted in the early 1990s, 'the contemporary Japanese approach to nuclear weapons instead reflects a sophisticated determination to preserve the flexibility and operational viability of the US deterrent extended to Japan, within the political constraints generated by that country's nuclear allergy'.[91] The highly secretive approach to nuclear transiting arrangements, the covert nature of undeclared US nuclear bases in Ichi Jima and Iwo Jima, and the 'emergency reintroduction' of nuclear weapons clause inserted into the Okinawa reversion agreement each testify to the sensitivity of Japanese governments with respect to public opinion.

In contrast with the desire to keep operational aspects of nuclear weapons cooperation secret, Japan had a strong desire for public US security assurances as part of extended nuclear deterrence. Since the 1960s, this has been an important element in the alliance from Japan's perspective. Following the Johnson administration's commitment that US allies in Asia would be defended against nuclear blackmail from China[92], extended nuclear deterrence in the US–Japan alliance was strengthened during the 1970s. In 1972, US Secretary of Defense Melvin Laird linked countering conventional military threats against the US and its allies to potential escalation to nuclear weapons use by the US.[93] These comments had direct relevance for Japan given the rising conventional threats it was facing from the USSR in the North Pacific. Washington's extension of the nuclear umbrella to Japan was confirmed publicly in 1975. Incorporated in a joint statement between President Ford and Prime Minister Miki, both sides 'recognized that the US nuclear deterrent is an important contributor to the security of Japan' and that 'the United States would continue to abide by its defense commitment under the Treaty of Mutual Cooperation and Security in the event of armed attack against Japan, whether by nuclear or conventional forces'.[94]

Despite the operational imperatives of nuclear transit arrangements disappearing with the end of the Cold War, Washington and Tokyo have nevertheless remained keen to narrow differences over nuclear policy, which did, however, become increasingly symbolic of broader debates and concerns about the future of the alliance. In this respect, the evolution of institutional alliance cooperation in relation to defence and security issues has been a crucial factor. Japanese anxiety during the 2010 NPR process catalysed a new form of nuclear weapons cooperation between Washington and Tokyo. Japanese elites were focused on eliciting declaratory commitments from the US regarding the nuclear umbrella, but they were also keen to create formal consultative arrangements, analogous to NATO's structured planning processes, to manage extended deterrence (discussed in greater detail below).[95] The receptiveness of the US to enhanced extended deterrence consultations with Japan following Tokyo's expressions of concern over the Obama administration's open-mindedness to proposals for a nuclear no-first-use commitment mirrored a desire by Washington to strengthen institutional arrangements that had served the alliance well in the past.

Nuclear strategy

For US nuclear strategy, Japan has been relevant primarily as an enabler of US deterrence and nuclear operations against the Soviet Union, China, and North Korea. Given the strong US force presence and geographic situation of Japan, deterrence and defence against Japan itself did not raise particular challenges for US nuclear strategy. Okinawa was a key base for US bombers from the start of the Cold War, and the movement of US nuclear assets through Japanese waters and airspace during the 1970s and 1980s was a central part of the Carter and Reagan administrations' more assertive force posture in the North Pacific to reinforce US readiness to fight a global war against the Soviet Union. The Reagan administration's strategy of horizontal escalation mandated a central role for US forces stationed in Japan to strike targets in the Soviet Far East in the event of war in Europe or the Middle East; a key operational component of this strategy was the capacity to destroy Soviet nuclear-armed submarines operating in the Pacific.[96] Japanese policymakers were closely attuned to US military strategy during this period, and this sharpened throughout negotiations with the Soviet Union over the INF treaty when Tokyo opposed the idea of a trading US F-16s based in Japan and the presence in the region of US aircraft carriers for the removal of Soviet SS-20 missiles from Asia.[97] Given the strong anti-nuclear sentiment in Japan, however, Japanese policymakers' most important view regarding nuclear strategy was perhaps that they demonstrated significant realism in not rejecting the concept outright. Despite strong Japanese rhetoric publicly on the issue of nuclear disarmament, in practice successive governments have not attempted to hold the nuclear powers seriously to account in international forums for their disarmament commitments. In fact, Japanese officials have focused on ensuring that pro-disarmament resolutions or statements that Japan supports do not endorse a timetable for the elimination of nuclear weapons. As a former senior Japanese arms control diplomat has argued, '[p]roposals such as "the elimination of nuclear weapons within a time bound framework" or a "nuclear abolition treaty" may undermine security, because one cannot foresee the security environment in which abolition will take place'.[98] Even in cases where Japan has led nuclear disarmament initiatives, Tokyo has been unenthusiastic about supporting recommendations in favour of constraining the policies or postures of nuclear powers. Japan's decision in 2017 not to sign the UN Nuclear Weapons Prohibition Treaty similarly reflects Tokyo's ambivalence towards arms control and disarmament initiatives that threaten the freedom of manoeuvre for the US with respect to how it integrates its nuclear forces into security alliance guarantees.[99]

In contrast with NATO allies, but consistent with its arm's length approach to extended deterrence, Japanese governments showed little concern with any specific changes of US nuclear strategy during the Cold War. One exception to this was (and remains) that Japanese policymakers are sensitive to any potential shift in US nuclear doctrine to a no-first-use posture. This reflects the view in Tokyo that, as an embodiment of the underlying US alliance commitment, the nuclear umbrella must provide for a first-use option in retaliation against non-nuclear aggression. This position can be traced to a formal statement by the Nakasone government in 1982 that endorsed a previous statement by the Reagan administration that the US reserved the right to use nuclear weapons against the Soviet Union if it attacked Japanese targets with conventional forces.[100] The view of successive Japanese governments since the early 1980s regarding this position has hardened as China's military modernisation has accelerated, and North Korea's appetite for conventional military provocations has grown as its nuclear and missile programmes have expanded. Even the co-chair of the 2009 International Commission on Nuclear Non-Proliferation and Disarmament, former Japanese Foreign Minister Yoriko Kawaguchi reportedly resisted proposals during the Commission's deliberations to recommend a no-first-use commitment on the part of the five nuclear weapons states.[101]

Domestic factors

Since the 1950s, successive Japanese governments have been confronted with domestic public opinion that remains highly dubious about the role of nuclear weapons in the US alliance. For opponents of the alliance with the US, nuclear weapons are a significant hazard, and the risks of Japan contributing to a nuclear war by supporting US nuclear strategy are morally unacceptable. The likelihood that Japan will be a nuclear target because of its role in American nuclear strategy is also a major reason for opposition to the alliance among the Japanese public. Even supporters of the US–Japan alliance display unease over the nuclear dimension of the alliance. Public support in Japan for the security treaty with the US increased from just over 40 per cent in the late 1960s to almost 70 per cent by the mid-1980s.[102] Although Japanese views of the US remain highly favourable,[103] Japanese opinion is much less favourably disposed to the nuclear umbrella. Polling by the NHK network undertaken in 2014 and 2015[104] showed that most respondents felt US extended nuclear deterrence was unnecessary for Japan's security, despite growing perceptions of threats emanating from North Korea and China. Moreover, more than two-thirds of Japanese oppose the US bringing nuclear weapons in to Japan despite calls from some Diet figures for the stationing of US tactical weapons on Japanese territory.[105]

Unlike South Korean elites, policymakers in Japan remain highly sensitised to domestic opinion when it comes to managing nuclear cooperation with the US. Historically, this distinction was in part due to the democratic nature of the Japanese polity, in contrast to South Korea's authoritarian system during the Cold War, but there can be little doubt that anti-nuclear norms are highly resilient in Japanese society.[106] This juxtaposed with the frequently pro-nuclear views among Japanese policymakers, exemplified most clearly by the disparity between public and elite views regarding the merits of the US nuclear umbrella. Ambivalence over nuclear weapons is also reflected in the gap between the willingness of Japanese elites to countenance a cost–benefit analysis of an indigenous nuclear programme and the overwhelming opposition among the public to nuclear acquisition.

From the 1950s onwards, US officials have recognised this elite-public gap and have tried to exercise sensitivity concerning the nuclear dimension of the alliance. The Nixon administration's decision to agree to a nuclear-free Okinawa, despite doubts expressed by the US Joint Chiefs of Staff and regional allies, is a salient example of this. Even under the hawkish Reagan administration, US officials were conscious of the need to place security cooperation and consultation on a more equal footing.[107]

The importance of Japan for US security

Outside of Europe, Japan was the single most important security ally for the US during the Cold War. Japan's emergence as a major international economic player in its own right during the 1970s reinforced its importance from Washington's perspective as a country with which the US had a close and rapidly expanding trade and investment relationship.[108] Japan's position as the world's third largest economy throughout the 1970s and second largest into the 1980s meant that it acquired growing clout in influential forums. While increasing trade tensions between the US and Japan came to characterise the bilateral relationship throughout the 1980s, Washington nevertheless saw Japan as its most important economic partner in its strategy of promoting Western economic interests during the latter stages of the Cold War.[109]

Japan's geographic location alone made it a highly valued American ally, as it hosted major military bases that provided the US with the ability to project its strategic presence in East Asia. In addition, Japan allowed the US to maintain a significant array of signals intelligence (SIGINT) facilities across the country that contributed directly to American nuclear war planning through the gathering of communications and electronic intelligence targeted at the Soviet Union, China, and North Korea.[110] The powerful imagery of Japan as 'an unsinkable aircraft carrier' originated from a characterisation by Yasuhiro Nakasone, but it was a compelling geostrategic reality for US planners preoccupied with containing Soviet and Chinese influence in Asia. As one US analyst pointed out during the late 1980s:

> Japan's geo-strategic position, close to Soviet territory and in close proximity to the major Siberian military bases of the Soviet Union, gives Japan a special strategic role unmatched by any other Asian country. Consequently, Japan's defense is inseparable for the defense of Asia's other democracies. If Japan decided to remain strategically neutral, the forward defense of the United States would have to retreat to Guam and Hawaii, leaving a rather vulnerable military presence in the Republic of Korea and an isolated presence in the Philippines.[111]

In addition, Tokyo's willingness in practice to defend US nuclear weapons policy internationally in spite of the country's domestic anti-nuclear norm made Japan a valuable ally from Washington's perspective. In seeking to preserve US possession of nuclear weapons by referring to extended deterrence as central to Japan's security – and by implication circumventing the need for Japan to acquire a nuclear inventory of its own – successive Japanese governments not only sought to preserve the legitimacy of the nuclear umbrella, they also demonstrated alliance loyalty to the US. As a major player in the UN system and possessing moral weight because of its Hiroshima and Nagasaki experiences, Japan's unwillingness to pursue nuclear disarmament measures seriously because of its alliance with the US may be a bone of contention among disarmament advocates, but it has undoubtedly been appreciated by policymakers in Washington.[112]

Access to information

Throughout the Cold War, the role of information in the US–Japan alliance aligns with the realist perspective that it has little relevance, as national interest and power are self-evident. An operational military relationship between Japan and the US did not start to take shape until the 1970s, and it was not until the 1980s under the Nakasone government that Japan embraced a defence and foreign policy posture that aligned with its status as a fully fledged US ally. Willingness to discuss bilateral burden sharing and reciprocal security obligations was a hallmark of this shift, which foreshadowed an intensification of information flows under the US–Japan alliance. However, this was largely confined to conventional military planning, with discussion of nuclear weapons limited to their generic role in Japan's security; Japanese officials had no role in developing operational guidelines for the employment of nuclear weapons from Japanese territory. In the area of nuclear weapons cooperation, one author has argued that Japan's approach was 'one of total reliance on American strategy'.[113]

The absence of a US–Japan integrated joint command structure meant that operational insights into American nuclear strategy (especially targeting policy) would have been hard to glean during the Cold War. Notwithstanding some designated areas where the SDF supported US nuclear operations in waters surrounding Japan during crisis scenarios, Tokyo had no direct involvement in nuclear planning or coordination at the level of policy. Moreover, as distinct from their South Korean counterparts, there is no evidence that Japanese officials requested any direct role in nuclear war planning. Unlike South Korea and NATO counterparts, there appears to have been no pressing desire among Japanese policymakers for access to technical or operational-level information about nuclear weapons. Instead, the focus was on the depth of US strategic commitments at the political level. In this respect, Japanese officials were content with a form of cooperation on nuclear weapons that remained arm's length in nature.

After the Cold War, however, the previously self-evident nature of the US interest in Japan's security diminished. Hence, Japan has sought closer institutional access to information about US nuclear policy – a desire that US administrations have generally been inclined to accommodate as a means of strengthening trust in the alliance. The creation of the bilateral EDD in 2011 is the most obvious example of where this has occurred. The Obama administration proved receptive to demands from Tokyo for an extended deterrence dialogue following the 2010 NPR. A hallmark of the EDD has been 'hardware' tours for Japanese officials of US nuclear weapons infrastructure. This has included visits to ICBM command posts, boarding nuclear-armed *Ohio*-class SSBNs, and visiting the research and development laboratories overseen by the US National Nuclear Security Administration.[114] However, US officials were explicit that this dialogue would take place within the existing framework of the SCC and not mimic NATO's Nuclear Planning Group as a stand-alone institution within the alliance. Furthermore, the EDD would be strictly consultative and not have any decision-making role with respect to nuclear planning, or discussion of shared nuclear command and control or joint deployment arrangements.[115] A State Department official has since confirmed that, in the case of Japan, the US rejected any bargaining within the EDD over the specific type of extended nuclear deterrence assurances conferred by the US.[116]

Conclusion

The US-Japan alliance has been marked by a high degree of stability since it came into effect in 1952. For most of the history of the alliance, Washington and Tokyo have worked hard to promote policy unity and cohesive intent on key strategic questions. On the nuclear front, aside from brief periods in the early 1970s and late 2000s, there has been little evidence of any meaningful policy divergence between Japan and the US. Although one could point to the occasional flirtation of Japanese governments with an indigenous nuclear option and juxtapose this with US non-proliferation policy, even here there is less difference than meets the eye. Over the course of many governments, Japan's approach has been framed consistently in terms of careful, strategic cost–benefit calculations, rather than doubts about US security guarantees.

Compared with some of its other alliance relationships, the US has demonstrated forbearance in dealing with Japanese policymakers when their preferences have diverged from those of Washington. This testifies to the strategic importance of Japan to the US, but it also reflects the deep political and economic ties between the two countries that have developed since the inception of the security alliance. Importantly, it also mirrors the institutional architecture that has been built up within the alliance over time.

Unlike most of the other cases covered in this book, the defence and security tracks of the US–Japan alliance at no point eclipsed the depth of the political relationship between the two countries. This may explain why Japanese apprehension over the potential of alliance abandonment has never been as acute as South Korea's anxiety.

During the Cold War, access to Japanese territory was an enabler of the US ability to conduct nuclear operations across the globe. The covert transit of US nuclear-armed platforms through Japan was complemented by the hosting of bases designed to support the ability of the US to project nuclear force in the event of a world war. Japan also played an important role in supporting US SIGINT facilities, and the SDF contributed to nuclear command and control exercises with their US counterparts in the 1980s. From Tokyo's perspective, reinforcing this cooperation were US extended nuclear deterrence reassurances that circumvented the need for Japan to consider seriously acquiring its own nuclear force. The nuclear umbrella was a central thread of the US–Japan security alliance, and the institutional frameworks that were initiated to create more operationally focused bilateral dialogue on extended deterrence in 2010 built on more than four decades of political and strategic cooperation between Washington and Tokyo.

In all of this, deep-seated contradictions have had to be managed by Japanese governments. The most obvious of these has been the strong anti-nuclear norms permeating Japanese society, and the growing role of nuclear weapons in the US–Japan alliance. The acute sensitivity of nuclear issues for successive governments in Tokyo has been reflected in attempts to maintain a low-key public profile with respect to nuclear cooperation in the US alliance. Washington has been cognisant of this, and US officials have remained attuned to the brittleness of public opinion in Japan regarding nuclear issues and its potential to undermine broader support for the alliance.

Notes

1 M. Jansen, *The Making of Modern Japan* (Cambridge, MA: Harvard University Press, 2000), chapter 19.

2 For discussion, see R. Samuels, *'Rich Nation, Strong Army': National Security and the Technological Transformation of Japan* (Ithaca, NY: Cornell University Press, 1994), chapter 5.

3 J. Dower, 'The San Francisco System: Past, Present, Future in US-Japan-China Relations', *Japan Focus: The Asia-Pacific Journal*, 1:8 (2014), https://apjjf.org/2014/12/8/John-W.-Dower/4079/article.html

4 S. Guthrie-Shimizu, 'Japan, the United States, and the Cold War: 1945–1960', in M. Leffler and O. Arne Westad (eds), *The Cambridge History of the Cold War*, Vol. 1: *Origins* (Cambridge: Cambridge University Press, 2010), 253.
5 Guthrie-Shimizu, 'Japan, the United States, and the Cold War', 264.
6 P. Katzenstein, *Cultural Norms and National Security: Police and Military in Postwar Japan* (Ithaca, NY: Cornell University Press, 1996), 143.
7 V. Cha, *Powerplay: The Origins of the American Alliance System in Asia* (Princeton, NJ: Princeton University Press, 2016), 154–155.
8 C. Johnson, *Blowback: The Costs and Consequences of American Empire* (New York: Metropolitan Books, 2000), 177.
9 R. Samuels, *Securing Japan: Tokyo's Grand Strategy and the Future of East Asia* (Ithaca, NY: Cornell University Press, 2007), 44.
10 Katzenstein, *Cultural Norms and National Security*, 104–108.
11 V. Cha, *Alignment Despite Antagonism: The US-Korea-Japan Security Triangle* (Stanford, CA: Stanford University Press, 1999), 72–73.
12 M. Yoshii, 'The Creation of the "Shock Myth": Japan's Reactions to America's Rapprochement with China, 1971–72', *Journal of American East Asian Relations*, 15 (2008), 131–146.
13 S. Akihiro, *The Self Defense Forces and Postwar Politics in Japan* (Tokyo: JPIC, 2017), 82–84.
14 A. Kurosaki, 'Nuclear Energy and Nuclear Weapon Potential: A Historical Analysis of Japan in the 1960s', *Nonproliferation Review*, 24:1/2 (2017), 52–54.
15 Y. Komine, 'Whither a 'Resurgent Japan': The Nixon Doctrine and Japan's Defense Buildup', *Journal of Cold War Studies*, 16:3 (2014), 98–99.
16 M. Green and K. Furukawa, 'Japan: New Nuclear Realism', in M. Alagappa (ed.), *The Long Shadow: Nuclear Weapons and Security in 21st Century Asia* (Stanford, CA: Stanford University Press, 2008), 351.
17 For a summary, see 'Japanese Defence Policy', *Survival*, 13:1 (1971), 2–8.
18 Komine, 'Whither a 'Resurgent Japan', 104–105.
19 'National Defense Program Outline, October 29 1976', http://worldjpn.grips.ac.jp/documents/texts/docs/19761029.O1E.html
20 Akihiro, *The Self Defense Forces and Postwar Politics in Japan*, 111.
21 'Guidelines for Japan-US Defense Cooperation: Report by the Subcommittee for Defense Cooperation, Submitted to and Approved by the Japan-US Security Consultative Committee, November 27 1978', https://japan2.usembassy.gov/pdfs/wwwf-mdao-defense-guidelines1978.pdf
22 Y. Komine, *Negotiating the US-Japan Alliance: Japan Confidential* (London and New York: Routledge, 2017), 224.
23 This cap obtained in practice until 1987 when it was breached by the Nakasone government in the annual defence budget. C. Haberman, 'Japan Formally Drops Military Spending Cap', *New York Times*, 25 January 1987, www.nytimes.com/1987/01/25/world/japan-formally-drops-military-spending-cap.html
24 T. Hasegawa, 'The Soviet Factor in US-Japanese Defense Cooperation, 1978–1985', *Journal of Cold War Studies*, 15:2 (2013), 79.

25 D. Oberdorfer, 'How to Make a Japanese Brouhaha', *Washington Post*, 20 March 1983, www.washingtonpost.com/archive/opinions/1983/03/20/how-to-make-a-japanese-brouhaha/0e508dd9–105b-4673–98aa-1e63fe8eae08/.

26 On the implications of the maritime strategy for US allies in Asia, see E. Olsen, 'The Maritime Strategy in the Western Pacific', *Naval War College Review*, 40:4 (1987), 38–49.

27 Samuels, *Securing Japan,* 90.

28 Akihiro, *The Self Defense Forces and Postwar Politics in Japan*, 141–142.

29 S. Smith, *Japan Rearmed: The Politics of Military Power* (Cambridge, MA: Harvard University Press, 2019), 44–46.

30 For a description of the respective changes, see Ministry of Defense, *Defence of Japan 2013*, www.mod.go.jp/e/publ/w_paper/2013.htmlwww

31 Ministry of Defense, 'National Defense Program Guidelines for FY 2014 and Beyond (Summary)', www.mod.go.jp/e/d_act/d_policy/national.htmlwww

32 Ministry of Defense, 'The Guidelines for Japan-US Defense Cooperation (September 23, 1997)', www.mod.go.jp/e/d_act/us/anpo/19970923.htmlwww

33 US Department of Defense, 'The Guidelines for US-Japan Defense Cooperation (April 27, 2015)', https://archive.defense.gov/pubs/20150427_–_GUIDELINES_FOR_US-JAPAN_DEFENSE_COOPERATION.pdf

34 E. Chanlett-Avery, 'The US-Japan Alliance', *Congressional Research Service Report*, RL33740, 13 June 2019, 27, https:// fas.org/ sgp/ crs/ row/ RL33740.pdf

35 B. Elias Mikalsen Gronning, 'Operational and Industrial Military Integration: Extending the Frontiers of the Japan-US Alliance', *International Affairs*, 94:4 (2018), 5.

36 See J. Wuthnow, 'US Minilateralism in Asia and China's Responses: A New Security Dilemma?', *Journal of Contemporary China*, 28:115 (2019), 133–150.

37 E. Chanlett-Avery, M. Manyin, B. Williams, and C. Cimino-Isaacs, 'US-Japan Relations in Focus', *Congressional Research Service*, 29 April 2020, https://fas.org/sgp/crs/row/IF10199.pdf

38 J. Przystup, 'The Enduring Relevance of the US-Japan Alliance', *INSS Strategic Forum*, July 2019, https://inss.ndu.edu/Portals/68/Documents/stratforum/SF-300.pdf?ver=2019–07–23–142433–990

39 H. Envall, 'What Kind of Japan? Tokyo's Strategic Options in a Contested Asia', *Survival*, 6:4 (2019), 119.

40 J. Welfield, 'Japan and Nuclear China: Japanese Reactions to China's Nuclear Weapons', *Canberra Papers on Strategy and Defence*, no. 9 (Canberra: Australian National University Press, 1970), 14–15.

41 M. Reiss, *Without the Bomb: The Politics of Nuclear Nonproliferation* (New York: Columbia University Press, 1988), 122.

42 T. Nakanishi, 'US Policy and Japan', *The Washington Quarterly*, 10:1 (1987), 82.

43 R. Samuels and J. Schoff, 'Japan's Nuclear Hedge: Beyond "Allergy" and Breakout', *Political Science Quarterly*, 130(3), 2015, 473–503.

44 M. Ota, 'Conceptual Twist of Japanese Nuclear Policy: Its Ambivalence and Coherence Under the US Nuclear Umbrella', *Journal for Peace and Nuclear Disarmament*, 1:1 (2018), 204.

45 Reiss, *Without the Bomb*, 133. A major feature of the specialist literature in the 1970s was the plethora of detailed studies examining the various pathways by which Japan could acquire a national nuclear weapons force and the accompanying deployment, posture, and targeting policies that would result. The most significant is J. Endicott, *Japan's Nuclear Option: Political, Technical, and Strategic Factors* (New York: Praeger, 1975).

46 J. Hymans, 'Veto Players, Nuclear Energy, and Nonproliferation: Domestic Institutional Barriers to a Japanese Bomb', *International Security*, 36:2 (2011), 172.

47 E. Solingen, *Nuclear Logics: Contrasting Paths in East Asia and the Middle East* (Princeton, NJ and Oxford: Princeton University Press, 2007), 57.

48 These were all common themes in commentary at the time of Japan's signature. See G. Quester, 'Japan and the Nuclear Non-Proliferation Treaty', *Asian Survey*, 10:9 (1970), 765–778.

49 The only other US agreement with similar provisions relates to the European EURATOM consortium. M. Montgomery, 'US, Japan Extend Nuclear Agreement', *Arms Control Today*, September 2018, www.armscontrol.org/act/2018–09/news-briefs/us-japan-extend-nuclear-agreement; D. Demetriou, 'US-Japan Nuclear Pact Extended Despite Concern Over Tokyo's Plutonium Stockpile', *Telegraph*, 18 July 2018, www.telegraph.co.uk/news/2018/07/18/us-japan-nuclear-pact-extended-despite-concern-tokyos-plutoniumstockpile/

50 Quoted in Cha, *Powerplay*, 157.

51 W. Burr and J. Kimball, *Nixon's Nuclear Specter: The Secret Alert of 1969, Madman Diplomacy, and the Vietnam War* (Lawrence, KA: University Press of Kansas, 2015), 19.

52 R. Norris, W. Arkin, and W. Burr, 'Where They Were: How Much Did Japan Know?', *Bulletin of the Atomic Scientists* (January–February 2000), 78–79.

53 Norris, Arkin, and Burr, 'Where They Were', 12.

54 Norris, Arkin, and Burr, 'Where They Were', 12.

55 H. Kristensen, R. Norris, and M. McKinzie, *Chinese Nuclear Forces and US Nuclear War Planning* (Washington, DC: Federation of American Scientists and the Natural Resources Defense Council, 2006), 134–135.

56 D. Ellsberg, *The Doomsday Machine: Confessions of a Nuclear War Planner* (New York: Bloomsbury, 2017), 79.

57 M. Bullard, 'Japan's Nuclear Choice', *Asian Survey*, 14:9 (1974), 849.

58 Komine, *Negotiating the US-Japan Alliance*, 35–36.

59 K. Ayako, 'The Sato Cabinet and the Making of Japan's Non-Nuclear Policy', *Journal of American-East Asian Relations*, 15 (2008), 46–47.

60 'Description of Consultation Arrangements Under the Treaty of Mutual Security and Cooperation with Japan, June 1960, https://nsarchive2.gwu.edu/nukevault/ebb291/doc01.pdf

61 M. Yamazaki, 'Nuclear Energy in Postwar Japan and Anti-Nuclear Movements in the 1950s', *Historia Scientiarum*, 19:2 (2009), 132–145.

62 In 1968, Sato combined the 'three principles' with the pursuit of a peaceful nuclear programme and nuclear disarmament, as well as the nuclear umbrella to form 'four pillars' of Japan's nuclear policy. See A. Kurosaki, 'Public Opinion, Party Politics and Alliance: The Influence of Domestic Politics on Japan's Reliance on the US Nuclear Umbrella, 1964–8', *The International History Review*, 42:4 (2020), 774-793.

63 Ota, 'Conceptual Twist of Japanese Nuclear Policy', 201.

64 Department of State, 'Memorandum from the Joint Chiefs of Staff to Secretary of Defense McNamara, JCSM-900–65, Washington, December 23, 1965', in *Foreign Relations of the United States: 1964–1968*, Vol. 29, Part 2; *Japan*, https://history.state.gov/historicaldocuments/frus1964–68v29p2/d65

65 H. Kim, 'The Sato Government and the Politics of Okinawa Reversion', *Asian Survey*, 13:110 (1973), 1024–1025.

66 Ayako, 'The Sato Cabinet and the Making of Japan's Non-Nuclear Policy', 48.

67 Komine, 'Okinawa Confidential', 838.

68 H. Kissinger, *The White House Years* (London: George Weidenfeld and Nicholson, 1979), 335.

69 'Japan Officially Gave US Consent to Bring in Nuclear Weapons Ahead of Okinawa Reversion Accord: Document', *Japan Times*, 14 August 2017, www.japantimes.co.jp/news/2017/08/14/national/history/japan-officially-gave-u-s-consent-bring-nukes-ahead-okinawa-reversion-accord-document/

70 Cha, *Alignment Despite Antagonism*, 75. Similarly, Japan remained concerned in the 1970s over US moves to withdraw its forces from the Korean Peninsula.

71 Quoted in Y. Komine, 'Okinawa Confidential, 1969: Exploring the Linkage between the Nuclear Issue and the Base Issue', *Diplomatic History*, 27:4 (2013), 838.

72 H. Kristensen, 'Japan Under the US Nuclear Umbrella', *Nautilus Institute for Security and Sustainability*, 21 July 1999, https://nautilus.org/supporting-documents/japan-under-the-us-nuclear-umbrella/

73 L. Hughes, 'Why Japan Will Not Go Nuclear (Yet); International and Domestic Constraints on the Nuclearization of Japan', *International Security*, 31:4 (2007), 87.

74 H. Kristensen, 'Declassified: US Nuclear Weapons at Sea', *Federation of American Scientists Blog*, 3 February 2016, https://fas.org/blogs/security/2016/02/nuclear-weapons-at-sea/

75 E. Heginbotham and R. Samuels, 'Active Denial: Redesigning Japan's Response to China's Military Challenge', *International Security*, 42:4 (2018), 144.

76 Green and Furukawa, 'Japan', 364.

77 According to Greg Kulacki, a senior analyst with the Union of Concerned Scientists, senior Japanese officials attending hearings of the Congressional Commission on the Strategic Posture of the United States in 2009 disseminated a paper recommending that US extended nuclear deterrence capabilities needed to be 'flexible, credible, prompt, discriminating and selective, stealthy and

demonstrable, and sufficient to dissuade others from expanding or modernizing their nuclear capabilities'. See N. Fujita, 'US Analyst: Japan's Nuke Stance Obstructs Arms Control', *The Asahi Shimbun*, 26 April 2018.

78 This followed an earlier announcement by the Bush administration to mothball the system. See H. Kristensen, 'Japan, TLAM/N, and extended deterrence', *Federation of American Scientists Blog*, 2 July 2009, available at: https://fas.org/blogs/security/2009/07/tlam/

79 N. Abe, 'No First Use: How to Overcome Japan's Great Divide', *Journal for Peace and Nuclear Disarmament*, 1:1 (2018), 145–146.

80 B. Roberts, 'Extended Deterrence and Strategic Stability in Northeast Asia', *NIDS Visiting Scholar Paper Series*, 1 (2013), www.nids.mod.go.jp/english/publication/visiting/pdf/01.pdf

81 M. Ota, 'Japan Warned Us Over Reductions to Nuclear Arsenal and Sought Flexible Deterrence, 2009 Memo Reveals', *Japan Times*, 4 April 2018, www.japantimes.co.jp/news/2018/04/04/national/politics-diplomacy/japan-warned-u-s-reductions-nuclear-arsenal-sought-flexible-deterrence-2009-memo-reveals/

82 T. Peng, 'China's Changing Japan Policy in the Late 1960s and Early 1970s and the Impact on Relations with the United States', *Journal of American-East Asian Relations*, 15 (2008), 153–158.

83 C. Hughes, 'Japan's "Resentful Realism" and Balancing China's Rise', *Chinese Journal of International Politics*, 9:2 (2016), 138.

84 Samuels, *Securing Japan*, 156–157.

85 J. Wit, D. Poneman, and R. Gallucci, *Going Critical: The First North Korean Nuclear Crisis* (Washington, DC: Brookings Institution Press, 2004), 290–291.

86 For analysis, see M. Rapp-Hooper, 'Decoupling is Back in Asia: A 1960s Playbook Won't Save These Problems', *War on the Rocks*, 7 September 2017, https://warontherocks.com/2017/09/decoupling-is-back-in-asia-a-1960s-playbook-wont-solve-these-problems/

87 M. Landler, 'As Next Trump-Kim Summit Nears, Japan Worries US Will Leave it in the Dark', *New York Times*, 23 January 2019, www.nytimes.com/2019/01/23/world/asia/shinzo-abe-north-korea-trump.html

88 T. Yoshihara and J. Holmes, 'Thinking About the Unthinkable: Tokyo's Nuclear Option', *Naval War College Review*, 63:2 (2009), 65.

89 Kristensen, 'Japan Under the US Nuclear Umbrella'.

90 Department of State, 'Telegram from the Embassy in Japan to the Department of State, Tokyo, June 5, 1968, 0700Z', in *Foreign Relations of the United States: 1964–1968*, Vol. 29, Part 2: *Japan*, https://history.state.gov/historicaldocuments/frus1964–68v29p2/d123

91 W. Tow, *Encountering the Dominant Player: US Extended Deterrence Strategy in the Asia-Pacific* (New York: Columbia University Press, 1991), 87.

92 L. Johnson, 'Remarks at the State Dinner at Parliament House, Kuala Lumpur, Malaysia, October 30, 1966', in *Public Papers of the Presidents, 1966, Book II*, available at: www.presidency.ucsb.edu/ws/index.php?pid=27971#axzz1n4DpGsuo

93 J. Van de Velde, 'Japan's Nuclear Umbrella: US Extended Nuclear Deterrence for Japan', *Journal of Northeast Asian Studies*, 7:4 (1988), 18.
94 G. Ford, 'Japan-US Joint Announcement the Press (by Prime Minister Takeo Miki and President Gerald R. Ford, Washington DC, August 6, 1975', in *Public Papers of the Presidents: Gerald Ford, 1975*, Book II (Washington, DC: US Government Printing Office, 1976), 1114.
95 B. Roberts, *The Case for US Nuclear Weapons in the 21st Century* (Stanford, CA: Stanford University Press, 2016), 206.
96 J. Epstein, 'Horizontal Escalation: Sour Notes of a Recurrent Theme', *International Security*, 8:3 (1983–84), 25.
97 D. Jones, 'Post-INF Treaty Attitudes in East Asia', *Asian Survey*, 30:5 (1990), 485.
98 Y. Amano, 'A Japanese View on Nuclear Disarmament', *Nonproliferation Review*, 9:1 (2002), 142.
99 'Japan Abstains as Nuclear Arms Ban Treaty Talks Start at UN', *Japan Times*, 28 March 2017. www.japantimes.co.jp/news/2017/03/28/national/japan-abstains-talks-start-u-n-nuclear-arms-ban-treaty/
100 M. Takubo, 'The Role of Nuclear Weapons: Japan, the US, and 'Sole Purpose', *Arms Control Today*, 5 November 2009, www.armscontrol.org/act/2009_11/Takubo
101 D. Flitton, 'Australia, Japan in Nuclear Rift', *Sydney Morning Herald*, 4 September 2009, www.smh.com.au/national/australia-japan-in-nuclear-rift-20090903-f9yw.html
102 Katzenstein, *Cultural Norms and National Security*, 148.
103 B. Stokes and K. Devlin, 'Views of the US and President Trump', *Pew Research Centre: Global Attitudes and Trends*, 12 November 2018, www.pewresearch.org/global/2018/11/12/views-of-the-u-s-and-president-trump/
104 M. Mochizuki, 'Three Reasons Why Japan Will Likely Continue to Reject Nuclear Weapons', *Washington Post*, 6 November 2017, https://www.washingtonpost.com/news/monkey-cage/wp/2017/11/06/japan-is-likely-to-retain-its-non-nuclear-principles-heres-why/
105 Mochizuki, 'Three Reasons Why Japan Will Likely Continue to Reject Nuclear Weapons'.
106 See M. Rost Rublee, *Nonproliferation Norms: Why States Choose Nuclear Restraint* (Athens, GA and London: University of Georgia Press, 2009), chapter 3.
107 Hasegawa, 'The Soviet Factor in US-Japanese Defense Cooperation', 98–99.
108 G. Curtis, 'US Policy Towards Japan from Nixon to Clinton: An Assessment', in G. Curtis (ed.), *New Perspectives on US-Japan Relations* (Tokyo: Japan Center for International Exchange, Tokyo, 2000), 3–6.
109 E. Vogel, 'Japanese-American Relations After the Cold War', *Daedalus*, 121:4 (1992), 35–38.
110 D. Ball and R. Tanter, 'US Signals Intelligence (SIGINT) Activities in Japan: 1945–2015', *Japan Focus: The Asia Pacific Journal*, 14:6 (2016), https://apjjf.org/2016/06/Ball.html

111 Van de Velde, 'Japan's Nuclear Umbrella', 20.
112 M. Halperin, 'The Nuclear Dimension of the U.S.-Japan Alliance', *NAPSNet Special Reports*, 21 December 2000, https://nautilus.org/napsnet/napsnet-special-reports/the-nuclear-dimension-of-the-u-s-japan-alliance/
113 Van de Velde, 'Japan's Nuclear Umbrella', 29.
114 T. Roehrig, *Japan, South Korea, and the United States Nuclear Umbrella: Deterrence After the Cold War* (New York: Columbia University Press, 2017), 109.
115 Interview with State Department official, Washington, DC, 16 July 2015.
116 Interview with State Department official, Washington, DC, 16 July 2015.

5

Assurance and abandonment: Nuclear weapons in the US–South Korea alliance

Situated in one of the most militarised regions in the world, South Korea has a long-standing relationship with nuclear weapons that is evident in three domains. The first is that South Korea initiated and subsequently shelved an indigenous nuclear weapons programme. Fearing abandonment and looking to reinforce South Korea's capacity for military self-reliance in the face of a hostile northern neighbour, the Park Chung-hee government created a secret bomb programme in the 1970s that was only terminated after the US threatened to review formally the bilateral alliance. Second, South Korea today confronts a nuclear-armed state with which it remains technically at war. North Korea's acquisition of nuclear weapons has changed the threat environment dramatically for South Korea and underscored the country's vulnerability to coercion from Pyongyang. Third, nuclear weapons have been an element in South Korea's alliance with the US, ever since the US first deployed tactical nuclear weapons on the Korean Peninsula in the late 1950s.

Despite hosting US nuclear weapons from 1958 to 1991, South Korea was essentially excluded from nuclear planning on the Korean Peninsula during this period. Until the late 1970s, and even beyond, the US–South Korea relationship was characterised by a transactional nature of interactions, underdeveloped bilateral security institutions, and a marked power asymmetry between Washington and Seoul. Only with the advent of deeper institutional ballast in the alliance under the Bush and Obama administrations, in the context of the growing North Korean nuclear threat, has there been closer consultation on nuclear weapons between Washington and Seoul.

The US–South Korea alliance

The US–South Korea alliance has its roots in armed conflict. US military engagement on the Korean Peninsula began after the Second World War, when American forces occupied the southern zone of the peninsula. The partitioning of the two Koreas in 1948 created the Republic of Korea (ROK), as well as the Democratic People's Republic of Korea (DPRK) in the Soviet-occupied zone north of the thirty-eighth parallel. Inter-Korean rivalries deepened under the respective leadership of the staunch anti-Communist ROK President Syngman Rhee and the hardline North Korean leader Kim Il-sung. Frequent military skirmishes across the border resulting from probing actions on both sides suggested that escalation to all-out military conflict was only a matter of time.

By 1949, however, the consensus in the US government was that, because of geostrategic demands elsewhere, combined with significant fiscal pressure domestically and a belief that North Korea would not launch a full-scale invasion, South Korea did not figure as a priority in US global planning. Moreover, as Stueck argues, 'reinforcing the predisposition for withdrawal was the lack of enthusiasm in Washington for the volatile, autocratic Rhee, who threatened to mobilise his troops and march north'.[1] The Truman administration scaled back the US military commitment to South Korea, withdrawing all American forces from the peninsula in mid-1949, though maintaining substantial military and economic assistance to Seoul.[2] In his famous 'defensive perimeter' speech in January 1950, US Secretary of State Dean Acheson omitted the Korean Peninsula from the list of theatres globally that the US was willing to defend with force. Occurring shortly after the withdrawal of US forces from South Korea, Acheson's speech was linked to the decision by Pyongyang to invade South Korea in June 1950, with the material backing of the Soviet Union.[3]

Fought to a bitter stalemate, the Korean War was the driving force behind the formation of the US–ROK alliance. Instituted under the Mutual Defense Treaty of 1953, the alliance would come to be defined by three key features. The first was a large-scale US military presence on the peninsula. The Korean War had witnessed the massive deployment of US ground, air, and naval assets to South Korea, but as soon as the conflict ended, the Eisenhower administration was looking for ways to reduce the number of ground forces stationed on the peninsula. As early as 1956, an assessment by the US National Security Council found that notwithstanding 'weakness in the air, the ROK, given adequate logistical support could repel aggression by North Korean forces alone'.[4] However, reducing conventional forces would later prove vexing for Washington, particularly during the Nixon and Carter administrations. Nixon had aimed to cut the US troop presence by half at the start of his administration[5], while Carter enunciated a plan during his 1976 presidential election campaign to withdraw all US military forces by 1982.[6] Yet, largely because of resistance within the US bureaucracy and upward reassessments of North Korean military strength, only one-third of US ground forces were withdrawn from South Korea between 1969 and 1981.[7]

The second key feature of the US–ROK alliance was that, until 1978, even in peacetime, all South Korean military forces were placed under US operational control. This reflected Washington's concerns that the ROK military would reignite a second Korea War if it were controlled exclusively by the Syngman Rhee government.[8] The creation of Combined Forces Command (CFC) in 1978 institutionalised a binational military command structure through which South Korean officers began to be involved in operational decision making. CFC arrangements established joint operational command of allied forces in peacetime, but preserved sole US command over American and ROK forces in wartime.[9] Not until 1994 did South Korea regain peacetime operational command over ROK forces, and in 2007 following protracted negotiations, the US agreed to transfer complete operational control to South Korea by 2012.[10] Yet, owing to persistent concerns in Seoul about the potential decoupling of the US from the security of the Korean Peninsula, the so-called 'operational control (OPCON) transfer' has been deferred repeatedly since 2007.[11]

The third key feature of the alliance was a dearth of institutional frameworks to coordinate the bilateral relationship. In contrast to NATO and the US–Japan alliance, the US–ROK alliance had few political–military institutions in its first two decades. It was not until 1971 that Washington agreed to a bilateral forum – the Security Consultative Mechanism (later changed to Security Consultative Meeting [SCM]) – to coordinate the political aspects of alliance management. While the Park Chung-hee government had agitated for closer political coordination of alliance matters following the re-emergence of serious North Korean provocations in the late 1960s, the SCM appears to have been a direct quid pro quo by the Nixon administration to reassure Seoul in the wake of Washington's unilateral announcement in 1970 of a 20,000 troop drawdown on the peninsula.[12] Many of the alliance insecurities on the part of South Korea and related fears of US abandonment in the 1960s and 1970s were a corollary of the under-institutionalised nature of the alliance.

Of all US alliances, none has featured entrapment and abandonment concerns so prominently and consistently as the alliance with South Korea. While the US remained anxious about the potential for entrapment under the leadership of Syngman Rhee, South Korea under the leadership of Park

Chung-hee (1963–79) exhibited serious fears of abandonment. South Korea provided the second-largest foreign troop contingent in support of the US in the Vietnam War, but remained apprehensive throughout the 1970s over the prospect of a US withdrawal from the Korean Peninsula. In the wake of the Guam Doctrine, the Nixon administration flagged its intention to withdraw an infantry division from South Korea, which was presented to Seoul as a fait accompli. Overlapping with a US–China rapprochement, increasing North Korean military provocations, and growing concern over US resolve and commitment in the face of looming defeat in Vietnam, Nixon's troop withdrawal plan was a factor in President Park's authorisation in 1971 of a covert South Korean nuclear weapons programme.[13] In a letter to Park in the same year, Nixon underscored the importance of US allies accepting burden sharing,[14] but a lack of serious consultation with Seoul in the lead-up to the withdrawal decision was probably just as damaging as the decision itself.

The Ford administration provided a brief period of reassurance for the Park government, with senior US officials conscious of the connection between Seoul's abandonment anxieties and South Korea's nuclear programme, which US intelligence agencies had detected in 1975.[15] The imperative of reassuring America's Asian allies following the fall of Saigon in April 1975 was especially important in South Korea's case, given Park's public and privately stated fears that North Korea would be emboldened by the US defeat to launch an invasion of the South.[16] Yet, the Carter administration reversed this positive turn in 1977 when it announced that US forces, including all nuclear forces, would be removed from South Korea by 1982. The Park government's poor human rights record reinforced Carter's personal determination to fast-track plans for a US pull-out, notwithstanding concerted opposition from within Congress, the Pentagon, and some senior administration officials.[17] It was only after the depth of this opposition became apparent, along with a revised intelligence assessment of North Korea's combat capabilities, that US withdrawal plans were deferred.[18]

Park's assassination in 1979 and the advent of the Reagan administration foreshadowed a more stable period in the US–ROK alliance. Seoul and Washington jointly affirmed a more equal alliance relationship, and the Reagan administration committed to maintaining US force levels, cancelled plans to withdraw tactical nuclear weapons, and supplied significant amounts of advanced weaponry to the ROK military.[19] Moreover, South Korea's gradual transition to democratic governance throughout the 1980s – culminating in the first democratic elections in 1987 – served to stabilise the alliance with the US, which in turn helped South Korea along the path to democratisation.[20]

The end of the Cold War in the late 1980s led to a significant improvement in the security situation on the Korean Peninsula with the conclusion of a landmark denuclearisation agreement between the two Koreas in 1991. South Korea's establishment of formal diplomatic relations with China and the USSR effectively weakened North Korea's strategic position on the peninsula and exposed further the massive gap between the two Koreas in terms of economic development, global engagement, and political maturity.[21] By the early 1990s, it seemed that the US–ROK alliance was entering a new phase where the threat environment would decline over time.

This optimism was punctured by dramatic revelations of North Korea's covert nuclear weapons programme and accompanying evidence of a highly ambitious ballistic missile development programme. The first Korean nuclear crisis in 1993–94 tested the US–ROK alliance in several respects, not least because of perceptions in Seoul that it was not being fully consulted by the Clinton administration, including on plans for a US preventive military strike against North Korea's nuclear assets. A similar dynamic was evident in the 2002–3 nuclear crisis, when the incoming South Korean President, Roh Moo-hyun, expressed concerns over potential entrapment in a US-led war against North Korea.[22] For its part, the Bush administration made no secret of its scepticism regarding efforts by Kim Dae-jung and Roh Moo-hyun to engage Pyongyang through the so-called 'Sunshine Policy'.[23]

Notwithstanding these periodic tensions, however, the US–ROK alliance was bolstered significantly under the Bush and Obama administrations, including through the creation of new subcommittees to coordinate defence and strategic policy under the framework of the US–ROK SCM.[24] The high point was the 'Joint Vision' declaration in 2009, which endorsed a highly ambitious future for the US–ROK alliance and accompanied the continuing expansion of alliance institutions. In the wake of North Korea's sinking of a South Korean navy vessel and artillery strikes against the island of Yeonpyeong in 2010, and amid signs of underlying tension between Seoul and Washington over how to respond to North Korean provocations,[25] the US and South Korea agreed to create a consultative body on extended deterrence (the Extended Deterrence Policy Committee [EDPC])[26] and more detailed arrangements for military cooperation at the tactical and operational levels.[27]

This was reinforced by the signing of a 'counter provocation plan' between the US and ROK militaries that envisaged 'a doctrine of disproportionate retaliation, delegated decision-making authority to tactical level commanders, unilateral military action, and even pre-emptive strikes under certain conditions'.[28] In essence, the plan codified more permissive rules of engagement and employment of higher-level military force in response to future North Korean provocations. In May 2013, the Chairman of the

ROK Joint Chiefs of Staff and the Commander of US Forces in Korea signed an upgraded combined readiness plan designed to implement the new initiative.[29] A subsequent offshoot of the counter provocation plan was the announcement in 2016 that South Korea would launch 'decapitation strikes' against senior North Korean leaders in the early stages of any conflict.[30]

The advent of the Moon Jae-in government in 2017 occurred as the Trump administration was particularly concerned about North Korea's emerging ability to strike the US mainland with nuclear weapons. Throughout 2017, there was a sense that Washington was moving closer to military action on the Korean Peninsula than it had since the 1993–94 nuclear crisis.[31] Displaying similar entrapment fears to those of previous ROK governments, the Moon administration successfully extracted a commitment from the US that South Korean approval would be required prior to any military strike being authorised on the peninsula.[32] In a year when Seoul and Washington proceeded with the deployment of terminal high-altitude area defence (THAAD) missile defence systems on South Korean territory in the face of acute pressure from Beijing, the Moon government sought to walk a fine line between reinforcing alliance commitments and achieving inter-Korean reconciliation. A series of high-level inter-Korean and US–North Korea summits throughout 2018 and early 2019 raised hopes that Pyongyang might be on the cusp of committing to a long-term denuclearisation plan, but such hopes had disappeared by the second half of 2019 as North Korea made it clear it would not be addressing its nuclear programme unless the US moved to reduce sanctions.[33]

This was accompanied by growing tensions in 2020 between the US and South Korea over negotiations on cost-sharing arrangements under the bilateral Status of Forces Agreements. President Trump's decision to scale down, and in some cases defer, US–ROK joint exercises in an attempt to signal good faith towards North Korea followed his repeated questioning in private of the strategic rationale for keeping US forces on the Korean Peninsula.[34] While not stating such doubts explicitly, Trump's concerns about the cost of maintaining US forces in South Korea echoed US rhetoric under the Nixon and Carter administrations, so in that sense were not new. Yet, from Seoul's perspective, Washington's demand for an unprecedented financial contribution to maintain US forces hardened the view of the Trump administration as excessively transactional in its approach to the alliance.[35]

Nuclear weapons in the US–ROK alliance

Nuclear weapons have cast a long shadow over the US–ROK alliance since the beginning of the Korean War. The Truman administration considered their use during the course of the conflict, at one point approving the transfer of custody to the US Air Force of nuclear cores to marry with unassembled devices located at airbases in Japan and Guam.[36] This was supplemented by thinly veiled threats against North Korea and China between 1951 and 1953 aimed at coercing both countries into entering armistice negotiations. Despite the inconclusive results of these threats and of the various actions by Washington to convey atomic resolve, the accepted wisdom in US policy circles at the time was that nuclear threats had proven effective in reaching the July 1953 armistice.[37] While the effectiveness of attempted US nuclear coercion may have been ambiguous at best, and at worst 'counterproductive, actually prolonging the war', US planners appear to have convinced themselves that nuclear weapons were central to security on the Korean Peninsula.[38]

This strategic logic complemented the more practical conclusion that the US could not afford to maintain a large-scale troop presence in South Korea after 1953. The emergence of the 'New Look' in American defence planning placed a premium on threats of 'massive retaliation' to shore up US global deterrence, thus offsetting the need for major conventional forces being deployed in key theatres throughout Europe and Asia. As the Eisenhower administration sought to reconfigure American commitments worldwide on this basis, the US aimed to pare back its overall force levels on the Korean Peninsula and persuade the South Korean government to develop its own armed forces. The minutes of a September 1956 NSC meeting note that 'the President commented with a sigh that we were surely spending an awful lot of money in Korea ... and went on to say that Korea would provide a very good laboratory case to assist us in determining what we should do about our expenditures on a worldwide basis'.[39] Against this background, in August 1957, the Eisenhower administration approved NSC 5702/2, which authorised the deployment of nuclear weapons to South Korea.[40]

Over the course of their thirty-three-year deployment in South Korea, US nuclear weapons were physically stationed at locations near the demilitarized zone (DMZ), Kunsan airbase in the southwest of the country, and Osan airbase south of Seoul.[41] In the context of a major reduction in US ground forces on the Korean Peninsula, the decision to deploy tactical nuclear weapons was supported by the Joint Chiefs of Staff as a military deterrent, but the deployment was also seen as a way of reassuring the South Korean government of a continuing US commitment.[42] Significantly, the deployment was a unilateral decision by the US with no input from the South Korean government; indeed, the approval of NSC 5702/2 had occurred without the direct knowledge of Seoul.[43] Yet, once the decision was conveyed to South Korea, Rhee expressed his gratitude to the Eisenhower administration, while requesting details around the timing and scope of the deployment.[44] In response, the

US ambassador to South Korea was instructed to inform Rhee that 'the 7th and 24th Divisions (comprised of 5 battalions armed with weapons with atomic capabilities) will be reorganised into Pentomic Divisions and the 100th Field Artillery Battalion (Honest John) and 663rd Field Artillery Battalion (280mm gun) will be introduced into Korea'.[45] Additional systems would be introduced in subsequent years, including three surface-to-surface missile systems between 1960 and 1963, at least two cruise missile systems in 1959 and 1961, the 155-mm howitzer in 1964, and atomic demolition munitions (ADMs) from the late 1950s.[46] In terms of warhead numbers, it is estimated that at the peak of US global nuclear deployments in Asia in 1967, 'among roughly 32,000 nuclear weapons ... slightly less than 1,000 US nuclear warheads were stationed in South Korea'.[47]

Although reported obliquely in the American media, the introduction into South Korea of nuclear artillery, nuclear-armed missiles, ADMs, and free-fall nuclear bombs on aircraft was never disclosed by any ROK government to the South Korean public. This was despite US Defense Secretary James Schlesinger's public acknowledgement in 1975 that American tactical nuclear weapons were stationed on the peninsula and that the US would consider using them in response to aggression 'that was likely to result in defeat in any area of very great importance to the US in Asia, including Korea'.[48] Right up until the withdrawal of nuclear weapons from South Korea in 1991, senior South Korean officials refused to confirm their presence, even when directly questioned on the issue. As late as 1987, under questioning in the National Assembly, the ROK Defence Minister stated implausibly that 'we cannot confirm or deny the existence or non-existence of nuclear weapons and even I have no knowledge of the matter'.[49] Given Washington's transparency about global nuclear deployments, including on the Korean Peninsula, it is likely that Seoul's public position was informed less by alliance considerations and more by a desire to avoid any detailed questioning on the mission, force posture, and command and control of nuclear weapons stationed on South Korean territory.

Stationing US nuclear forces on the Korean Peninsula did not, however, address South Korean fears of abandonment. The Park Chung-hee government embarked on a covert programme to acquire a South Korean nuclear weapons capability in 1971, following US confirmation it would be withdrawing 20,000 troops from the peninsula. Authorised under the cover of strict secrecy, 'Project 890' was an initiative controlled by the President's office and created the Agency for Defence Development and the Weapons Exploitation Committee to coordinate development of a nuclear weapons programme as part of a broader military modernisation effort.[50] Military modernisation under the *Yulgok* programme of the Park government began in earnest in 1974 and was inextricably linked to the imperative of greater self-reliance in South Korea's defence capabilities.[51] Project 890 was underpinned by a dual endeavour to acquire nuclear reprocessing technology with a view to generating weapons grade fissile material, and an ambitious missile development programme, which included reverse engineering the Nike-Hercules missile first deployed by the US on the peninsula in the early 1960s.[52]

By 1975, the US had concluded that South Korea was attempting to acquire nuclear forces through the development of a major reprocessing facility with assistance from Western European and Canadian suppliers.[53] As Scott Snyder notes: 'External observers easily put the pieces together as ethnic Korean nuclear scientists, including from the US and Canada, suddenly began travelling to Korea and as the Park government negotiated deals to obtain reprocessing and heavy water technology and equipment from France and Canada.'[54] In response, the Ford administration threatened to review formally the US–ROK alliance and exerted significant pressure on third-party suppliers not to transfer nuclear technology or equipment to South Korea. Although initially resisting American pressure, the Park government abandoned its nuclear programme when it became clear that South Korea would be forced to absorb major economic costs, in addition to the possible end of the US alliance, if it maintained its course.[55]

Rather than mirroring any specific strategic or operational logic about how nuclear weapons could be used against North Korea, the South Korean nuclear programme was symptomatic of deep anxieties over the reliability of continuing US security commitments. In an August 1975 meeting with his US counterpart, the South Korean Defence Minister, Suh Jyong-chul, pointedly observed that Kim Il-sung 'knows about the [Mutual Defense] Treaty and your statements of support, but he may ask, as a result of Vietnam, whether this commitment is reliable'.[56] The Guam Doctrine's endorsement of sweeping troop reductions was seen as presaging a more general US pull-back from Asia. Coupled with the Nixon administration's shock rapprochement to China and a resurgence of North Korean strategic confidence as US fortunes declined in the region, from Seoul's perspective, a post-Vietnam US withdrawal appeared very much on the cards. As one account has noted, 'South Korea feared a US retreat from Asia more deeply than other Asian countries because it had witnessed, up close, the consequences of faltering US support and retreat in Vietnam, despite having committed 50,000 troops to the Vietnam War'.[57]

As outlined earlier, the Carter administration's announcement that it would withdraw all US forces from South Korea by 1982 triggered renewed consternation in Seoul, notwithstanding earlier attempts by the Ford administration to reaffirm US security commitments under the alliance. The fact that US nuclear weapons were part of the withdrawal plans under Carter made the intended pull-out of American forces all the more disconcerting for the Park government, which had terminated South Korea's short-lived nuclear programme. By 1978, however, the US was already moving to reassure Seoul of its military commitment under the alliance. The creation of CFC was central in binding operationally the two countries' militaries, and while there is no evidence of greater South Korean involvement in planning involving nuclear weapons, US officials acknowledged privately that greater reassurance under the US nuclear umbrella was required.[58] In what appears to have been an endeavour to do exactly that, the frequency of US nuclear-capable submarine port visits to South Korea spiked dramatically between 1977 and 1980, with fourteen visits by eight SSBNs in 1979 alone.[59] The high-profile use of strategic nuclear assets to supplement the presence of tactical nuclear weapons on the peninsula was no doubt designed to underscore the credibility of extended nuclear deterrence during a period of uncertainty within South Korea, and more broadly in Asia, about US strategic commitments in the post-Vietnam era.

The return of the US–ROK alliance to relative stability during the 1980s meant that nuclear issues assumed a low profile for much of the decade. Increasing confidence on the part of South Korea as it continued to accelerate well ahead of North Korea across all economic and social indicators was also reflected in the military realm, where most assessments concluded that any invasion by the North could be defeated by South Korean conventional forces alone.[60] Improving bilateral relations with China, an emerging détente with Pyongyang, and explicit reassurances from then-US President George H. W. Bush that extended nuclear deterrence would remain in place, promoted a degree of confidence in South Korea that contributed to an acceptance that US nuclear weapons would be withdrawn in 1991.[61] The removal of all nuclear weapons from South Korea was seen as an important step in North Korea complying with its international non-proliferation commitments by ratifying the NPT (Pyongyang had signed the treaty in 1985) and allowing Seoul to conclude a joint denuclearisation agreement with the North, which was signed in March 1992.[62] As Choi and Park have written, the withdrawal of US nuclear weapons from South Korea marked the transition from 'ground-based nuclear deterrence to offshore nuclear deterrence'.[63]

The nuclear crises of 1993–94 and 2002–3 and the subsequent evolution of North Korea's nuclear weapons programme after its first nuclear test in 2006 saw South Korean anxieties over extended deterrence surge once again. While the Bush and Obama administrations agreed to make increasingly explicit references to the nuclear umbrella in successive SCM joint communiqués, Seoul was also keen for the US to rotate nuclear-capable strategic assets through the peninsula in the wake of periodic North Korean nuclear and missile testing, as well as a high level of conventional military provocations.[64] This included the DPRK's artillery strike in late 2010 on the South Korean island of Yeongpyeong, which, as already noted, severely tested the Obama administration's capacity to reassure Seoul. The Lee Myung-bak and Park Geun-hye governments sought to be involved in regular round-table consultations with the US on detailed aspects of extended nuclear deterrence within the alliance. A product of the 2010 NPR, the Obama administration agreed to the creation of the EDPC involving annual high-level consultations on the strategic and operational attributes of the nuclear umbrella as well as periodic visits of South Korean officials to US Strategic Command, nuclear weapons facilities, and other elements of America's nuclear infrastructure.[65]

Successive North Korean nuclear tests since 2006 have been accompanied by requests from Seoul for reassurance from Washington that the nuclear umbrella remains part of Washington's overall security commitments under the Mutual Defense Treaty. These reassurances have been forthcoming and, notwithstanding periodic tensions, the Obama and Trump administrations continued to engage their South Korean counterparts in operational-level dialogue regarding the spectrum of US extended deterrence options. South Korean strategic planners have been especially concerned about what they see as Pyongyang's penchant for limited military force below the nuclear level on the assumption that the US and ROK will not retaliate because they fear nuclear escalation.[66] This was underscored for South Korean planners following the 2010 Yeongpyeong attacks when the US sought to de-escalate as Seoul pushed for a tougher response to North Korea's provocation. Deliberations over how the US and South Korea might respond to future 'grey zone' provocations from Pyongyang has been a major feature of the extended deterrence dialogue between Washington and Seoul since 2010.[67]

Notwithstanding deeper formal consultation on nuclear policy between Seoul and Washington since the 2000s, calls have also emerged within South Korea in recent years for the reintroduction to the country of US tactical nuclear weapons, and in some conservative sectors the reconstitution of the ROK's earlier nuclear weapons programme.[68] While by no means reflecting a consensus of opinion within the South Korean government, some voices in favour of considering the reintroduction of tactical nuclear weapons have included senior members of the Moon Jae-in Cabinet.[69] Public opinion on the issue remains divided, although Presidents Lee Myung-bak, Park Geun-hye, and Moon Jae-in have each ruled out requesting the redeployment of US nuclear weapons or the resuscitation of the ROK's indigenous weapons programme.[70]

Tracing nuclear weapons cooperation

Threat assessment and prioritisation

Perceptions of external threat have been a strong influence on dynamics in the US–South Korean alliance. Since its creation in 1948, South Korea has been preoccupied with countering the North Korean threat. In addition to seeking US support through the alliance, successive ROK governments have maintained ambitious national defence modernisation programmes. Indeed, a recurring feature of the alliance has been attempts by Washington to restrain South Korean leaders from escalating crises with the North through large-scale retaliation in response to North Korean provocations. However, South Korean governments keen to engage Pyongyang have combined strong defence readiness with a commitment to the alliance. Under the Roh Moo-hyun administration, for example, South Korea embarked on an ambitious defence reform programme that had the net effect of increasing expenditure on the ROK military during Roh's term in office.[71]

One of the hallmarks of the US–ROK alliance has been the periodic gap between Seoul and Washington over the perception of the threat from North Korea. This reflected Seoul's local fixation, as distinct from a more global US perspective, as well as different assessments of North Korean capabilities and intentions. For most of the Cold War, Seoul was more focused than Washington on the nature and extent of the military threat from North Korea. Under Park Chung-hee in particular, but also under Syngman Rhee, South Korean policymakers were frustrated that their US counterparts did not share the same sense of urgency regarding the threat of a North Korean invasion. This was especially evident during the 1970s when South Korean concerns about US disengagement from the peninsula were at their height and when the Park government took steps to achieve greater strategic autonomy through an indigenous missile capability, more sophisticated conventional forces, and its short-lived nuclear weapons programme.

To some extent, substantive policy differences in the alliance have been contingent on particular administrations in power at any given time in Seoul and Washington. Notwithstanding the Nixon administration's lack of consultation with Park Chung-hee regarding Washington's troop withdrawal plan, Republican administrations have tended to enjoy more conducive relations with Seoul. This was mainly because of the sharper-edged policy towards North Korea by Republican presidents compared to their Democratic counterparts. Political and policy alignment was at its strongest under the Ford and Reagan administrations, and weakest under the Carter administration, which was openly critical of Park's authoritarianism and itself more receptive to dialogue with Pyongyang.

Since the 1990s, however, the gap in threat perceptions between Washington and Seoul has narrowed. This appears to have been due to the development of more robust institutional coordination in the alliance regarding North Korea policy, including the establishment under the G. W. Bush administration of high-level ministerial consultations between the State Department and ROK Ministry of Foreign Affairs.[72] This in turn has complemented the strong existing cooperation between the Pentagon and the Ministry of National Defence and has filled an important gap in the non-military side of the alliance.

In contrast to earlier decades, when US policymakers had either dismissed or played down Seoul's anxieties regarding the North Korea threat, Pyongyang's determination to acquire nuclear weapons has remained a grave concern to the US. At the same time, the effect of partisan alignment has been inverted somewhat since the 1980s, as successive progressive administrations in Seoul have sought direct diplomatic engagement with North Korea. The Kim Dae-jung and Roh Moo-hyun governments overlapped with the Bush administration, which was highly sceptical towards their Sunshine Policy. By contrast, the tough policy approach towards North Korea of the Lee Myung-bak and Park Geun-hye governments was in close alignment with the Obama administration, despite concern in Washington over Seoul's willingness to escalate the 2010 crisis with North Korea.

For its part, South Korean threat perceptions have also broadened during the 2000s. Politically, there is a persistent tension between Seoul and Tokyo over strategic and territorial issues that has occasionally, much to Washington's frustration, been manifested in major tensions between South Korea and Japan.[73] But Seoul has also become suspicious of China's strategic weight and Beijing's proclivity to exert pressure against its Asian neighbours. This was brought home to South Korean policymakers by China's highly negative reaction to the deployment of THAAD anti-missile systems in 2017 and Beijing's targeting of the South Korean economy in response.[74] Although North Korea's acquisition of nuclear weapons, coupled with the expanding combat radius of its missile strike force, continues to sit at the forefront of South Korea's contemporary threat perception, Seoul's concerns about China brought it into closer alignment with the broader regional perspective on strategic stability that characterises the US view of Northeast Asia and the purpose of its forces there.

Policy objectives regarding nuclear weapons cooperation

Attempts by Syngman Rhee to sabotage the 1953 armistice negotiations, and his subsequent desire to 'go north' after the armistice was signed, proved to be a major irritant in early US–ROK relations. During the Cold War, the

US was thus keen to retain sole control over operational military decision making on the Korean Peninsula, as reflected in the OPCON arrangements that were in place until 1994. US planners were also focused on preserving flexibility to undertake nuclear strikes not just against North Korea, but also against China. This was reflected in targets assigned to the US SIOP and aircraft of the Eighth Tactical Fighter Wing at Kunsan airbase that were on heightened readiness from 1974 as part of the US regional posture for executing nuclear strikes against China.[75] However, US policymakers had neither the interest nor the reason to bring South Korea into nuclear weapons planning and coordination; any reassurances by Washington appear to have been aimed at doing just enough to dissuade South Korea from itself going nuclear or dissuading Seoul from initiating a military first-strike against North Korea. This reflects very strong realist attributes in the alliance.

Given the limited control that Seoul had in the alliance even over the use of its own forces in wartime, South Korea's policy objectives in regard to the use of nuclear weapons specifically have been less pronounced than in other US alliances. While it is unclear whether governments in Seoul ever had preferences for specific contingencies of nuclear use that differed from the US, South Korea was in any event shut out of any bargaining with the US over the purpose of nuclear weapons deployed on its soil.

After the Cold War and the withdrawal of US nuclear weapons from the peninsula, Seoul became more interested in shaping visible demonstrations of the continued US nuclear commitment. South Korea's demand for, and Washington's provision of, explicit public statements of extended nuclear deterrence was a feature of the alliance's response to successive North Korean nuclear tests from 2006. These assurances were embedded in US–ROK communiqués issued following annual SCM meetings and reaffirmed during peaks of heightened tensions on the peninsula. As noted, these assurances accompanied the increasingly regular rotation of US nuclear-capable assets through the peninsula initiated under the Bush administration.

Nuclear strategy

From the 1950s to the 1970s, the US strategy for defending against a North Korean invasion involved an assumption that nuclear weapons would be used early in any conflict. A 1967 planning document drafted by the Pentagon stated that 'the twelve ROK Army and two US divisions in South Korea [have] keyed their defense plans almost entirely to the early use of nuclear weapons'.[76] The deployment pattern of US tactical nuclear weapons north of Seoul was consistent with a strategy that assumed early first-use in the event of a North Korean invasion. An assessment prepared in 1970 by the US NSC noted that 'US field commanders judge that a North Korean invasion force would attack along the three principal invasion routes used in 1950 with the bulk of the force (about 6 divisions) targeted on Seoul'.[77] One analysis of various invasion scenarios in the late 1990s identified 'only two main natural axes of potential attack near Seoul … the Chorwon and Munsan corridors each about 15 kilometres wide in some places'.[78] While it seems nuclear weapons, in particular ADMs, were regarded as well suited to defending in such terrain, by the 1970s it became clear that 'as the metropolitan Seoul city limits [had] expanded, these weapons could not be used in proximity to the capital, given the blast damage and fallout that would likely occur'.[79] Atomic demolition munitions were eventually withdrawn from the Korean Peninsula around the mid-1980s,[80] although longer-range missile systems were retained until 1991, probably with a view to continuing to hold targets within North Korea (and China) at risk in any conflict scenario.[81]

Seoul's interest in US nuclear strategy during the Cold War hinged on anxiety over the North Korean conventional military threat. By the 1970s, however, South Korea appears to have come to the same conclusion as the US, namely that the use of tactical nuclear weapons in a second Korean War remained a remote prospect and that there were few if any realistic battlefield contingencies where nuclear use could contribute to the defence of South Korea. Nevertheless, existential fears in Seoul ran deep, and the mooted withdrawal of tactical nuclear weapons by the Carter administration, along with removal of all US ground forces from the peninsula, provoked serious apprehension in Seoul.

Whereas questions about US forward-based nuclear weapons in South Korea during the Cold War focused on the manner of their possible use, discussion about their possible reintroduction to South Korea relates to concerns about how to substantiate US extended nuclear deterrence. The reintroduction of tactical nuclear weapons has been ruled out by the US since 1991, despite Donald Trump going on the record as a presidential candidate to say he would be comfortable with a South Korean nuclear weapons capability.[82] Although senior political figures in South Korea occasionally signal their support for reintroducing tactical nuclear weapons, successive ROK Presidents since the 1990s have also confirmed that existing arrangements whereby the US regularly rotates nuclear-capable assets through ROK territory remains sufficient for them in terms of physical hardware reassurance.[83] However, current and former policymakers in Seoul have privately expressed a desire to explore joint operational planning on nuclear weapons and potential nuclear sharing arrangements.[84] Although the US has remained unsympathetic to these views, the Trump administration's decision to push ahead with the production of the B61-12 gravity nuclear bomb for the European theatre and its endorsement of lower-yield nuclear options at least suggests the US retains options should it review its future posture on the Korean Peninsula.[85] For this reason, the 2018 NPR was received positively in Seoul.[86]

Domestic factors

In contrast to other US alliances, the South Korean public remained relatively non-committal during the Cold War with respect to nuclear issues. There were very few anti-nuclear protests or public opinion polls demonstrating strong views one way or the other regarding nuclear weapons, including their role in the US alliance. This can be attributed to three possible explanations. The first is that the authoritarian political system in the ROK inhibited meaningful domestic debate on foreign policy or defence; debating the pros and cons of nuclear weapons on South Korean territory was no exception to this. Before the 1990s, governments in Seoul rarely invoked public opinion when commenting on nuclear weapons in an alliance context, and there is negligible evidence of such opinion in published polling. The second explanation is an absence of common public knowledge that nuclear weapons were in fact deployed on South Korean territory after 1958. As noted, senior South Korean officials refused to comment on the matter right up until the withdrawal of nuclear forces in 1991, despite the US in the mid-1970s acknowledging the presence of nuclear weapons on ROK territory. The third possible explanation is that due to the immediate and operationally focused nature of the North Korean threat, the overwhelming majority of South Koreans were prepared to endorse all measures, including the nuclear umbrella, to counter what was seen as an existential security theat.

All of these explanations are plausible in accounting for the South Korean public's relative detachment from nuclear issues for most of the Cold War period. Yet, each successive North Korean nuclear test after 2006 has led to calls for South Korea to review its non-nuclear status, as well as to explore the reintroduction to the peninsula of US tactical nuclear weapons to counter Pyongyang's emerging nuclear force. In a 2013 poll by the Asan Institute after North Korea's third nuclear test, two-thirds of respondents supported an indigenous nuclear weapons programme, with majority support across those who identified as progressives and conservatives as well as all age groups.[87] At the height of tensions on the peninsula in 2017, polling revealed that 60 per cent of South Koreans believed that the country should acquire its own nuclear force, while over two-thirds of respondents supported redeploying US nuclear weapons to the ROK.[88] More recent evidence indicates that this support is persistent.[89] While domestic opinion on nuclear matters is very different in South Korea from most other US allies, this has yet to have significant influence on alliance dynamics.

The importance of South Korea for US security

For much of the Cold War, South Koreans chafed under the assumption that the US did not sufficiently value or respect the ROK as an ally. Indeed, Dean Acheson's omission of South Korea from his 1950 defence perimeter speech is sometimes identified as giving the green light to North Korea to invade in June that year. Writing in the late 1970s, Chae Jin-Lee observed that 'South Korean leaders know that the United States regards its alliance with Japan as more important than that with South Korea and that Japan's own national security is guaranteed by the US nuclear umbrella'.[90] Although the reference to Japan undoubtedly reflected an underlying sense of grievance in relation to the colonial period, it also mirrored a popular view that South Korea had been treated as a second-class ally by Washington.

There were certainly some grounds for this perspective. Compared to the US–Japan alliance, consultation in the US–ROK alliance was underdeveloped, and successive US administrations had taken decisions regarding the alliance that were unilateral and high handed. The Nixon and Carter announcements concerning planned US force drawdowns caught Seoul unprepared, and the Syngman Rhee and Park Chung-hee governments were barely consulted about the status of US nuclear weapons on South Korean territory. Such a peremptory approach to alliance management would have been unthinkable in the US–Japan or NATO contexts, and by the 1980s there was a popular view among ROK policymakers 'that South Korea should look out for its own interests and be prepared for a contingency that US security assistance might not be as readily forthcoming as in the past'.[91]

For most of the post-Korean War period until the 1980s, successive US administrations saw the US–ROK alliance through the prism of entrapment. US forces deployed to the peninsula continued to train to defend South Korea against North Korean aggression, but in Washington the political commitment to Seoul was uneven. The country's importance to the US as an ally grew after the end of the Cold War, however, with the emerging North Korean nuclear threat and China's increasing influence in Asia elevating South Korea's geopolitical significance from Washington's perspective.[92] As the North Korean nuclear capability has grown to a level that can impose catastrophic costs on other US allies in Asia, and potentially on the continental US, administrations have sought to strengthen the bilateral alliance with Seoul. Deployment of US THAAD systems on South Korean territory reinforces defences against North Korea beyond Seoul. Regardless of whether they accurately reflect the capability of the THAAD system, Beijing's complaints that South Korea enables the US to observe its missile tests to acquire targeting information reflect a US motive in leveraging the alliance to advance its interests against China.[93] A collapse of the DPRK and potential Chinese intervention to stabilise and occupy the northern part of the peninsula remains a plausible scenario of concern to the US, as does a reunified Korea with a major nuclear and missile inventory.[94] In both of these scenarios the US would look to play a major role, and the alliance with South Korea would be a key enabler for leveraging US strategic influence on the peninsula.

Access to information

Because historically the US–ROK alliance has been defined by joint preparation to fight a second Korean War, the South Korean military acquired some insight into nuclear planning that other allies of the US in Asia did not. Although excluded from US decision making in regard to the posture, deployment, and use of nuclear weapons, South Korea nevertheless gained insights into US nuclear war plans. As Peter Hayes has outlined, from the late 1960s onwards, the South Korean military participated in nuclear exercises with US forces and was briefed 'with sanitised versions of the American Standard Operating Procedures for nuclear war in Korea'.[95] On the surface, including South Korean forces in US nuclear exercises appeared to emulate NATO's model of multinational nuclear coordination. However, there is no evidence that South Korean involvement in these exercises went beyond carefully stage-managed simulations, and it appears that the ROK military had little option but to consent given overall US operational control of allied forces on the peninsula.[96] It is telling that when the South Korean military formally requested a direct role in nuclear war planning on the peninsula in the early 1970s, this was firmly rejected by Washington.[97]

Although South Korea acquired limited knowledge of US plans for nuclear use on the Korean Peninsula, there are fewer grounds to conclude that Seoul gained similar detailed knowledge on the relationship between nuclear weapons stationed on its territory and the US SIOP, including aircraft at Kunsan assigned to strike Chinese targets. As with other US nuclear assets deployed on South Korean territory, successive governments in Seoul had little knowledge about how these might be used in a wartime situation, let alone influence over nuclear strike missions. This remained the case until the removal of all US nuclear weapons from South Korea in 1991.

While access to information, in line with realist assumptions, thus played little role in the alliance during the Cold War, the creation of the US–ROK EDPC in 2010 occurred around the same time as the creation of an analogous arrangement in the US–Japan alliance and was, as one former senior Obama administration official observes, the result of South Korean (and Japanese) pressure for 'more NATO-like' extended deterrence arrangements.[98] Although both sides emphasised publicly the conventional military focus of the EDPC, in private Seoul was reportedly keen to explore in greater depth the nuclear planning side of the alliance, and specifically the circumstances in which the US would consider employing nuclear weapons. One US official closely involved in interacting with South Korean officials at the time has recalled that 'they were constantly looking for evidence of where the nuclear dimension came into play'.[99] As the EDPC evolved after 2010, both sides agreed to deepen the institutional architecture around extended deterrence with the bifurcation in 2016 of the EDPC into the Extended Deterrence Strategy and Consultation Group (EDSCG) and the Deterrence Strategy Committee (DSC); this had the stated aim of broadening agency involvement on both sides and focusing on more detailed policy issues.[100] Notwithstanding a thickening of this institutional architecture, US officials have been steadfast in reiterating that these consultative arrangements would not replicate NATO's nuclear-planning arrangements.[101]

Conclusion

For most of its existence, the US–South Korea alliance has combined close military cooperation with a lack of institutional underpinnings on the political side. Although the consultative mechanism of the SCM was put in place in the late 1960s, the US did not really embrace genuine political consultation with Seoul until the 1980s, and excluded South Korea from military planning (even relating to the employment of its own forces) until 1978. Part of the reason for this was the authoritarian nature of the Park Chung-hee administration, but Washington also feared entrapment in a second Korean conflict because of what it saw as Seoul's propensity to match Pyongyang's aggressive posturing. Moreover, Washington's political treatment of Seoul, particularly during the 1970s, revealed disdain for South Korean preferences, which was at odds with the close nature of the military relationship. Until the 1980s, the US–ROK alliance could therefore be described as a military rather than security alliance; that is, one prepared to wage war, but ill-equipped to provide reassurance and thus security for its junior member. Not until the 1990s did the alliance's political-security consultation and coordination mechanisms start to replicate the institutionalised nature of the military relationship.

The role of nuclear weapons in the alliance was a one-sided affair during the Cold War. The initial deployment of US nuclear weapons in South Korea stemmed from the Eisenhower administration's desire to avoid a repetition of the costs in blood and treasure to the US resulting from the Korean War. This rationale dominated until the 1970s, when the Ford administration tried to leverage extended nuclear deterrence (along with a threat to review the alliance) as a means of assurance to persuade the Park Chung-hee government to terminate its nuclear programme. As North Korea's nuclear weapons programme has given Pyongyang greater coercive potential on the peninsula, South Korean policymakers have become more focused on solidifying nuclear weapons cooperation in the US–ROK alliance. For its part, the US has been willing to use nuclear reassurance and deterrence as key instruments in managing its alliance with South Korea, on the crucial proviso that nuclear weapons cooperation is undertaken on Washington's terms.

South Korea consented to station US tactical nuclear systems on its territory and at times even participated in stage-managed US exercises involving nuclear weapons, but Seoul was never part of the deliberations or decision making with respect to how these systems would be used in any conflict. While South Korea embarked upon its own weapons programme under Park Chung-hee, this owed more to anxiety over the perceived credibility of US conventional security assurances in the wake of the Guam Doctrine and less to being shut out of deliberations over how tactical nuclear weapons would be used in a second Korean War.

The withdrawal of US nuclear weapons from the Korean Peninsula in 1991 presaged an era in which South Korean decision makers became more focused on the credibility of US nuclear assurances in the alliance. In one sense this was not surprising; removing American tactical nuclear systems from South Korea's primary strategic theatre inevitably raised questions over the credibility of the US nuclear umbrella in a crisis. To paraphrase Thomas Schelling, US nuclear weapons on ROK territory rendered the nuclear umbrella inherently more credible, as distinct from threats and assurances that had to be made credible once these weapons were removed.[102]

Short-lived euphoria in Seoul over the end of the Cold War and the Joint Declaration on the Denuclearisation of the Korean Peninsula soon gave way to rising alarm at the prospect of a nuclear-armed North Korea. The creation of a subcommittee as part of the SCM process devoted exclusively to extended deterrence confirmed a desire on the part of Seoul for more structured dialogue on the nuclear umbrella at an operational level. For their part, the Obama and Trump administrations have endorsed institutionalising this extended deterrent dialogue because they regard it as a reassurance mechanism to bolster alliance cohesion, but also as a means of reinforcing deterrence in the eyes of Pyongyang.[103]

Although South Korean policymakers continue to raise questions privately about the long-term commitment of the US to the alliance, this is a far cry from the existential anxiety that characterised the Park Chung-hee government. On nuclear issues specifically, the growing institutionalisation of the US–ROK alliance has reflected an increasing alignment of expectations between Washington and Seoul, but it has also served to underscore the narrowing differences on substantive questions relating to threat assessments and the promotion of greater access to information for South Korea as the junior alliance partner.

Notes

1 W. Stueck, 'The Korean War', in M. Leffler and O. Arne Westad (eds), *The Cambridge History of the Cold War*, Vol. 1: *Origins* (Cambridge: Cambridge University Press, 2010), 276.

2 J. Schnabel and R. Watson, *The Joint Chiefs of Staff and National Policy*, Vol. III, Part 1: *1950–1951, The Korean War* (Washington, DC: Office of the Chairman of the Joints Chiefs of Staff, 1998), 12–13.

3 Schnabel and Watson, *The Joint Chiefs of Staff and National Policy*, 17.

4 Department of State, 'Memorandum of Discussion at the 297th Meeting of the National Security Council, Washington, September 20, 1956', in *Foreign Relations of the United States: 1955–1957*, Vol. XXIII, Part 2: *Korea, 1955–1957*, https://history.state.gov/historicaldocuments/frus1955–57v23p2/d169

5 Department of State, 'Memorandum from President Nixon to the President's Assistant for National Security Affairs (Kissinger), Washington, November 24, 1969', in *Foreign Relations of the United States: 1969–1976*, Vol. XIX, Part 1: *Korea, 1969–1972*, https://history.state.gov/historicaldocuments/frus1969–76v19p1/d45

6 J. Wood, 'Persuading a President: Jimmy Carter and American Troops in Korea', Unpublished Paper, 1996, https://nsarchive2.gwu.edu//NSAEBB/NSAEBB431/docs/intell_ebb_002.PDF

7 S. Harrison, *Korean Endgame: A Strategy for Reunification and US Disengagement* (Princeton, NJ: Princeton University Press, 2002), 179.

8 See V. Cha, *Powerplay: The Origins of the American Alliance System in Asia* (Princeton, NJ: Princeton University Press, 2016), chapter 5.

9 J. Hornung, *Modelling a Stronger US-Japan Alliance: Assessing US Alliance Structures* (Washington, DC: Centre for Strategic and International Studies, 2015), 10–11.

10 B. B. Bell, 'The Evolution of Combined Forces Command', Presentation to the 4th Korea Foundation Global Seminar, Washington, DC, 8–11 June 2012, www.brookings.edu/wp-content/uploads/2012/09/69-Bell-Evolution-of-Combined-Forces-Command.pdf.

11 J. Kim, 'Military Considerations for OPCON Transfer on the Korean Peninsula', *Council on Foreign Relations Blog*, 20 March 2020, www.cfr.org/blog/military-considerations-opcon-transfer-korean-peninsula

12 V. Cha, *Alignment Despite Antagonism: The US-Korea-Japan Security Triangle* (Stanford, CA: Stanford University Press, 1999), 110–115.

13 Seung-Young Kim, 'Security, Nationalism, and the Pursuit of Nuclear Weapons and Missiles: The South Korean Case, 1970–82', *Diplomacy & Statecraft*, 12:4 (2001), 54–56.

14 Department of State, 'Letter from President Nixon to Korean President Park, Washington, November 29, 1971', in *Foreign Relations of the United States: 1969–1976*, Vol. XIX, Part 1: *Korea, 1969–1972*, Washington, DC, 2010, https://history.state.gov/historicaldocuments/frus1969–76v19p1/d115
15 P. Hayes and Chung-in Moon, 'Park Chung-hee, the CIA and the Bomb', *Global Asia*, 6:3 (2011), 46–58.
16 For discussion, see L. Choi, 'The First Nuclear Crisis in the Korean Peninsula, 1975–76', *Cold War History*, 14:1 (2014), 71–90.
17 Wood, 'Persuading a President', 103–105.
18 Department of Defense, 'Charts re. Reporting on North Korean Military Strength, June 8, 1979, Top Secret', *US National Security Archive,* https://nsarchive2.gwu.edu//dc.html?doc=3696533-Document-06-Charts-re-Reporting-on-North-Korean
19 S. Snyder, *South Korea at the Crossroads: Autonomy and Alliance in an Era of Rival Powers* (New York: Columbia University Press, 2018), 47.
20 M. Seth, *A Concise History of Modern Korea: From the Late Nineteenth Century to the Present*, 2nd edition (Lanham, MD: Rowman and Littlefield, 2016), 220–221.
21 For background on South Korea's normalisation of relations with China and the Soviet Union, see Snyder, *South Korea at the Crossroads*, 58–65.
22 H. French, 'South Korea's President-Elect Rejects Use of Force Against North Korea', *New York Times*, 17 January 2003, www.nytimes.com/2003/01/17/world/threats-responses-korean-peninsula-south-korea-s-president-elect-rejects-use.html
23 Yong-Sup Han, 'The Sunshine Policy and Security on the Korean Peninsula: A Critical Assessment and Prospects', *Asian Perspective*, 26:3 (2002), 37–69.
24 Hornung, *Modeling a Stronger US-Japan Alliance*, 9.
25 E. Ramstad, 'Firing Drill Increases Tensions in Korea', *Wall Street Journal*, 20 December 2010, www.wsj.com/articles/SB10001424052748704138604576029240348016046
26 J. Lewis, 'Extended Deterrence Policy Committee', *Arms Control Wonk*, 19 October 2010, www.armscontrolwonk.com/archive/203057/extended-deterrence-policy-committee/
27 White House Office of the Press Secretary, 'Joint Vision for the Alliance of the United States of America and the Republic of Korea, June 16, 2009', https://obamawhitehouse.archives.gov/the-press-office/joint-vision-alliance-united-states-america-and-republic-korea
28 V. Jackson, *Rival Reputations: Coercion and Credibility in US-North Korea Relations* (Cambridge: Cambridge University Press, 2016), 186.
29 Sang-hun Choe, 'US and South Korea Make Plans for Defense', *New York Times*, 25 March 2013, www.nytimes.com/2013/03/26/world/asia/us-and-south-korea-sign-plan-to-counter-north.html
30 J. Johnson, 'South Korean Plans to Kill Kim Likely to Reinforce North's View that Nukes Are Needed', *Japan Times*, 11 September 2016, www.japantimes.co.jp/news/2016/09/11/asia-pacific/

south-korean-military-floats-plan-decapitation-strikes-decimate-norths-leadership-report/#.WYuuIHcjFPM

31 For analysis of the 2017 Korean peninsula crisis, see V. Jackson, *On the Brink: Trump, Kim, and the Threat of Nuclear War* (Cambridge: Cambridge University Press, 2019), especially 132–148.

32 A. Fifield, 'No American Strike in North Korea Without My Consent, Says South's President', *Washington Post*, 17 August 2017, www.washingtonpost.com/world/asia_pacific/no-american-strike-on-north-korea-without-my-consent-says-souths-president/2017/08/17/775290e8-8332-11e7-82a4-920da1aeb507_story.html

33 A. Jeong, 'North Korea Test-Fires Projectiles, Aims to Pressure US on Sanctions Relief', *Wall Street Journal*, 28 November 2019, www.wsj.com/articles/north-korea-test-fires-projectiles-aims-to-pressure-u-s-on-sanctions-relief-11574939934

34 Sung-han Kim and S. Snyder, 'Denuclearizing North Korea: Time for Plan B', *Washington Quarterly*, 42:4 (2020), 86.

35 P. Stewart and I. Ali, 'Exclusive: Inside Trump's Standoff with South Korea Over Defense Costs', *Reuters*, 11 April 2020, www.reuters.com/article/us-usa-southkorea-trump-defense-exclusiv/exclusive-inside-trumps-standoff-with-south-korea-over-defense-costs-idUSKCN21S1W7

36 B. Cumings, *The Korean War: A History* (New York: The Modern Library, 2011), 156–157.

37 For discussion, see R. Dingman, 'Atomic Diplomacy During the Korean War', *International Security*, 13:3 (1988/89), 50–91.

38 R. Betts, *Nuclear Blackmail and Nuclear Balance* (Washington, DC: Brookings Institution, 1987), 44.

39 Department of State, 'Memorandum of Discussion at the 297th Meeting of the National Security Council, Washington, September 20, 1956', in *Foreign Relations of the United States: 1955–1957*, Vol. XXIII, Part 2: *Korea, 1955–1957*, https://history.state.gov/historicaldocuments/frus1955–57v23p2/d169

40 Department of State, 'Memorandum of Discussion at the 334th Meeting of the National Security Council, Washington, August 8, 1957', in *Foreign Relations of the United States: 1955–1957*, Vol. XXIII, Part 2: *Korea, 1955–1957*, https://history.state.gov/historicaldocuments/frus1955–57v23p2/d239

41 H. Kristensen and R. Norris, 'A History of US Nuclear Weapons in South Korea', *Bulletin of the Atomic Scientists*, 73:6 (2017), 350–351.

42 Department of State, 'Memorandum of Discussion at the 326th Meeting of the National Security Council, Washington, June 13, 1957', in *Foreign Relations of the United States: 1955–1957*, Vol. XXIII, Part 2: *Korea, 1955–1957*, https://history.state.gov/historicaldocuments/frus1955–57v23p2/d221

43 B. Cumings, 'On the Strategy and Morality of American Nuclear Policy in Korea, 1950 to the Present', *Social Science Japan Journal*, 1:1 (1998), 64.

44 Lee Jae-bong, 'US Deployment of Nuclear Weapons in 1950s South Korea and North Korea's Nuclear Development: Toward Denuclearisation of the Korean Peninsula', *The Asia-Pacific Journal*, 7:3 (2009), https://apjjf.org/-Lee-Jae-Bong/3053/article.pdf

45 Lee Jae-bong, 'US Deployment of Nuclear Weapons in 1950s South Korea and North Korea's Nuclear Development'.

46 Office of the Assistant to the Secretary of Defense, 'History of the Custody of Deployment of Nuclear Weapons: July 1945 through September 1977', February 1978, https://nsarchive2.gwu.edu//dc.html?doc=6532113-National-Security-Archive-Doc-01-Office-of-the; and Kristensen and Norris, 'A History of US Nuclear Weapons in South Korea', 350.

47 Se Young Jang, 'The Evolution of US Extended Deterrence and South Korea's Nuclear Ambitions', *Journal of Strategic Studies*, 39:4 (2016), 506.

48 Quoted in J. Hong-nam, *America's Commitment to South Korea: The First Decade of the Nixon Doctrine* (Cambridge: Cambridge University Press, 2009), 88.

49 Quoted in Lee Jae-bong, 'US Deployment of Nuclear Weapons in 1950s South Korea and North Korea's Nuclear Development', 3.

50 Se Young Jang, 'The Evolution of US Extended Deterrence and South Korea's Nuclear Ambitions', 513–514.

51 For background, see Hyung-A Kim, 'Heavy and Chemical Industrialisation, 1973–1979: South Korea's Homeland Security Measures', in Hyung-A Kim and C. Sorensen (eds), *Reassessing the Park Chung Hee Era, 1961–1979: Development, Political Thought, Democracy, and Cultural Influence* (Seattle, WA: University of Washington Press, 2011), 29–31.

52 Seung Young-Kim, 'Security, Nationalism, and the Pursuit of Nuclear Weapons and Missiles', 62.

53 Department of State, 'State Department Telegram (195214) to US Embassy South Korea: "ROK Nuclear Fuel Reprocessing Plans", 16 August 1975, Secret', https://nsarchive2.gwu.edu//dc.html?doc=5798497-National-Security-Archive-Doc-03-State

54 Snyder, *South Korea at the Crossroads*, 44–45.

55 Choi, 'The First Nuclear Crisis', 82–84.

56 'Memoranda of Conversations between James R. Schlesinger and Park Chung-hee and Suh Jyong-chul, August 26, 1975', History and Public Policy Program Digital Archive, Gerald R. Ford Presidential Library, National Security Adviser Presidential Country Files for East Asia and the Pacific, Box 9, Korea (11), obtained by Charles Kraus, http://digitalarchive.wilsoncenter.org/document/114633.pdf?v=240ba63526da6f1f845710c0d685600f

57 J. Pollack and M. Reiss, 'South Korea: The Tyranny of Geography and the Vexations of History', in K. Campbell, R. Einhorn, and M. Reiss (eds), *The Nuclear Tipping Point: Why States Reconsider Their Nuclear Choices* (Washington, DC: Brookings Institution, 2004), 263–264.

58 A. Lanoszka, *Atomic Assurance: The Alliance Politics of Nuclear Proliferation* (Ithaca, NY: Cornell University Press, 2018), 128.

59 H. Kristensen, 'When the Boomers Went to South Korea', *Federation of American Scientists Blog*, 4 October 2011, https://fas.org/blogs/security/2011/10/ssbnrok/

60 This strategic optimism was captured in the country's inaugural defence white paper released publicly in 1988. See Tai Young Kwon and Young Sun Song, 'The First ROK Defense White Paper: Its Significance and Important Contents', *Korean Journal of Defense Analysis*, 1:1 (1989), 193–211.

61 See D. Oberdorfer, *The Two Koreas: A Contemporary History* (Reading, MA: Addison-Wesley, 1997), 259–260.

62 The Joint Declaration prohibits North and South Korea from manufacturing or deploying nuclear weapons on the Korean Peninsula. Pyongyang has never acknowledged the departure of US nuclear weapons from the peninsula. J. Pollack, 'Denuclearization of the Korean Peninsula: Reviewing the Precedents', *Arms Control Wonk*, 10 June 2018, www.armscontrolwonk.com/archive/1205354/denuclearization-of-the-korean-peninsula-reviewing-the-precedents/

63 K. Choi and Joon-Sung Park, 'South Korea: Fears of Abandonment and Entrapment', in M. Alagappa (ed.), *The Long Shadow: Nuclear Weapons and Security in 21st Century Asia* (Stanford, CA: Stanford University Press, 2008), 392.

64 High-profile overflights of US B-52 and B-2 platforms were a prominent feature of the US-ROK response to the North Korean nuclear tests in 2013 and 2016. See J. Solomon, J. Barnes, and A. Gale, 'North Korea Warned: US Flies Stealth Bombers Over Peninsula in Show of Force', *Wall Street Journal*, 29 March 2013, www.wsj.com/articles/SB10001424127887323501004578389162106323642; and T. Munroe and J. Kim, 'US Flies B-52 Over South Korea After North's Nuclear Test', *Reuters*, 11 January 2016, www.reuters.com/article/us-northkorea-nuclear/u-s-flies-b-52-over-south-korea-after-norths-nuclear-test-idUSKCN0UN0Y420160111

65 T. Roehrig, *Japan, South Korea, and the United States Nuclear Umbrella: Deterrence After the Cold War* (New York: Columbia University Press, 2017), 130–134.

66 D. Kim, N. Wright, and K. Lee, 'The United States Needs a Gray-Zone Strategy Against North Korea', *Foreign Policy*, 14 May 2019, https://foreignpolicy.com/2019/05/14/the-united-states-needs-a-gray-zone-strategy-against-north-korea-missile-test-nuclear/

67 B. Roberts, 'Deterrence and Détente on the Korean Peninsula', *Council on Foreign Relations Blog*, 22 April 2019, www.cfr.org/blog/deterrence-and-detente-korean-peninsula

68 Byong-Chul Lee, 'Don't be Surprised When South Korea Wants Nuclear Weapons', *Bulletin of the Atomic Scientists*, 23 October 2019, https://thebulletin.org/2019/10/dont-be-surprised-when-south-korea-wants-nuclear-weapons/

69 A. Fifield, 'South Korea's Defense Minister Suggests Bringing Back Tactical US Nuclear Weapons', *Washington Post*, 4 September 2017, www.washingtonpost.com/world/south-koreas-defense-minister-raises-the-idea-of-bringing-back-tactical-us-nuclear-weapons/2017/09/04/7a468314-9155-11e7-b9bc-b2f7903bab0d_story.html?utm_term=.6757fc92bc40

70 D. Smeltz, K. Friedhoff, and L. Wojtowicz, 'South Koreans See Improved Security, Confident in US Security Guarantee', Chicago Council on Global Affairs, 18

January 2019, www.thechicagocouncil.org/research/public-opinion-survey/south-koreans-see-improved-security-confident-us-security-guarantee www

71 In-Bum Chun, 'Korean Defense Reform: History and Challenges', *Brookings Institution Report*, 31 October 2017, www.brookings.edu/research/korean-defense-reform-history-and-challenges/

72 Snyder, *South Korea at the Crossroads*, 139.

73 S. Denyer, 'Japan-South Korea Ties "Worst in Five Decades" as US Leaves Alliance Untended', *Washington Post*, 9 February 2019, www.washingtonpost.com/world/asia_pacific/japan-south-korea-ties-worst-in-five-decades-as-us-leaves-alliance-untended/2019/02/08/f17230be-2ad8–11e9–906e-9d55b6451eb4_story.html?noredirect=on&utm_term=.2981e3dd2dfc

74 M. Stiles, 'Upset Over a US Missile Defense System, China Hits South Korea Where It Hurts, in the Wallet', *Los Angeles Times*, 28 February 2018, www.latimes.com/world/asia/la-fg-china-south-korea-tourism-20180228-htmlstory.html

75 Kristensen and Norris, 'A History of US Nuclear Weapons in South Korea', 351.

76 Quoted in P. Hayes, *Pacific Powderkeg: American Nuclear Dilemmas in Korea* (New York: Lexington Books, 1991), 47.

77 Department of State, 'Memorandum from Laurence E. Lynn, Jr., of the National Security Council Staff to the President's Assistant for National Security Affairs (Kissinger), Washington, February 26, 1970', in *Foreign Relations of the United States: 1969–1976*, Vol. XIX, Part 1: *Korea, 1969–1972*, https://history.state.gov/historicaldocuments/frus1969–76v19p1/d53

78 M. O'Hanlon, 'Stopping a North Korean Invasion: Why Defending South Korea is Easier than the Pentagon Thinks', *International Security*, 22:4 (1998), 140.

79 Roehrig, *Japan, South Korea, and the United States Nuclear Umbrella*, 61.

80 M. Bird, 'Nuclear History Note: US Atomic Demolition Munitions, 1954–1989', *RUSI Journal*, 153:2 (2008), 67.

81 D. Rosenbaum, 'US to Pull A-Bombs from South Korea', *New York Times*, 20 October 1991, www.nytimes.com/1991/10/20/world/us-to-pull-a-bombs-from-south-korea.html

82 'Highlights from our Interview with Donald Trump on Foreign Policy', *New York Times*, 26 March 2016, www.nytimes.com/2016/03/27/us/politics/donald-trump-interview-highlights.html

83 A. Woolf and E. Chanlett-Avery, 'Redeploying US Nuclear Weapons to South Korea; Background and Implications in Brief', *Congressional Research Service Report*, R44950, 14 September 2017, https://crsreports.congress.gov/product/pdf/R/R44950/3

84 See D. Kim, 'How to Keep South Korea from Going Nuclear', *Bulletin of the Atomic Scientists*, 9 March 2020, https://thebulletin.org/2020/03/how-to-keep-south-korea-from-going-nuclear/; and C. Work, 'Alternative Futures for the US-ROK Alliance: Will Things Fall Apart?', *38 North*, May 2020, www.38north.org/2020/05/cwork050720/

85 See S. Aishwarya, 'USAF Completes Flight Tests of B61–12 Gravity Bombs from F15-E', *Air Force Technology*, 30 August 2017, www.

airforce-technology.com/news/newsusaf-completes-testing-of-b61–12-gravity-bombs-on-f-15e-strike-eagle-5913501/; and J. Borger, 'US Nuclear Weapons: First Low-Yield Warheads Roll Off the Production Line', *Guardian*, 28 January 2019, www.theguardian.com/world/2019/jan/28/us-nuclear-weapons-first-low-yield-warheads-roll-off-the-production-line

86 M. Williams, 'The 2018 Nuclear Posture Review: Reception by US Allies in the Asia-Pacific', *CSIS Next Generation Nuclear Network*, 23 May 2018, https://nuclearnetwork.csis.org/2018-nuclear-posture-review-reception-u-s-allies-asia-pacific/

87 'The Fallout: South Korean Public Opinion Following North Korea's Third Nuclear Test', *Asan Institute for Policy Studies Brief*, 24 February 2013, http://en.asaninst.org/contents/issue-brief-no-46-the-fallout-south-korean-public-opinion-following-north-koreas-third-nuclear-test/

88 M. Ye Hee Lee, 'More than Ever, South Koreans Want Their Own Nuclear Weapons', *Washington Post*, 13 September 2017, www.washingtonpost.com/news/worldviews/wp/2017/09/13/most-south-koreans-dont-think-the-north-will-start-a-war-but-they-still-want-their-own-nuclear-weapons/?utm_term=.e8776cdfa10a

89 See L. Sukin, 'Credible Nuclear Commitments Can Backfire: Explaining Domestic Support for Nuclear Weapons Acquisition in South Korea', *Journal of Conflict Resolution*, 64:6 (2020), 1011–1042.

90 Chae-Jin Lee, 'The Direction of South Korea's Foreign Policy', *Korean Studies*, 2 (1978), 120.

91 H. Sungjoo, 'South Korea and the United States: The Alliance Survives', *Asian Survey*, 20:11 (1980), 1085.

92 In a reversal of Seoul's abandonment fears during the 1970s, during the 1993–94 nuclear crisis the Kim Young-sam government genuinely feared entrapment in a US-led war resulting from the Clinton administration authorising a first-strike on North Korea. For a discussion, see J. Wit, D. Poneman, and R. Galluci, *Going Critical: The First North Korean Nuclear Crisis* (Washington, DC: Brookings Institute, 2004), chapter 9.

93 R. Watts, '"Rockets' Red Glare": Why Does China Oppose THAAD in South Korea, and What Does it Mean for US Policy?', *Naval War College Review*, 71:2 (2018), 88.

94 For a detailed discussion of one specific Chinese intervention scenario, see O. Skylar Mastro, 'Conflict and Chaos on the Korean Peninsula: Can China's Military Help Secure North Korea's Nuclear Weapons?', *International Security*, 43:2 (2018), 84–116.

95 P. Hayes, 'American Nuclear Hegemony in Korea', *Journal of Peace Research*, 25:4 (1988), 357.

96 Hayes, 'American Nuclear Hegemony in Korea', 357.

97 Hayes, 'American Nuclear Hegemony in Korea', 357.

98 B. Roberts, *The Case for US Nuclear Weapons in the 21st Century* (Stanford, CA: Stanford University Press, 2016), 206.

99 Interview with US official, Washington, DC, 16 July 2015.

100 US Embassy and Consulate in Korea, 'Joint Statement of the 2016 United States-Republic of Korea Foreign and Defense Ministers' Meeting, Washington DC, October 19, 2016', https://kr.usembassy.gov/joint-statement-2016-united-states-republic-korea-foreign-defense-ministers-meeting/

101 Interview with US official, Washington, DC, 3 September 2019.

102 T. Schelling, *Arms and Influence* (New Haven, CT: Yale University Press, 1966), 36.

103 Interview with US official, Washington, DC, 3 September 2019.

6

Informal bargaining: Nuclear weapons cooperation and the US–Australia alliance

Of all America's alliances in Europe and Asia, the one with Australia is the least impacted by nuclear issues. The US has never deployed nuclear weapons on Australian soil and, aside from a very brief period in the late 1950s, there have been few pressures from Australia for such a deployment. The US nuclear umbrella features in Australia's strategic guidance, but not in public pronouncements by US officials or in joint communiqués at annual Australia–US Ministerial Meetings. Yet, successive Australian governments have taken nuclear weapons cooperation with Washington very seriously. For most of the Cold War, Australia was intimately involved in supporting the US global nuclear command and control network through hosting key US installations, while conservative (Coalition) and centre-left (Labor) governments in Australia regard extended nuclear deterrence as a key ingredient in the country's long-term security.

This chapter investigates the nature and scope of nuclear weapons cooperation between the US and Australia since the 1950s. Unlike the other cases examined in this book, Australia has had a highly informal process of engagement with the US on nuclear weapons. The setting of this interaction has varied between bilateral, trilateral (before the US suspended its formal security commitment to New Zealand under the ANZUS treaty), and multilateral (under the Southeast Asia Treaty Organization [SEATO]) frameworks, and often in parallel, which was a cause as well as consequence of the relative lack of institutional frameworks in the first decades of the US–Australia alliance. Notwithstanding the close relationship with the US in managing the so-called 'joint facilities' that have embedded Australia in US nuclear strategy since the 1960s, Australia–US nuclear weapons cooperation has been characterised by a lack of structured interaction. Rather than being a product of US reticence, this has largely been due to a lack of demand from Australia for robust institutional cooperation that stems from a preference for maintaining strategic distance from Washington when it comes to nuclear weapons.

The Australia–US alliance

The security alliance between Australia and the US dates to 1951, when the ANZUS treaty was concluded in the context of Australia's early commitment of forces to the war in Korea, and the US desire to enter into a peace treaty with Japan.[1] Entering into force the following year, ANZUS was a tripartite agreement that included New Zealand, and complemented the close integration of Australia's defence planning and policy with the UK's defence presence in Malaya and Singapore operating within the Commonwealth framework. Recognising the limits of British power in the Pacific, Australia had coveted a formal security alliance with the US since at least end of the Second World War,[2] especially after the US signed the North Atlantic Treaty in 1949. However, although Australia had provided critical territory to help prosecute the Pacific War against Japan, its geographic position was now far less relevant for US global strategy. Nor did Washington have any interest in giving greater priority to Southeast Asia, a theatre that mattered far less to the US than it did to Australia.[3] Instead, the main benefit of the ANZUS treaty for Washington, apart from encouraging Australia's consent to the peace treaty with Japan and committing Australia to support the US in Asia, was to facilitate Australia's military commitment to the British defence of the Middle East.[4]

Geographically isolated from its allies, faced with the uncertain consequences of decolonisation of the countries to its north, and conscious that British and US strategic priorities lay elsewhere, Australia tried to gain insight into US strategic plans and US recognition of the importance of Southeast Asia for its own security. As early as 1952, Australia unsuccessfully sought to be included in NATO planning.[5] In the early ANZUS Council meetings during the 1950s, Australian officials tried to persuade their US counterparts that a direct link between the countries' military chiefs of staff was required, but senior levels of the US military demurred. Of particular concern to senior American military officials was the proposal for a combined military staff and a standing military liaison group.[6] When the State Department convinced the US Joint Chiefs of Staff (JCS) to agree to staff talks, the Chairman of the JCS General Omar Bradley suggested that these be held in Hawaii, as the Australians 'will get tired of hanging around with nothing to do'.[7]

Initially, the conclusion of the ANZUS treaty actually reinforced Australia's focus on the defence of the British Commonwealth.[8] The 1951 Radford–Collins agreement between the US and Australian navies formalised the geographic and organisational separation of peacetime surveillance and wartime protection of shipping between the Commonwealth in Southeast Asia, and the US national effort in the Pacific.[9] While Australia decided to accord Southeast Asia priority over the Middle East in its own defence effort from 1953, the 'Five Power' talks between the US, the UK, France, Australia, and New Zealand failed to agree on a basic strategy for the defence of the region.[10]

In 1954, the collapse of the French position in Indo-China gave political utility in US eyes to a defence organisation for the region, since it would include non-Anglo-Saxon regional countries. It also gave the US political cover both domestically and internationally for responding to Communist aggression in the way it saw fit. The UK, Australia, New Zealand, and France agreed to join the US, Pakistan, Thailand, and the Philippines as members of SEATO.[11]But when Australia developed joint defence plans and prepared to deploy forces in Malaya, the US made clear it would not provide support to this commitment.[12] Indeed, Australia was told by John Foster Dulles that the US was prepared to defend Western Europe because it was such a valuable asset, but it would not support Australia's attempts to do the same in Southeast Asia.[13]

Growing scepticism in Australia over the extent of the US commitment under ANZUS had thus been reinforced by the SEATO experience as well as concern over Washington's lack of support for the UK during the 1956 Suez crisis.[14] And yet it was only through closer integration with the US that Australia could hope to achieve greater influence and insight; by 1956 Washington had agreed to regional defence planning in SEATO, mainly to reassure the organisation's Southeast Asian member states. That year, the Menzies government made a conscious decision to give SEATO priority over the Commonwealth defence framework, and in 1957, Prime Minister Menzies announced that Australia would henceforth standardise its acquisition of military equipment with the US rather than the UK, noting that 'having regard to ANZUS and SEATO and to our geographical situation, Australian participation in any future war must be in close association with the forces of the United States'.[15] As Peter Edwards has noted, 'beginning with guided missile destroyers for the Royal Australian Navy and F111 strike aircraft for the Royal Australian Air Force, purchases of major equipment from this time onwards were generally sourced from, and facilitated interoperability with, the United States'.[16] But Australian defence planners knew that, unlike in NATO, no US forces were allocated against SEATO plans.[17]

Moreover, the United States had limited its obligations under SEATO to the defence against Communist threats alone.[18] But a significant strategic concern to Australia was Indonesia, which under President Sukarno skilfully maintained relations with Moscow, Washington and Beijing, while waging low-level warfare against the Dutch in West Papua, and the new Federation of Malaysia. When Australia committed forces to assist Britain in the defence of Malaysia against Indonesia's confrontation, it looked to US support under ANZUS against possible escalation, including along the shared border with Australia's then-colony, Papua New Guinea.

These attempts to secure US guarantees culminated in the Kennedy administration's refusal to furnish a commitment that US ground forces would be dispatched to support Australia in the event that confrontation with Indonesia escalated to direct armed conflict. The fraught nature of consultations with Washington as tensions rose with Jakarta took the Menzies government by surprise. In particular, Canberra was taken aback by the legalistic and highly caveated interpretation of America's ANZUS obligations; the US would only act with air and naval support in the event of Australian forces being subjected to a direct attack by Indonesia, but explicitly not in cases of 'subversion, guerrilla warfare or indirect aggression'.[19] Despite generic levels of reassurance, US officials made it clear that they would not commit to anything in advance. Mirroring classic entrapment concerns, the Kennedy administration counselled the Menzies government to focus on de-escalating tensions with Indonesia and avoiding armed conflict.[20] This had the effect of chastening Australian expectations regarding US commitments under ANZUS, while at the same time underscoring the operational limitations of the treaty in practice. In a very real sense, this dual realisation drove the policy settings of Australia's approach to the alliance from the early 1960s to the early 1970s. The Australian Defence Committee advised the government in 1963 that 'the degree of obligation which America feels to Australia under ANZUS could be influenced by the contributions which Australia makes to the common defence'.[21] The Kennedy administration's approach of bypassing SEATO on decisions concerning the US commitment to the Vietnam War effectively rendered the organisation moribund.[22] Australia's decision to join the US-led coalition in Vietnam can only be understood when placed in this context; as one of only a handful of troop contributing countries, Australia saw an opportunity to enhance its standing in Washington by demonstrating its commitment as a loyal ally. Like South Korea, rather than reflecting confidence in its alliance with the US, Australia's Vietnam contribution betrayed a degree of insecurity in the US commitment. Senior Australian policymakers calculated that by supporting the US militarily in Southeast Asia, future US administrations would be more sympathetic to Australian requests for tangible American support in prospective Southeast Asian contingencies.[23]

Australia's Vietnam commitment brought the US and Australian militaries closer together in operational terms. Working with US forces in naval, ground, and air combat operations meant that all three Australian services became closely aligned with their US counterparts in tactics, techniques and procedures.[24] At the same time that combat operations were escalating, a new element of the alliance took shape in the form of major US intelligence and communication facilities that were being constructed on Australian soil to take advantage of the country's geographic position. The Northwest Cape submarine communication facility became operational in 1967 and supported the operation of US Polaris SSBNs in the Indian Ocean. It was followed by approval of the Pine Gap and Nurrungar satellite ground stations, which provided support for the US early warning and signals intelligence programme that took shape in the 1960s.[25] These facilities were one of the few ways in which Australia could make a practical contribution to vital US interests, and their highly secretive expansion continued even as tensions grew between the Nixon administration and the new Whitlam Labor government after 1972.[26]

By the early 1970s, Australia's strategic situation was transformed by the combined effects of the Guam doctrine of 1969, the ascent to power by Suharto in Indonesia, the end of the Vietnam War, the creation of the Association of Southeast Asian Nations (ASEAN), and emerging Western rapprochement with China. In effect, the Cold War ended for Australia as an immediate, local security concern. Australia's post-Vietnam defence policy instead focused on the continental defence of Australia from future regional threats, and a new modus vivendi emerged in the alliance where Australia regarded looking after itself and its region as its main contribution. Australia offered the US military use of facilities in Australia to support air and naval deployments in the Indian Ocean, including training facilities for B-52 aircraft,[27] and contributed maritime patrol aircraft and submarines to the monitoring of Soviet ship movements in Southeast Asia. However, it declined an invitation to participate in the US Rapid Deployment Force for the Middle East in 1980,[28] and although periodic exercises with the US continued, the equipment of the Australian Defence Force from the late 1970s and well into the 1990s reflected the much less sophisticated forces of possible adversaries in its immediate region.

Now it was Australia that became quite comfortable with a relationship in which both allies side-stepped what their treaty commitments might mean in practice,[29] as defence 'self-reliance' became linked politically with the emancipation of Australia from its colonial roots, and limited to an 'independent' foreign policy in Asia. Providing a review of the alliance that had been requested by the new Hawke government in 1983, the Defence Committee wrote that attempting to increase the scope of US commitments to support Australia would not only be unlikely to succeed, it would also 'allow US (and NZ) influence to intrude on what are ... essentially national Australian activities'.[30] The US suspension of its security guarantee to New Zealand in 1985 led to the dissolution of the ANZUS Council, and the creation in 1986 of annual Australia–US Ministerial (AUSMIN) meetings that provided Australia with a bilateral channel to deal directly with the US.[31] At the same time, however, Australia's strategic aspiration of self-reliance was reinforced in the landmark 1987 Defence White Paper,[32] which made explicit that Australia had to take responsibility for defending its northern approaches and dealing with low-level contingencies within the framework of the alliance. Uncertainty about the post-Cold War order in Asia, especially after the 1995–96 Taiwan Strait crisis, and Australia's relative economic decline in the region, meant that Australia valued and sought to reinforce an enduring US strategic commitment to Asia, even if its support remained primarily diplomatic rather than military in nature.

With the attacks of 9/11, which occurred as Prime Minister John Howard was visiting Washington, the alliance entered a new phase. Australia invoked the ANZUS treaty for the first time. Its early and strong support for the US-led war on terrorism, as well as its decision to join the US coalition of the willing that invaded Iraq in 2003, placed Australia in a favourable position to negotiate within the alliance, particularly on accessing high-end US defence capabilities, bolstering intelligence cooperation, and attracting high-profile support in the White House and Congress for Australia's economic and political interests, including a bilateral free-trade agreement.[33] Embedding Australian military personnel into US combatant commands became a regular feature of alliance cooperation, although operational cooperation focused on the Middle East rather than Australia's own regional neighbourhood.

When the Obama administration decided in 2011 to 'pivot' to the Indo-Pacific to maintain US strategic influence on the region, Australia responded favourably despite its growing economic dependence on China. In 2012, Canberra agreed to the US–Australia 'Force Posture Initiative', including a rotational deployment of US Marines to Darwin, additional pre-positioning of equipment, space surveillance sensors, and increased US Air Force operations from Australian bases, which the government explicitly framed as support to the 'pivot' as a whole.[34] However, implementation remained hampered by lengthy negotiations on cost sharing,[35] as well as Australia's political reluctance to signal a closer involvement in US long-range offensive operations.[36] Yet, as relations with China have become more antagonistic since 2016 over its island-building in the South China Sea, Beijing's expansion of influence in the South Pacific, and its interference in Australian domestic politics, Australia's reticence regarding closer alliance cooperation has abated. In a notable step, Canberra announced in 2020 that it would invest $1.1 billion at RAAF base Tindal south of Darwin, which will enable the operation of RAAF tankers as well as US long-range bombers from the airfield.[37]

Nuclear weapons in the US–Australia alliance

In the 1950s, the ANZUS alliance had little relevance to US nuclear strategy, as the US did not commit forces to the defence of Australia or New Zealand, and both countries were so geographically remote from China and the Soviet Union that they played no role in the support of the SAC's long-range bomber operations. However, understanding US atomic strike plans was important for Australia's own defence policy, particularly regarding planning for the defence of Malaya as part of the Commonwealth Strategic Reserve.[38] Even before ANZUS came into force, the Australian Defence Committee recommended that the Menzies government request consultations with Washington on the nature of US nuclear strike plans against China.[39] However, despite endorsing (in 1954) a highly detailed nuclear targeting list of hundreds of industrial–urban complexes within China, the Eisenhower administration resisted requests by Australian officials for consultations on the topic.[40]

Some of these barriers to access began to lift as Australia received briefings on the general outlines of US war plans against China at ANZUS and SEATO staff planning meetings in 1955. In 1956, the SEATO Council endorsed the recommendation that nuclear weapons be incorporated more explicitly into planning assumptions about how a war would be fought against China in the region,[41] which reflected the increased reliance on tactical nuclear weapons in US and UK strategy at the time. Australia's planners acknowledged the utility of nuclear weapons for interdiction and long-range bombing. They were, however, less convinced than their US and UK counterparts that nuclear weapons could directly substitute for conventional forces in Southeast Asia's geographic context, especially as an increased emphasis on nuclear weapons in UK policy coincided with significant reductions in UK forces overall in Malaya.[42] Hence, greater allied reliance on nuclear weapons actually reinforced Australia's focus on conventional defence capability because, as the Defence Committee argued in 1956: 'If ... adequate conventional forces are not maintained by the Western Powers to meet the requirements of cold and limited war, it may be possible for the Communist powers to achieve their aims despite the maintenance by the Western Powers of the thermo-nuclear deterrent'.[43]

There is no evidence that Australia exercised any real influence over the nature of US nuclear planning in Southeast Asia. Yet, affirmation within SEATO that US (and UK) nuclear weapons would be used in the region's defence provided Australia with an important degree of reassurance. This was reflected in the 1956 Strategic Basis guidance endorsed by the Menzies government, which noted that:

> Planning can reasonably proceed on the basis that Australian forces engaged in operations in conjunction with UK and US forces, in accordance with common treaty obligations, will be supported by nuclear action by the UK and US, when circumstances require such support. This is inherent in the SEATO strategic concepts developed to date for the defence of South East Asia in limited war, and can be expected similarly to apply in other cases as plans are developed to meet other situations ... The form of support might well be by making available for service with our forces elements armed with and capable of using nuclear weapons or by making such weapons available to our forces *in the field* under certain operational circumstances.[44]

As early as 1955, the Australian Chief of the Air Staff noted in a Defence Committee meeting that Australia 'already had the planes that could deliver nuclear bombs and that if somebody else provided the bombs the Australian Air Force could use them',[45] and in classified guidance and selected public statements, the Menzies government continued to preserve the possibility of acquiring nuclear weapons from Australia's allies, including the US. Senior figures in the Menzies government, including the Prime Minister, sent feelers to Washington as well as London regarding arrangements that would allow the potential future transfer of tactical nuclear weapons to Australia for use in a wartime contingency.[46] Mostly, however, these discussions were kept informal and at the military level. Following changes to the US Atomic Energy Act in 1958 that allowed Washington to transfer nuclear weapons to allies for potential use on their delivery systems, the chief of the US Air Force had assured his Australian counterpart that nuclear bombs could be stored on Australian soil under US control.[47] As Wayne Reynolds notes, 'information was sent to Australia between November 1959 and December 1960 on the feasibility of equipping RAAF Canberra bombers with the USAAF Mark 7 atomic bombs, along with copies of US aircrew delivery manuals and maintenance instructions for special stores'.[48]

However, there is no evidence that concrete plans were ever put in place. Australia's defence effort overall focused on what it saw as Western weakness in conventional forces in Southeast Asia for limited war contingencies, not global war involving nuclear weapons; in any case, the Kennedy administration was much less keen than the Eisenhower administration on dispersing US nuclear weapons to US allies, given the desire for US political control over nuclear use inherent in its strategy of flexible response. Moreover, Menzies himself was ultimately only lukewarm about the prospect of Australia acquiring nuclear weapons from the US (and UK),[49] as he also strongly believed that the stability of the global nuclear order hinged on limiting possession of nuclear weapons to the great powers.[50]

As the prospect of the US transferring nuclear weapons to Australia dissipated during the 1960s, Australian policymakers focused more squarely on the role of extended nuclear deterrence in the alliance. This focus intensified following China's first nuclear test in 1964. Australian officials believed that possessing the bomb would embolden China to undertake riskier strategic behaviour, including coercing smaller non-nuclear states. Indeed, it was at this point that Australian deliberations over acquiring a national nuclear capability began to gain momentum within government. Even prior to the Chinese test, the Menzies government had refused to provide the UN with a commitment that Australia would refrain from acquiring nuclear weapons.[51] It had also authorised the purchase of the new-generation F-111 fighter-bomber from the US, motivated in part by the aircraft's nuclear-capable systems and its long-strike strike capability.[52] By 1965, the State Department was assessing that although Australia 'will probably continue to rely on the US nuclear shield ... the growth of a Chinese or Indonesian threat might lead Australia to want to acquire such weapons itself, rather than being militarily dependent on the United States'.[53] Consideration of a threshold weapons capability for Australia peaked under the Gorton government in the late 1960s, the logic of which was reinforced by growing doubts about US resolve to defend its Asian allies in the wake of the Guam Doctrine in 1969. In defiance of US officials who were keen to shore up allies' support for the NPT and an accompanying global system of nuclear safeguards, Australia remained reluctant to ratify the NPT or conclude an International Atomic Energy Agency safeguards agreement until the Whitlam government came to power in 1972.[54]

Paradoxically, Cold War anxiety about the credibility of the US nuclear umbrella peaked just as Australia was becoming physically embedded in the American global military communications network. The creation in 1967 of the Northwest Cape submarine communication facility and the Pine Gap and Nurrungar satellite ground control and processing stations (both becoming operational in 1970) were significant milestones in Australia–US alliance cooperation during the Cold War.

Australia also played a key role in supporting the free passage of US nuclear-armed platforms in its immediate region. Responding to long-standing pressures in the South Pacific for agreement on a nuclear-free zone, the Hawke government played a leading role in negotiating the South Pacific Nuclear-Free Zone (SPNFZ) treaty in 1985. Although the Reagan administration was privately critical of Australia for not discouraging regional support for a nuclear-free zone in the first place, in the final text the Hawke government successfully safeguarded US nuclear transit rights in the region through ports and airfields, including Australia.[55] While the US did not endorse the treaty, in a submission to Cabinet, Australia's Foreign Minister Bill Hayden underscored the lack of any impact on US nuclear operations in the region, even noting that the SPNFZ was 'designed to maintain the security advantages afforded to the Southwest Pacific through the ANZUS treaty and the US security presence in the region'.[56] But in terms of cooperation that strengthened the role of nuclear weapons in the alliance, it was the hosting of the joint facilities that proved far and away the most important.

The Northwest Cape facility provided very low frequency communications for US nuclear-missile-firing submarines traversing the Indian and Southwest Pacific Oceans, whereas the function of the Pine Gap and Nurrungar facilities was to provide early warning of missile launches globally, monitor missile telemetry, and sweep up telecommunications across a wide range of the earth's surface.[57] Australia's commitment of territory and personnel in support of these bases was designed to deepen the alliance in a practical sense, but the effect was that Australia provided direct support to the operation of US nuclear forces. Opponents of the facilities argued that by hosting them, Australia was endorsing US first-strike planning while ensuring the country would be a nuclear target in the event of war. Advocates of the bases maintained that by supporting US nuclear strategy, Australia was making a critical contribution to the alliance, which outweighed any associated risks.

Notwithstanding the bases being named 'Joint Facilities' in 1974, it took some time for this shared authority to be achieved in practice. In 1980, Australian personnel were granted full access to all areas of the Pine Gap facility and an Australian was appointed chair of the committee that determined the day-to-day focus of the satellites controlled at Pine Gap.[58] But it was not until 1986 that Australia reached an agreement with the US to embed senior Australian personnel in all decision-making functions across the three facilities, including having an Australian citizen appointed to the newly created post of deputy chief of facility.[59]

These changes were announced by Prime Minister Hawke in 1988 – 'to ensure greater integration of Australian personnel in both the operation and the management of the Joint Facilities'[60] – but they were essentially the result of the persistence of then Defence Minister Kim Beazley, who insisted that all decisions at the facilities be taken with 'the full knowledge and concurrence' of Australia. According to former Deputy Secretary of the Department of Defence, Paul Dibb, Beazley's insistence on full knowledge and concurrence was initially resisted by the Reagan administration because no other US ally had proposed such arrangements for American bases on its territory; however, the argument that operational secrecy could be preserved while assuaging sovereignty concerns among the Australian public 'won the Americans over'.[61] Notably, however, the implementation agreement, which incorporated detailed 'administrative arrangements', took some fifteen months to negotiate. A subsequently declassified report prepared in 1990 by the US Space Command referred to the 'controversy' surrounding the negotiations, which indicates there was a period of intensive bargaining between Australian and US officials on the specific terms and conditions of the classified arrangements.[62]

By embedding Australia operationally into the US global nuclear command and control network, the Joint Facilities served to increase Australia's strategic value in the eyes of Washington during the Cold War. Senior Australian policymakers learned to live with thinly veiled nuclear threats from Soviet officials; the Fraser government in 1980 felt these were sufficiently credible to commission a highly classified intelligence analysis of the impact of a nuclear attack on Australia.[63] Despite the likelihood, which has been publicly acknowledged by policymakers since the Hawke government,[64] that the presence of the bases made Australia a Soviet, and possibly Chinese, nuclear target, successive governments argued that this was justified because of the contribution the facilities made to deterrence stability and the national technical means of verification underpinning nuclear arms control and disarmament.[65]

Yet, any such attack would have de facto been an attack on the US itself, happening to take place in Australia by virtue of it being 'a suitable piece of real estate'[66] for the facilities. Hence, although Australia was subject to a nuclear threat during the second part of the Cold War, the implications were very different from those for other US allies. Australia was spared the political agonies and strategic doubts of those US allies in Europe and Northeast Asia that had to depend on, but could never be quite certain of, US support against a Soviet attack. Therefore unlike other US allies, Australia has never sought formal public assurances of American extended nuclear deterrence, and the very existence of the US nuclear umbrella in relation to Australia has been assumed by observers and policymakers rather than confirmed through public statements from Washington.

Australian policymakers were intent on making more explicit reference to the nuclear umbrella after the end of the Cold War than before.[67] Growing uncertainty over future US strategic commitments in Asia led to a view among Australian policymakers that a public affirmation of the value placed on US extended nuclear deterrence as a key element of US strategic engagement in Asia was necessary. For the first time, Australian governments thus began openly referring to the US nuclear umbrella, but did so in terms that reflected the limited role it sought to give nuclear weapons overall, in line with the support for nuclear disarmament that would lead the Keating Labor government to create the Canberra Commission on the Elimination of Nuclear Weapons in 1995. In the 1993 Strategic Review, which laid the groundwork for the 1994 Defence White Paper, the Keating government implied a 'sole-purpose' approach to US extended deterrence, as Australia stated it would only depend on the US nuclear umbrella for defence against threats that were nuclear:

> During the Cold War, Australia was a member of the Western strategic community committed to nuclear deterrence. In part, this involved a risk of nuclear threat to Australia, principally because of our hosting of joint Defence facilities. We judged the risk to be acceptable, because of our overriding interest in supporting our US ally to maintain the system of nuclear deterrence and because the Joint Facilities contributed to stability and supported arms control and disarmament measures. The risk has now dissipated, but nuclear weapons still exist in the arsenals of a number of states. Australia continues to depend on the United States for security against any future nuclear threat.[68]

Former senior Australian Defence Department official Hugh White – who was involved in preparing the 1993 Strategic Review and subsequent White Paper – has confirmed that the insertion of explicit reference to the nuclear umbrella was discussed informally with US officials at the Pentagon who indicated 'they would get back to us if they had a problem'.[69]

Despite the essence of this statement being repeated in successive Australian strategic guidance documents since the mid-1990s,[70] no US administration has publicly endorsed the Australian position on extended nuclear deterrence. Notwithstanding a fleeting mention in the 2019 US National Defense Authorization Act,[71] coverage of Australia under the nuclear umbrella is absent from public pronouncements by US officials and in annual AUSMIN communiqués. At the same time, however, Washington has publicly endorsed the overall strategic vision outlined in Defence planning guidance where references to the nuclear umbrella have appeared. The private briefings given to senior US officials on drafts of Defence White Papers provide an opportunity for input into the final version, so it is notable that the distinct Australian approach to statements about the nuclear umbrella has remained unchanged since 1993.

Notwithstanding Australia's established commitment to nuclear disarmament and its track record on global arms control, successive conservative and centre-left governments maintained careful support for US extended nuclear deterrence under the Obama and Trump administrations. While some elements of the Labor Party have expressed support for a global nuclear ban treaty, Australia has refused to support the Treaty on the Prohibition of Nuclear Weapons, with official statements noting that such support 'would be inconsistent with our US alliance obligations'.[72] This position was a logical corollary of Australia's earlier submissions to the 2009 Congressional Commission on America's Strategic Posture and the 2010 NPR, which underscored the importance of avoiding the decoupling of US and allied interests. In a statement prepared for the Congressional Commission, Australia's Defence Department noted that '[i]n order to maintain confidence in extended deterrence, the US will need to make clear that it would respond in kind to nations that employ nuclear weapons against friends and allies of the US, even when there is no existential threat to the US itself'.[73]

Tracing nuclear weapons cooperation

Threat assessment and prioritisation

Despite strong rhetorical support for the role of values in the alliance, the alignment and differences regarding the perception of threats between Australia and the US has always mirrored abandonment and entrapment concerns arising from their own national priorities. Australia's remote physical location and experience of the fall of Singapore in 1942 meant that it was primarily concerned in the 1950s with the defence of Southeast Asia in limited and global war, and sought to substantiate the role of US nuclear weapons in this theatre. However, the region was typically a third-order priority for its allies, and the US was unwilling to compromise its relationship with Jakarta over Dutch, British, and Australian conflicts with Indonesia that had little to do with the spread of Communism.

China was identified as a nuclear threat in the mid-1960s, but not until the early 1980s did Beijing introduce an ICBM (the DF-5) into service with the capacity to strike Australian territory.[74] This did not prevent scepticism about the value of US nuclear commitments within the Australian government being linked with doubts about the broader endurance of the US–Australia alliance. This was particularly salient under the Gorton government in the late 1960s that was sympathetic to the view that 'threats to use nuclear weapons are credible only in instances where they are tied to vital national interests ... offers by the United States to "extend" nuclear deterrence to their allies are inherently implausible'; this contrasted with the Menzian view that nuclear weapons were too important to be entrusted any actors other than the great powers.[75] While it was no coincidence that deliberations under the Gorton government about a potential Australian threshold nuclear weapons capability aligned with the Guam Doctrine, Canberra's concerns focused mainly on the resolve of the US to address threats on the Asian mainland rather than its willingness to defend the Australian continent as such.

From the 1970s, Australia remained a committed member of the Western community of nations in the Cold War and supported the US global role in providing strategic stability in Asia. The possibility of Soviet nuclear strikes against the Joint Facilities was a reality for Australian policymakers that they accepted as part of this support, but as a direct and imminent concern to Australian defence, the Cold War had ended with the war in Vietnam. The concept of 'self-reliance' that was (and remains, in various forms) central to Australia's defence policy since the early 1970s was instead a direct reflection of the limits of US assistance that Australia could expect in any regional conflict.

In spite of effusive public references to the US alliance, even today Australian policymakers are privately uncertain about the threshold for US intervention in the defence of Australian interests. This wariness was reinforced by the East Timor experience in 1999 when senior Australian policymakers were surprised by initial US reluctance to take on a major supporting role in the International Force East Timor (INTERFET) mission, with some expressing concerns about the credibility of existing US security commitments under the alliance.[76] In the post-Cold War era and in the context of China's rise as a major military power as well as it being Australia's most important trading partner, Australian policymakers continued to regard possible Australian support to the US through the lens of Australia's own narrow interests, rather than through the lens of the expansive geographic scope of the ANZUS treaty that encompasses the whole 'Pacific area'. Foreign Minister Alexander Downer, in comments on Taiwan in 2004, and Defence Minister David Johnston, in comments on the East China Sea in 2014, explicitly highlighted that the ANZUS treaty created no legal obligation for Australia to provide military assistance in case of an attack on US forces.[77] With the increasing assertiveness of China's push for regional dominance since 2016, Australia is now increasingly also seeing a more forceful political and military containment of China as in its interest – but the conclusion of the Hawke Cabinet in 1983 that the 'coincidence of [US and Australian] interest, rather than the provisions of the ANZUS Treaty, provides the basis for co-operation' between both countries informs perceptions of current policymakers.[78]

Policy objectives regarding nuclear weapons cooperation

Policy objectives of Australia and the US in relation to nuclear weapons have consistently reflected their broader objectives for the relationship, and the fact that neither ally ever identified a specific strategic role for nuclear weapons in the alliance. In the 1950s, Australia's enquiries about US atomic strike plans were just one element of its general attempt to gain more insights into US global planning and priorities. US reluctance to provide this information was likewise consistent with its general attitude that regarded Australia as a high maintenance ally with inflated expectations about joint military planning under ANZUS. Informal discussions about the possible transfer of US nuclear weapons to Australian forces in wartime during the 1950s must be seen in this context; for neither was there a clear rationale for a national role in nuclear operations in Australia's defence policy, nor did the US do anything to push Australia to 'modernise' its forces along these lines in the way it lobbied its NATO allies at the time.

The establishment of the Joint Facilities was based on a coincidental alignment of US interest in the geographic position of Australia, and Australia's interest in making contributions to US security as a way of building up strategic capital with a somewhat evasive ally. By the 1980s, Australia's objectives regarding the Joint Facilities focused on its ability to exploit the information gathered for its own defence, and more general considerations of sovereignty that the US was ultimately willing to concede to avoid a recurrence of the split with New Zealand over issues of nuclear weapons policy. Sensitive to the potentially brittle nature of support within the governing Labor Party for the Joint Facilities, and conscious of Australia's continuing support for the regional transit of American nuclear platforms against the background of the SPNFZ negotiations, Washington learned to live with the Hawke government's view that 'support for deterrence was on the explicit basis [Australia] would vigorously push ahead with [its] arms control agenda'.[79] Opposition to SDI was part of this agenda, as was Australia's vocal support for a comprehensive nuclear test ban treaty and reluctance to support US MX missile testing on Australian soil.[80]

Given this varied and highly contextual nature of the policy objectives regarding nuclear weapons in the alliance, one Australian expert has argued that the informal nature of discussions on nuclear weapons between both allies 'helped to make the security relationship between the two countries much less fraught than it might otherwise have been'.[81] Personal relationships and informal bargaining between key players have played an important role, and this has been especially salient with respect to the Joint Facilities and extended nuclear deterrence. Rather than issue requests through formal channels for assurances in relation to the nuclear umbrella,

Australian officials have chosen instead to broach the topic informally with US counterparts and invoke unilaterally an extended nuclear deterrence commitment within the framework of the alliance without receiving public confirmation from Washington. Similarly, the search for greater Australian sovereign authority over the joint facilities in the 1980s was driven largely by the influence and determination of Defence Minister Kim Beazley, who insisted on revised arrangements within the institutional framework of the bilateral alliance. But even in this regard, the nature of exchanges reflects the lack of political–military institutions or structure in the alliance overall,[82] and Australian policymakers' general reluctance to enter into detailed discussions with Washington that could encourage unwanted planning assumptions on the part of the US.[83]

Nuclear strategy

Australia's direct engagement with US nuclear strategy has been minimal, and at no point has there been any need for Washington and Canberra to come to an agreement on strategy relating to the use of nuclear weapons. In the 1950s, Australian staff officers working in SEATO had different views than their US and UK counterparts about the tactical utility of nuclear weapons in Southeast Asia – influenced undoubtedly by the failure of British air power to prevent the fall of Singapore in 1942 – but the limited relevance of nuclear weapons for the counterinsurgency conflicts that came to dominate actual operations in Southeast Asia meant that Canberra never had to form clear policy positions on specific points of nuclear strategy.

During the 1980s there was controversy about the Reagan administration's high-profile embrace of nuclear war-fighting doctrine and the implications of this for Australia. However, this was essentially confined to public discourse, and there appears to have been little friction behind closed doors between Australian and US officials on this point. This is not to say that Australian policymakers were uninterested in the topic – government ministers were acutely aware that key sections of their constituency were exercised about the role of the Joint Facilities in supporting American nuclear strategy – but Australian governments were content to highlight the role of the Joint Facilities in verifying arms control and strengthening deterrence, and acknowledging the stabilising role of mutually assured destruction between both superpowers in very general terms.

While cultivating a global role for Australia since the early 1970s as a leading advocate of non-proliferation and arms control, governments in Canberra have remained attuned to the option of a national nuclear force in the event Australia's security environment seriously deteriorates. The following assessment contained in the 2009 Defence White Paper captures well the inherent ambiguity in Australia's position:

> No requirement is seen now for Australia to acquire nuclear weapons. However, the increased likelihood of nuclear proliferation, and the possible requirement to keep the lead-time for Australia matched with contingent developments in other countries call for a review periodically of Australia's potential for development of nuclear weapons, against the possibility that the country might be forced to consider turning to them for protection at some indeterminate time in the future.[84]

The various scenarios canvassed in which an Australian government might review the country's non-nuclear status include a massive loss of confidence in the credibility of the US security alliance.[85]

In this sense, the role of American extended deterrence, and in particular the nuclear umbrella, remains a factor in Australian nuclear policy, but one that is also characterised by a high-level, generalised view. Even during the 1950s, Australia's emphasis on the role of nuclear weapons in US extended deterrence was because of their perceived importance for the US strategic commitment to Asia in general, rather than any need for assistance on Australia's part. Australia's ambivalence over the Carter administration's plans to dramatically reduce US forces in South Korea and withdraw its nuclear weapons was an offshoot of concern in Canberra that this was potentially the first step in a broader US pull-back from Asia in the wake of defeat in Vietnam.[86] Australia's affirmations of the role of extended nuclear deterrence since 1993 are an expression of this concern. However, as Canberra did not set out a preferred position on a specific issue of nuclear policy, the emphasis on a sole-purpose view of nuclear weapons inherent in Australian formulations that contrasts with US policy remained of little consequence. Beyond the implicit agreement on the value of nuclear deterrence, Washington and Canberra have never sought to define a common view on nuclear deterrence.

Domestic factors

The most prominent nuclear issue in Australian public opinion historically has been whether the country should export uranium, and more recently the question of whether Australia should explore nuclear power to offset long-term energy security risks.[87] Notwithstanding thinly veiled nuclear threats from North Korea against Australia,[88] and periods of political tension with a nuclear-armed China, public opinion polls do not indicate any support for an Australian nuclear weapons capability,[89] despite a resurgence of interest in the topic among some experts.[90] There is no evidence of any push for the introduction of US nuclear weapons to Australia, a trend that has remained consistent since the 1960s. Recent public opinion polling shows greater confidence than in the past in Australia's ability to defend itself, and perception of China as a security threat is lower than what it was during the Vietnam War.[91] Although public support for the US alliance has fluctuated according to contingent events (such as the unpopularity of the Iraq invasion in 2003), a clear majority of the Australian public consistently rates the alliance as positive for Australia's security.[92]

This support seems to have been based on the presumption that Australia relies on US 'protection' for its security and that US intervention would be forthcoming if Australia's security were ever seriously threatened. However, the nuclear dimension of the alliance has been more nuanced. During the Cold War, there was a consistent thread of anti-nuclear sentiment in Australian public opinion, which overlapped with criticism of the US alliance.[93] Between the early 1970s and late 1980s, most of this anti-nuclear sentiment focused on the presence of the Joint Facilities on Australian soil as well as continued Australian support for the transit of American nuclear platforms following New Zealand's refusal to allow nuclear-capable vessels to enter the country's ports. Anti-nuclear sentiment in Australia reached its height in the early to mid-1980s, when it became apparent that Pine Gap, Nurrungar, and Northwest Cape would play an important role in the employment of US strategic nuclear forces.[94]

Although never a majority view in public opinion, opposition to Australia hosting US bases was politically tricky for Labor governments in particular. During a visit to Washington in early 1974, then-Labor Deputy Prime Minister Lance Barnard assured senior US officials as follows: 'I don't want any possible debate in Australia about these bases. They make a significant contribution to US and Australian security and to world peace. I want to get them accepted by the public and not a subject of debate.'[95] While the Hawke government's negotiation of formal arrangements with Washington to ensure Australia's full knowledge and concurrence of operations at the Joint Facilities was largely framed in sovereignty terms, neutralising criticism from the left wing of the Labor Party was also a major factor. US policymakers recognised that compromise in this area was necessary to promote the Labor government's scope domestically to 'sell' the arms control and disarmament function of the joint facilities. In accepting the Hawke government's refusal to be involved in the research and development of SDI, for example, the Reagan administration agreed to Canberra's request that it announce to the Australian public that the Joint Facilities were not actively engaged in SDI research and development.[96]

The importance of Australia for US security

From the US perspective, a major benefit of the alliance lies in Australian political support for US policies elsewhere: the ANZUS treaty itself was a price for Australian agreement to the peace treaty with Japan, and in general Australia is seen as one of Washington's most loyal and least troublesome allies.[97] Australian support for the US on some issues on which Washington has found itself isolated internationally (Vietnam, Iraq) has strengthened the view among American policymakers that Australia is a highly dependable ally.[98] This is a perception that Australia has attempted to reinforce and link to its own strategic priorities by arguing that it provides an important leadership role in the South Pacific in particular.

A second major benefit, though more contextually dependent, is access to Australian territory. Removed from the main centres of conflict in Eurasia, Australia was (and remains) particularly relevant for space related facilities, such as satellite communications at Pine Gap, or a space surveillance radar installed on the Northwest shelf as part of the 2012 Force Posture Initiative, in addition to seismic equipment monitoring global nuclear tests. In the 2010s, the increasing reach of Chinese missile capabilities also rekindled US interest in Australia as a base area for operations in the wider Indo-Pacific,[99] which in addition to increased air force cooperation as part of the Force Posture Initiative have led to proposals being floated for home porting a US carrier strike group in Western Australia,[100] and potentially stationing future intermediate range missiles in northern Australia.[101]

Ultimately, however, Australia's contributions to US strategic interests on the global stage are seldom essential, and successive US administrations have been careful to limit their security commitments to Australia to avoid potential entrapment. Throughout the Cold War, Washington made it clear that although it was willing to provide generic security assurances under ANZUS, detailed commitments were off the table. Arthur Tange, who occupied a series of senior defence and foreign policy positions within the Australian bureaucracy, recalled the tone of high-level conversations with US officials in the mid-1960s:

> I retained a memory of the blunt warning that I heard [Secretary of State] Dean Rusk give to [Australian Foreign Minister] Hasluck in 1964. During the discussion of worsening relations between Malaysia and Indonesia, Hasluck volunteered to inform the Americans before committing Australian forces in support of Malaysia. Responding to the inherent assumption that such a deployment would trigger an expectation of American military support, Rusk pointedly said that the United States would expect that [by then] Australia would have introduced conscription and full mobilisation, and added 'there is

> no residuum of responsibility falling on the United States that is reached at a certain point'.[102]

Insecurity over whether the US would come to Australia's assistance was also evident in extreme scenarios painted by senior Australian policymakers, especially in the wake of China's first nuclear test in 1964. In a top-secret note to Prime Minister Gorton in 1968, the head of the Prime Minister's Department posed the rhetorical question: 'Will the Americans come to our aid, under ANZUS, with nuclear weapons in the event of a threat to Australia by Chinese nuclear weaponry? This year; next year; in twenty-four years from now? Will they?'[103]

Access to information

A key theme in the preceding analysis is that the role of nuclear weapons in the US–Australia alliance has generally been rather abstract. Hence, Australia seeking specific information regarding US nuclear capabilities or strategy, and American control of that information, has played a limited and only intermittent role in the alliance. The first such case was the mid-1950s, when US refusal to release information about US nuclear strike plans against China was a convenient way of stalling the planning of Australia, New Zealand, and the UK for the defence of Malaya. This was a commitment that the US did not support, as the response by Admiral Radford, Chairman of the JCS, made clear when Australia submitted these plans for his consideration.[104] The second, more enduring case relates to the specific activities undertaken at the Joint Facilities in Australia, which Australia sought to understand for sovereignty reasons more than because of any specific concern about the detail of US operations. Hence, the Whitlam government insisted on Australian Navy personnel being present in the control room of the Northwest Cape facility.[105] Yet, this did not guarantee that Australia was properly consulted on key changes at any of the facilities. In 1978, it became publicly apparent that the United States had not informed Australia of the planned installation of a new satellite antenna at North West Cape, which led Defence Minister James Killen to comment that the US was not showing Australia 'the proper courtesy'.[106] This provided an important background for the subsequent concerted push under the Hawke government's for US agreement to Australia's 'full knowledge and concurrence' with all operations at the Joint Facilities.

In relation to extended deterrence, Australia today is the only major US ally that claims applicability of the nuclear umbrella but does not have a formal nuclear policy consultation process with Washington. The reason for this appears to have more to do with a lack of demand on the Australian side than an unwillingness on the part of the US.[107] Discussions about deterrence arise as part of Australia's engagement with US Indo-Pacific Command, Strategic Command, and the US Defense and State Departments, but Australia's takeaways from these discussions do not always align in detail and emphasis.[108] Moreover, Australian understandings of US policy do not always align with Japanese understandings, as conveyed by Tokyo.[109] Many Australian policymakers today therefore do not believe that US thinking about the role of nuclear weapons in managing great power conflict in Asia is sufficiently specific for Australia to understand the implications of emerging alliance cooperation on long-range conventional or nuclear strike.[110] But they are also aware that there is little experience in Canberra in developing policy on nuclear deterrence,[111] nor are there threats to Australia that would vindicate a push by policymakers for more explicit commitments from the US. Hence, sustained discussions that might bring about leadership focus in Canberra on questions of the details of US nuclear policy, and which might lead to demand for more detailed discussions akin to those that exist in US alliances in Europe and with Japan and South Korea have yet to develop.

Conclusion

The role of US nuclear weapons in Australia's US alliance is defined by a paradox: although successive Australian governments have valued the long-term reassurance provided by US extended nuclear deterrence, the alliance lacks institutional architecture to manage nuclear weapons cooperation. This is in contrast to other US alliances in Asia and Europe and can be attributed to two key reasons. The first, and most obvious, is that there is no demand from Australia for the introduction of purpose-built institutions dealing with nuclear issues. Unlike NATO members and Japan and South Korea, Australian policymakers have never seen the US nuclear umbrella through the prism of operational defence considerations. Put another way, Australia's relatively benign threat environment has not led to demand for structured interaction with the US over how nuclear weapons should be managed within the alliance. The second reason is that the US–Australia alliance overall has little institutional depth. A major hallmark of the alliance is the high degree of informal bargaining that determines the nature of security cooperation. In an alliance that foregrounds personal connections, values, and even sentimentality over detailed management structures, and has to accommodate a history of very explicit limits of alliance cooperation with regard to regional threats to Australia, there appears to be little appetite in either country for creating new formal institutions.

Nevertheless, in spite of the paucity of institutional structure within the US–Australia alliance, Australia as the junior partner has had some influence over the nuclear weapons cooperation that has, in fact, taken place. As this chapter has shown, Australian governments during the 1970s and 1980s negotiated progressively greater authority in the day-to-day operations of the US bases operating on national territory, and Australia gained the consent of the Reagan administration to join the SPNFZ treaty, despite US concern about anti-nuclear public sentiments at the time. Uniquely among US allies in Asia and Europe, Australian policymakers chose not to formally request an extended nuclear deterrence commitment from the US, instead inserting language into strategic guidance to that effect, following informal consultations with US officials. With the exception of failing to achieve consistent insights into US nuclear planning during the 1950s, Australian governments have largely realised their objectives with respect to nuclear weapons cooperation even in the absence of institutional mechanisms. To a large extent, this reflects the limited demands that Australia has placed on the US in relation to nuclear matters. However, it also indicates that external balancing and power asymmetries, while present in every US alliance, have had limited influence in shaping nuclear weapons cooperation in the US–Australia alliance.

Notes

1 K. Calder, 'Securing Security Through Prosperity: The San Francisco System in Comparative Perspective', *Pacific Review*, 17:1 (2004), 149.
2 See G. St J. Barclay, *Friends in High Places: Australian-American Diplomatic Relations Since 1945*, (Melbourne: Oxford University Press, 1985); and D. Ball, 'The Strategic Essence', *The Australian Journal of International Affairs*, 55:2, 2001, 235–248.
3 P. Dennis, 'Major and Minor: The Defense of Southeast Asia and the Cold War', in K. Neilson and R. Haycock (eds), *The Cold War and Defense* (New York: Praeger, 1990), 144–145.
4 See H. Umetsu, 'The Birth of Anzus: America's Attempt to Create a Defense Linkage between Northeast Asia and the Southwest Pacific', *International Relations of the Asia-Pacific* 4:1 (2004), 171–196.
5 H. Brands, 'From ANZUS to SEATO: United States Strategic Policy Towards Australia and New Zealand, 1952–1954', *International History Review*, 9:2 (1987), 250–270.
6 Brands, 'From ANZUS to SEATO', 254–255.
7 Brands, 'From ANZUS to SEATO', 254.
8 Dennis, 'Major and Minor', 145.

9 A. Brown, 'The History of the Radford-Collins Agreement', Royal Australian Navy, Sea Power Centre, www.navy.gov.au/history/feature-histories/history-radford-collins-agreement

10 P. Lowe, *Contending with Nationalism and Communism: British Policy Towards Southeast Asia, 1945–65* (Houndmills: Palgrave Macmillan, 2009), 83–84.

11 D. Lee, 'Australia and Allied Strategy in the Far East, 1952–1957', *Journal of Strategic Studies*, 16:4 (1993), 516–522.

12 Lee, 'Australia and Allied Strategy in the Far East', 526–527.

13 Lee, 'Australia and Allied Strategy in the Far East', 527.

14 G. Pemberton, *All the Way: Australia's Road to Vietnam* (Sydney: Allen and Unwin, 1987), 57–58.

15 Pemberton, *All the Way*, 59.

16 P. Edwards, *Permanent Friends? Historical Reflections on the Australia-American Alliance*, Lowy Institute for International Policy, Paper No. 8 (2005), 19.

17 M. Jones, 'The Radford Bombshell: Anglo-Australian-US Relations, Nuclear Weapons and the Defence of South East Asia, 1954–1957', *Journal of Strategic Studies*, 27:4 (2004), 636–662.

18 Dennis, 'Major and Minor', 148.

19 P. Edwards, with G. Pemberton, *Crises and Commitments: The Politics and Diplomacy of Australia's Involvement in Southeast Asian Conflicts, 1948–1965* (Sydney: Allen and Unwin in association with the Australian War Memorial, 1992), 280.

20 Edwards and Pemberton, *Crises and Commitments*, 280.

21 Defence Committee, 'Australia's Strategic Position, 4 February 1963', in S. Frühling (ed.), *A History of Australian Strategic Policy Since 1945* (Canberra: Commonwealth of Australia, 2009), 305.

22 Pemberton, *All the Way*, 150–151.

23 Edwards and Pemberton, *Crises and Commitments*, 248–249.

24 J. Blaxland, 'US-Australian Military Cooperation in Asia', in P. Dean, S. Frühling, and B. Taylor (eds), *Australia's American Alliance* (Melbourne: Melbourne University Press, 2016), 125.

25 See D. Ball, *A Suitable Piece of Real Estate: American Installations in Australia* (Sydney: Hale and Iremonger, 1980), 50–82.

26 See J. Curran, *Unholy Fury: The US Alliance and the Nixon-Whitlam Crisis* (Melbourne: Melbourne University Press, 2015).

27 H. Albinski, *The Australian-American Security Relationship: A Regional and International Perspective* (St Lucia: University of Queensland Press, 1982), 135–136.

28 Cabinet Decision No. 12644(FAD), 26 August 1980; NAA A12909, 4317.

29 S. Frühling, 'Wrestling with Commitment: Geography, Alliance and the ANZUS Treaty', in P. Dean, S. Frühling, and B. Taylor (eds), *Australia's American Alliance* (Melbourne: Melbourne University Press, 2016), 13–35.

30 Defence Committee, *Review of ANZUS*, NAA A13977, 13 September 1983, 170.

31 W. Tow, 'ANZUS: Regional Versus Global Security in Asia', *International Relations of the Asia Pacific*, 5:1 (2005), 203.
32 See Department of Defence, *The Defence of Australia 1987: Presented to Parliament by the Minister for Defence, the Honourable Kim Beazley MP* (Canberra: Australian Government Publishing Service, 1987); and *Review of Australia's Defence Capabilities: Report to the Minister for Defence by Mr Paul Dibb* (Canberra: Australian Government Publishing Service, 1986).
33 A. Tidwell, 'The Role of "Diplomatic Lobbying" in Shaping US Foreign Policy and Its Effects on the Australia-US Relationship', *Australian Journal of International Affairs*, 71:2 (2017), 191–192.
34 Department of Foreign Affairs and Trade, 'AUSMIN Joint Communique, 12 August 2014', www.dfat.gov.au/geo/united-states-of-america/ausmin/Pages/ausmin-joint-communique-2014
35 M. Crane, 'Boosting the US Presence in Northern Australia: Slowly But Surely', *The Strategist*, 21 March 2019, www.aspistrategist.org.au/boosting-the-us-presence-in-northern-australia-slowly-but-surely/
36 When a senior US official 'misspoke' in 2015 about deploying B-1 bombers to Australia as a direct reaction to Chinese moves in the South China Sea, Australia was adamant that the initiative was 'not directed at any one country'. P. Dorling, 'B-1 Bombers Coming to Australia to Deter Beijing's South China Sea Ambitions: US', *Sydney Morning Herald*, 15 May 2015, www.smh.com.au/world/b1-bombers-coming-to-australia-to-deter-beijings-south-china-sea-ambitions-us-20150515-gh23zl.html
37 M. Doran, 'Federal Government Spends $ 1.1 Billion on Northern Territory Airbase, Expanding Reach into the Indo-Pacific', *ABC News Online*, 21 February 2020, www.abc.net.au/news/2020–02–21/federal-government-spends-1.1-billion-on-top-end-air-base/11986904
38 Lee, 'Australia and Allied Strategy in the Far East', 526–527; and Jones, 'The Radford Bombshell', 642–649.
39 C. Leah, 'Deterrence Beyond Down Under: Australia and US Security Guarantees Since 1955', *Journal of Strategic Studies*, 39:4 (2016), 525.
40 For analysis, see M. Jones, 'Targeting China: US Nuclear Planning and "Massive Retaliation" in East Asia, 1953–1955', *Journal of Cold War Studies*, 10:4 (2008), 37–65.
41 Jones, 'The Radford Bombshell', 651–653.
42 Jones, 'The Radford Bombshell', 653–656.
43 Defence Committee, 'Strategic Basis of Australian Defence Policy, 11 October 1956', in S. Frühling (ed.), *A History of Australian Strategic Policy Since 1945* (Canberra: Commonwealth of Australia, 2009), 225.
44 Defence Committee, 'Strategic Basis of Australian Defence Policy, 11 October 1956', 208 (emphasis in original).
45 W. Reynolds, 'The Wars that were Planned: Australia's Forward Defence Posture in Asia and the Role of Tactical Nuclear Weapons, 1945–1967', *Australian Journal of International Affairs*, 53:3 (1999), 304.

46 J. Walsh, 'Surprise Down Under: The Secret History of Australia's Nuclear Ambitions', *Nonproliferation Review*, 5:1 (1997), 3–6.
47 W. Reynolds, *Australia's Bid for the Atomic Bomb* (Melbourne: Melbourne University Press, 2000), 206.
48 Reynolds, *Australia's Bid for the Atomic Bomb*, 206.
49 Walsh, 'Surprise Down Under', 6–7.
50 C. Leah and R. Lyon, 'Three Visions of the Bomb: Australian Thinking About Nuclear Weapons and Strategy', *Australian Journal of International Affairs*, 64:4 (2010), 453–454.
51 'Letter Sent by the Minister for External Affairs to the Acting Secretary-General of the United Nations Concerning Resolution 1664, 15 March 1962', tabled in *Commonwealth Parliamentary Debates* (House of Representatives), 5 April 1962, 1381.
52 I. Bellany, *Australia in the Nuclear Age: National Defence and National Development* (Sydney: Sydney University Press, 1972), 62–63.
53 Department of State, 'Addendum INR Contribution to NIE 4–65 Likelihood of Further Nuclear Proliferation', 4 November 1965, https://nsarchive2.gwu.edu/NSAEBB/NSAEBB155/prolif-11b.pdf
54 Australian interest in a potential nuclear weapons program was also stoked by the view that such a capability would suit Australia's geo-strategic circumstances. The year before John Gorton assumed the prime ministership, a senior official in the Prime Minister's office noted the following in a top-secret memo: 'The only circumstances in which Australia would be interested in a nuclear capacity would be for its own self-defence against invasion. As far into the future as we can see, invasion of the mainland can only be by ship-borne forces. The geography of Australia lends itself uniquely to the use of a nuclear weapon in its self-defence. Drop an atom bomb on Europe and you will take away millions of lives; drop an atom bomb on the Coral Sea and the only effect will be a bit of radio-active debris.' Memorandum from Allan Griffith to Peter Lawler, 'Australian Nuclear Policy', 16 May 1967, NAA: A1209, 1965/6470, A1209.
55 A. O'Neil, 'Australia and the South Pacific Nuclear Free Zone Treaty: A Reinterpretation', *Australian Journal of Political Science*, 39:3 (2004), 567–583.
56 Cabinet Submission No. 2806 and Cabinet Decision No. 5512/ID and No 5563, folio 9; NAA A14039, 2806, 29 April 1985.
57 For the authoritative accounts of the Cold War functions of Pine Gap and Nurrungar, see D. Ball's *A Base for Debate: The US Satellite Station at Nurrungar*. Sydney: Allen and Unwin, 1987; and *Pine Gap: Australia and the US Geostationary Signals Intelligence*. Sydney: Allen and Unwin, 1988. Nurrungar was decommissioned in 1999 and its existing functions were transferred to the Pine Gap facility. Northwest Cape became an Australian facility in 1993 and 'in July 2008 a treaty was signed for US access to and use of the Australian facility for a period of 25 years'. S. Smith, 'Ministerial Statement

(Defence): Full Knowledge and Concurrence', *Commonwealth Parliamentary Debates* (House of Representatives), 26 June 2013, 7072.

58 Ball, D. *'Pine Gap': Testimony of Professor Des Ball to the Joint Standing Committee on Treaties*, 9 August 1999, 3–4.

59 Smith, 'Ministerial Statement', 7073.

60 'Parliamentary Statement by the Prime Minister on the Joint Facilities, 22 November 1988', https://pmtranscripts.pmc.gov.au/sites/default/files/original/00007438.pdf

61 P. Dibb, *Into the Wilderness of Mirrors: Australia and the Threat from the Soviet Union in the Cold War and Russia Today* (Melbourne: Melbourne University Press, 2018), 59.

62 United States Space Command, 'Background Paper on Australian Implementing Arrangement – Deputy Commander Controversy, April 19, 1990', https://nsarchive2.gwu.edu//NSAEBB/NSAEBB235/20.pdf

63 Dibb, *Into the Wilderness of Mirrors*, 61–62.

64 The Hawke government acknowledged this as part of their public defence of the Joint Facilities, beginning with: Department of Foreign Affairs, 'Uranium, the Joint Facilities, Disarmament and Peace' (Canberra: Australian Government Publishing Service, 1984).

65 This view unified all governments from the early 1970s onwards. For a policy "insider" analysis, see K. Beazley, 'Sovereignty and the US Alliance', in P. Dean, S. Frühling, and B. Taylor (eds), *Australia's American Alliance* (Melbourne: Melbourne University Press, 2016), 209–216. The latest Australian government statement on the facilities is C. Pyne, "Ministerial (Defence) Statement: Australia-United States Joint Facilities", *Commonwealth Parliamentary Debates* (House of Representatives), 20 February 2019, 1087–1088.

66 This is the iconic title of Desmond Ball's book *A Suitable Piece of Real Estate,* which was crucial in publicising the role of the joint facilities in Australia.

67 S. Frühling, 'The Fuzzy Limits of Self-Reliance: US Extended Deterrence and Australian Strategic Policy', *Australian Journal of International Affairs*, 67:1 (2013), 26.

68 Department of Defence, *Strategic Review 1993* (Canberra: Defence Centre Publishing, 1993), 7.

69 Quoted in A. O'Neil, *Asia, the US and Extended Nuclear Deterrence: Atomic Umbrellas in the Twenty-First Century* (London and New York: Routledge, 2013), 113.

70 Although successive statements have maintained the consistency of the sole purpose logic, they have varied in their intensity. In unusually blunt language, the 2009 Defence White Paper stated that 'the protection afforded by extended nuclear deterrence under the US alliance has over the years removed the need for Australia to consider more significant and expensive defence options', while the most recent Defence White Paper in 2016 understatedly observed that 'only the nuclear and conventional military capabilities of the United States can offer effective deterrence against the possibility of nuclear threats against

Australia'. See Department of Defence, *Defending Australia in the Asia-Pacific Century: Force 2030* (Canberra: Commonwealth of Australia, 2009), 50; and Department of Defence, *Defence White Paper 2016* (Canberra: Commonwealth of Australia, 2016), 121.

71 Under section 1255 of the Act, Congress used generic terms to endorse Australia's coverage under the nuclear umbrella in accordance with 'US treaty obligations and assurances'. See US Congress, *John S. McCain National Defense Authorization Act for Fiscal Year 2019*, www.congress.gov/bill/115th-congress/house-bill/5515/text

72 Department of Foreign Affairs and Trade, 'Australia and Nuclear Weapons', www.dfat.gov.au/international-relations/security/non-proliferation-disarmament-arms-control/nuclear-issues/Pages/australia-and-nuclear-weapons

73 Department of Defence, 'Draft Presentation to the Congressional Commission on the Strategic Posture of the United States', 12 February, 2009, 2.

74 Federation of American Scientists, 'DF-5', https://fas.org/nuke/guide/china/icbm/df-5.htm

75 Leah and Lyon, 'Three Visions of the Bomb', 461.

76 See M. Cohen and A. O'Neil, 'Doubts Down Under: American Extended Deterrence, Australia, and the 1999 East Timor Crisis', *International Relations of the Asia Pacific*, 15:1 (2015), 27–52.

77 See N. Bisley and B. Taylor, *Conflict in the East China Sea: Would ANZUS Apply?* (Sydney: Australia-China Relations Institute, UTS, 2014), 15–18.

78 Cabinet Decision DER no 634, NAA A13977, 30 May 1983, 170.

79 B. Hayden, *Hayden: An Autobiography* (Sydney: Harper Collins, 1996), 384.

80 K. Beazley, '"America First" and Australia's Strategic Future', in P. Dean, S. Frühling, and B. Taylor (eds), *After American Primacy: Imagining the Future of Australia's Defence* (Melbourne: Melbourne University Press, 2019), 129.

81 R. Lyon, 'Australia: Back to the Future?', in M. Alagappa (ed.), *The Long Shadow: Nuclear Weapons and Security in 21st Century Asia* (Stanford: Stanford University Press, 2008), 433.

82 For elaboration, see S. Frühling, 'Is ANZUS Really an Alliance? Aligning the US and Australia', *Survival*, 60:5 (2018), 199–218.

83 Conversation with Australian and US officials, Canberra, June 2019 and Washington, DC, September 2019.

84 Department of Defence, *Defending Australia in the Asia-Pacific Century*, 50.

85 For discussion, see S. Frühling, 'Never Say Never: Considerations About the Possibility of Australia Acquiring Nuclear Weapons', *Asian Security*, 6:2 (2010), 146–169.

86 This was the clear message conveyed to US authorities by the Fraser government. See Hubert Humphrey and John Glenn, *US Troop Withdrawal from the Republic of Korea: A Report to the US Senate Committee on Foreign Relations* (Washington, DC: US Government Printing Office, 1978), 17–18.

87 See M. Clarke, S. Frühling, and A. O'Neil, *Australia's Nuclear Policy: Reconciling Strategic, Economic, and Normative Interests* (Aldershot: Ashgate, 2015).

88 A. Tillett, 'North Korea Threatens Australia with "Disaster" Over Opposition to Nuke Program', *Australian Financial Review*, 15 October 2017, www.afr.com/news/north-korea-threatens-australia-with-disaster-over-opposition-to-nuke-program-20171015-gz14zj
89 See, e.g., R. Morgan, 'Australians View Terrorism and War as the Most Important Problems Facing the World After Terrorist Incidents and Rising Global Tensions', 14 July 2017, www.roymorgan.com/findings/7263-issues-facing-the-world-terrorism-verbatims-mid-2017–201707141606
90 For background, see S. Frühling, "A Nuclear-armed Australia? Contemplating the Unthinkable Option', *Australian Foreign Affairs*, 4 (2018), 71–91.
91 D. Chubb and I. McAllister, 'Public Attitudes Towards the Future Defence of Australia', in P. Dean, S. Frühling, and B. Taylor (eds), *After American Primacy: Imagining the Future Defence of Australia* (Melbourne: Melbourne University Press, 2019), 28–43.
92 Since 2005, the Lowy Institute annual poll has shown that a consistent majority of respondents believe the US alliance is either 'very important' or 'fairly important' for Australia. The lowest overall support rating was 63% in 2007 and the highest was 87% in 2012. See Lowy Institute for International Policy, 'Importance of the US Alliance', https://lowyinstitutepoll.lowyinstitute.org/australia-us-relations/
93 For the most cogent articulation of this link, see J. Camilleri, *ANZUS: Australia's Predicament in the Nuclear Age* (Melbourne: Macmillan, 1987).
94 On the dynamics underlying Australian anti-nuclear activism in the 1980s, see J. Strauss, 'What Did We Want? Debates within the Australian Nuclear Disarmament Movement in the 1980s', *Labour History*, 115 (2018), 145–165.
95 Department of State, 'Memorandum of Conversation: Secretary Schlesinger's Meeting with Deputy Prime Minister Barnard of Australia, January 9, 1974', in *Foreign Relations of the United States: 1969–1976*, Vol. E-12*: Documents on East and Southeast Asia, 1973–1976*, https://history.state.gov/historicaldocuments/frus1969–76ve12/d45
96 Beazley, 'Sovereignty and the US Alliance', 215.
97 See J Curran, *Fighting with America: Why Saying No to the US Wouldn't Rupture the Alliance* (Sydney: Penguin Random House, 2016).
98 J. Katz and K. Quealy, 'Which Country is America's Strongest Ally? For Republicans, it's Australia', *New York Times*, 3 February 2017, www.nytimes.com/interactive/2017/02/03/upshot/which-country-do-americans-like-most-for-republicans-its-australia.html
99 J. Thomas, Z. Cooper, and I. Rehman, *Gateway to the Indo-Pacific: Australian Defense Strategy and the Future of the Australia-US Alliance* (Washington, DC: CSBA, 2013).
100 N. O'Malley, 'US Bid for Multi-billion Dollar Nuclear Aircraft Carrier Strike Group in Perth', *Sydney Morning Herald*, 1 August 2012, www.smh.com.au/politics/federal/us-bid-for-multibillion-dollar-nuclear-aircraft-carrier-strike-group-in-perth-20120801–23emq.html

101 C. Mills Rodrigo, 'Prime Minister Says US Won't Deploy Missiles in Australia', *The Hill*, 5 August 2019, https://thehill.com/policy/defense/456150-prime-minister-says-us-wont-deploy-missiles-in-australia

102 Sir A. Tange, *Defence Policy-Making: A Close-Up View, 1950–1980*. Ed. P. Edwards (Canberra: ANU Press, 2008), 40.

103 Quoted in J. Hymans, *The Psychology of Nuclear Proliferation: Identity, Emotions, and Foreign Policy* (Cambridge: Cambridge University Press, 2006), 128.

104 Jones, 'The Radford Bombshell', 648–649.

105 Ball, *A Suitable Piece of Real Estate*, 56.

106 Quoted in Ball, *A Suitable Piece of Real Estate*, 57. The Fraser Cabinet 'noted that the US Government had not properly consulted the Australian Government ... and had shown a lack of regard for the relationship between the two countries by not doing so'. It decided that the Foreign Minister would discuss the issue with the US ambassador. Cabinet Decision No. 5367, 16 May 1978, NAA A13075, 5367.

107 Authors' discussions with US officials, Washington, DC, 19 September 2019.

108 Even many European policymakers come to different conclusions about the emphasis that the United States places on the ability to fight a limited nuclear conflict from US declaratory policy, and from observing US doctrinal concepts of escalation management. Interviews in Berlin, London, and Paris, September 2019.

109 Interviews with Australian policymakers, August 2019.

110 Interviews with Australian and US policymakers, August and September 2019.

111 See A. Townshend, D. Santoro, and B. Thomas-Noone, 'Revisiting Deterrence in an Era of Strategic Competition: Outcomes Report from the Inaugural US-Australia Indo-Pacific Deterrence Dialogue', US Studies Centre, University of Sydney, 8 February 2019, www.ussc.edu.au/analysis/revisiting-deterrence-in-an-era-of-strategic-competition

7

Understanding the drivers of nuclear weapons cooperation

Nuclear weapons have been central to US alliance management in the post-1945 world. Successive administrations in Washington have sought to use nuclear weapons as a means of bolstering the credibility of US global security commitments. Yet, rather than simply being passive recipients of US nuclear reassurances, US allies in Europe and Asia have actively bargained with Washington over the substance of the US nuclear weapons posture in relation to their territory and alliance. Although these negotiations occurred in the context of the political relationship and alliance policy overall, they have often been shaped by the institutional framework existing in the alliance, and led to changes that have had significant consequences for political relations and the functioning of the alliance. The prime example is the Nuclear Planning Group (NPG), which arose from the need to manage the strategic consequences of NATO's then-existing cooperation on nuclear weapons, and was a key element leading to a more inclusive and political alliance than it had been previously.

This book has shown that non-nuclear allies of the US exert an important degree of influence on nuclear issues, which has grown over time. When the US first began deploying its nuclear forces on the territory of allies in the 1950s, the nature of conversations about deterrence and reassurance were largely one way. The Eisenhower administration's drive to save costs associated with stationing significant conventional forces overseas dovetailed with a belief that nuclear weapons could simultaneously deter adversaries and reassure allies through a strategy of massive retaliation. But US allies had little input into this logic, and the United States deliberately sought to restrict allied involvement and information about operational plans from allies in NATO (with the partial exception of the UK and France) as well as in Asia. During the 1960s, the rise of flexible response made many US allies anxious about the credibility of nuclear reassurances, but it also occurred in a context where countries in Europe and Asia emerged from the post-war reconstruction phase stronger and more self-confident in economic, political and military terms. As NATO agreed on the new strategic concept and created the NPG, Japanese elites successfully pressed their US counterparts for structured interactions within the alliance over nuclear transit, even though Tokyo did not always insist on being consulted when nuclear weapons entered Japan's territorial waters or airspace. In the 1980s, Washington agreed to a co-equal role for Australia in managing the (until then) only nominally 'Joint Facilities'; in the 2000s, US nuclear weapons remained in Europe more despite than because of the views of senior US commanders about their military utility; and in the 2010s, the creation of structured extended deterrence dialogues in the cases of South Korea and Japan means that Australia now is the only major US ally without such a dedicated forum.

Explaining nuclear weapons cooperation

However, the ability of US allies to influence nuclear weapons cooperation has been far from uniform. Indeed, the case studies in this book have shown that there is frequent, and at times notable, variation in nuclear weapons cooperation between the US and its allies, which persists to this day. The analysis of nuclear weapons cooperation in this book avoided unit-level analysis of states' interests that simply assumes alliances are the dependent variable in relation to the independent variable of state behaviour. The book challenged traditional realist accounts by bringing institutional theory into the analysis of alliance behaviour. By establishing that there are two competing theoretical explanations of cooperation within alliances – realism and institutionalism – we outlined two distinctive hypotheses that were to be tested through detailed empirical analysis in the book's case studies:

Hypothesis 1 (H1): Nuclear weapons cooperation reflects the external balancing and power asymmetries between the US and its ally.

Hypothesis 2 (H2): Nuclear weapons cooperation reflects the structured interaction and organised practices inherent in individual alliances.

Underlying H1 is the assumption that nuclear weapons cooperation is exclusively threat based and that the US as the more powerful alliance partner will dominate the way in which nuclear weapons cooperation is undertaken as well as its substantive outcomes. By contrast, H2 assumes that the internal dynamics of alliances and the formal and informal institutions within them have an independent influence on nuclear weapons cooperation and outcomes.

In each of the cases examined in the book, we used six distinctive frames to capture the aims of allies and the sources of influence underlying nuclear weapons cooperation. What did each frame reveal about the applicability or otherwise of the two hypotheses in explaining the role of nuclear weapons in US alliances? Also, what did they reveal about the variation across alliances regarding nuclear weapons cooperation?

Threat assessment

Realism considers external threat perception as the main factor driving alliance cooperation, whereas institutionalism regards allies as a form of epistemic community, which means perceptions are mediated by alliance interaction. The case studies make it clear that achieving consensus among allies about the precise nature of threats and how best to counter them can be a major challenge. Throughout the Cold War, NATO occasionally struggled to achieve unity regarding the nature and scope of the Soviet threat, and since the end of the Cold War perceptions of the threat from Russia have differed between newer NATO member states and more established members of the alliance. The key Asian alliances of the US have also been characterised by periodic gaps in threat assessment. For a range of historical reasons and because of geographical proximity, Japan has tended to be more clear-cut than the US about the perceived threat from China, and it was only under the Trump administration that Washington and Tokyo's respective threat assessments about China converged. Although the US–ROK alliance was purpose built to counter the North Korean threat, Seoul and Washington have often diverged at the political level over the extent to which Pyongyang threatens their respective security interests. At different times, both alliance partners have exhibited fears of entrapment as a result of the other being more inclined towards military action in response to diverging perceptions of imminent threat. For their part, South Korean elites have feared abandonment periodically since the formal creation of the alliance in 1953. South Korea's experience as a US ally aligns most closely with realist theory insofar as it has confronted the alliance security dilemma more acutely than any other case examined in this book.

The assessment of threats by the US and its allies has been pivotal in shaping choices about nuclear weapons cooperation. Not surprisingly, the importance of nuclear weapons has been more intense and focused in situations where the US and its allies have converged in their assessment of threats and where such threats are seen as posing an immediate risk, as was the case in NATO, South Korea, and to a lesser extent Japan during the Cold War. By contrast, Australia's regionally focused threat perception and the global perspective of the US had almost no intersection during the 1950s and 1960s, and hence Australia was remarkably unsuccessful during these decades in achieving its objectives in either ANZUS or SEATO. Nuclear weapons have had little role in the relatively benign security situation confronting Australia from the 1970s to the present day.

However, the importance of nuclear weapons did not automatically lead to cooperation between the US and its allies. With the notable exception of NATO, no alliance has confronted more direct and credible military threats than the US–ROK alliance, yet for most of its existence nuclear weapons cooperation between Seoul and the US has been largely non-existent. Notwithstanding the highly integrated operational relationship between the two countries' armed forces, when the South Koreans requested greater formal involvement in US nuclear planning in the 1970s, they were rebuffed, and at the political level, there was no evident discussion about the US nuclear weapons stationed on South Korean territory and the role they would play in any war against North Korea.

Instead, periods of deepening cooperation on nuclear weapons in US alliances have often coincided with periods where the US and its allies prioritised the same threats, but diverged in their assessments and came to different conclusions about the implications for the alliance. The US–German and NATO analyses of the ability to defend Western Europe with conventional means during the 1960s paved the way for the adoption of 'flexible response' in NATO, but also brought with it a greater commonality in the understanding of the operational and strategic consequences of nuclear weapons use between the allies. Indeed, the concept of flexible response and the creation and work of the NPG that followed can be seen as an exercise in managing enduring, though ultimately insoluble, differences between the allies through institutionalised cooperation. US–Japanese negotiations on nuclear weapons in the context of the return of Okinawa, which occurred against the background of strategic uncertainty about the future shape of Asia in the post-Vietnam era, is another example.

This is not a uniform pattern, however. Significant differences about the assessment of the North Korean threat under the Nixon and Carter administrations were of significant concern to South Korea, which had few avenues of influence with Washington on the matter at that time; instead, Seoul resorted to starting a covert nuclear weapons programme. Only after the removal of US nuclear weapons from South Korea in 1991, the development of a more institutionalised US–ROK alliance between two now democratic states, and the emergence of a serious nuclear and missile threat from North Korea did Washington and Seoul agree on structured interaction covering the nuclear dimension of their alliance. Pyongyang's proven short- and medium-range missile strike capabilities have heightened Japanese and South Korean anxieties about North Korea since the country's first nuclear test in 2006, and led to the creation of formal deterrence dialogues with the US from 2010. By contrast, US anxiety spiked in 2017 when North Korea demonstrated through testing that it had acquired an ICBM capability that could reach the US mainland, so that threat assessments in Washington, Seoul, and Tokyo about North Korea tended to converge under the Trump administration. This was despite concern among South Korean and Japanese elites that Washington might aspire to cut a deal with Pyongyang that eliminates North Korea's ICBM capabilities but does nothing to inhibit its short- and medium-range missile force.[1]

Overall, the extent to which differences in threat perception between the US and its allies account for variation in nuclear weapons cooperation between alliances has thus been nuanced. Realist focus on the importance of external threats is a strong explanation for the existence of alliances in the first place, and of US commitment to them. But within that broad scope, attempts to come to joint understandings between the allies have facilitated, and been facilitated by, the development of closer cooperation on nuclear weapons in most alliances.

Policy objectives regarding nuclear weapons cooperation

From a realist perspective, the policy objectives of allies regarding nuclear weapons cooperation arise from material costs and relative benefits of such cooperation, while an institutionalist approach emphasises their endogenous nature and reflection of aims and values of the alliance overall. During the Cold War, two factors emerge as consistently important US objectives in shaping nuclear weapons cooperation in its alliances. First, the preservation of US control over US warheads was deemed critical so that no form of cooperation crossed the line that allies could override a US presidential decision about the use of nuclear weapons. Even if the physical implementation of that control was at times somewhat tenuous in the case of NATO nuclear sharing during the 1950s, it was (and remains) a fundamental precept of US policy in line with realist assessments of the importance of nuclear use decisions. Second, from the perspective of US military planning and operations, the provision of 'places and bases' by allies to enable the US to project global strategic power has been a central objective. Of all the allies examined in this book, Germany was the only one during the Cold War that did not play a role in physical preparations for US nuclear operations that would have extended geographically and in objectives beyond the immediate defence of the ally itself: from SAC bases in Norway and Okinawa, to aircraft at Kunsan on alert to strike China and the submarine communications and satellite stations in Australia, almost all US allies had a direct role in US nuclear operations beyond their immediate neighbourhood. While political support from allies is highly regarded in Washington (particularly when it comes to supporting the US in prosecuting unpopular causes), and although force contributions and higher defence spending are seen as key measures of allied commitment, it is the material value provided by bases, port access, and transiting arrangements for US forces that have been most valued by American policymakers, and which they sought to preserve in whatever manner nuclear weapons cooperation evolved within each alliance. This is a quintessentially realist calculation.

Within those bounds, however, the US has in many ways been remarkably accommodating of the various policy objectives regarding nuclear weapons cooperation that allies have advanced within the alliances. Perhaps somewhat surprisingly, these policy objectives did not always reflect the strategic importance of nuclear weapons. In the US–ROK alliance, South Korea's junior status in relation to nuclear weapons has not stood out much from its historically subordinate role in the alliance as a whole, and hence managing nuclear weapons never emerged as an area of particular focus for Seoul's interactions with the US. In Japan's case, the US and Japan both benefited from a mantle of secrecy over the presence and transit of US nuclear weapons. Both allies also placed particular importance on US pronouncements of extended nuclear deterrence guarantees (complemented, after 1991, with occasional strategic bomber visits) that have little or no financial or material implications for the US.

In Europe, Norway's carve-out from nuclear sharing and Germany's desire for influence on the specific decisions and planning on nuclear use were more challenging objectives – not just because the potential cost to the US of acceding to these allies' demands may have been much higher, but also because these allies' objectives were manifold, and defined at a more granular level than those in US alliances in Asia. Managing these often unresolvable challenges was a major driver behind the institutionalisation of the NATO alliance. Finding a modus vivendi with Norway's 'screening' restrictions became easier under flexible response, but rested largely on the development of implicit and explicit detailed understandings in NATO's integrated military commands about what allied presence was acceptable to Oslo. However, accommodating West Germany's objectives was even harder, both because the material consequences of giving in to its demands on, for instance, early first use of nuclear weapons, but also because German objectives themselves were inherently in conflict with each other, particularly in relation to the limitation of damage from NATO reliance on nuclear weapons.

Institutionalisation through the NPG became an important means for allies to manage such ultimately insoluble conflicts in a way that did not threaten the political viability of the alliance as a whole. In doing so, nuclear weapons cooperation assumed a political importance in its own right: the concept of nuclear burden sharing, which has no equivalent in any other alliance, over time became divorced from the very material connotations of the Cold War, and has today become a key political element of the identity of NATO as a nuclear alliance.

Nuclear strategy

Through a realist prism, nuclear strategy is the translation of capability into power in the form of outcomes; allies are therefore expected to focus on the consequences for their own security of different strategies. In contrast, an institutionalist perspective holds that this translation is an interpretive, ideational framework rather than mechanistic relationship, and hence that a 'strategy' gives political meaning to allied defence preparations.

At a global level, the changes in US nuclear strategy and nuclear policy more broadly – from the adoption of massive retaliation and introduction of tactical nuclear weapons to economise on the cost of defending allies in the 1950s, to the change to flexible response aimed at minimising the risk of retaliation against North America, to the desire to reduce the salience of nuclear weapons in the post-Cold War era – have reflected the calculated cost and benefit to the US of the use of nuclear weapons for deterrence and in war. Where differences with allied preferences proved most acute was when the *global* view of the US came into conflict with the *local* consequences for the ally. For reasons of their geographic situation, South Korea and Japan were largely comfortable with US nuclear strategy during the Cold War. Flexible response was more in tune with Norway's desire to take into account the scenario of limited conflict on NATO's flanks than the earlier concept of massive retaliation. In its desire to emphasise the role of intercontinental nuclear warfare for deterrence, West Germany was uncomfortable both with the nuclearisation of NATO's defence of Western Europe in the 1950s, and the move to delay nuclear escalation under flexible response.

Within those situations, however, there is also strong evidence that allies possess and continue to project very different interpretations of the use of nuclear weapons in their alliances, and have sought to frame cooperation in a way that allowed for these differences to continue. The way NATO adopted flexible response in its strategic concept of 1967 was so malleable that it allowed distinctive interpretations between the allies to continue, which the allies sought to reduce, but never fully resolved through negotiations on nuclear force structure and political guidelines until the end of the Cold War. Norway's approach of using the prospect that it might allow allied nuclear weapons onto its territory to stabilise the 'Nordic balance' was enabled by allied acceptance of its special status, even if allies did not make it their own. Likewise, Australia's view of the utility of nuclear weapons was and remains more geostrategic than operationally focused. It deliberately excludes conventional threats from the nuclear umbrella, which is at odds with US nuclear policy that does not endorse a sole-purpose doctrine. Australia's peculiar approach to confining references to extended nuclear deterrence to its own policy documents means that it can voice its support for the US nuclear umbrella in general, without being forced to reconcile its views in detail with those of the US.

Domestic factors

For realists, domestic factors are extraneous to alliance dynamics, while institutionalists see alliances as reinforcing elite cooperation even in the face of public opposition. With the exception of South Korea until the late 1980s, all the cases examined in this book have been democracies for the duration of their respective alliances with the US. Public opinion has therefore been a prominent factor in shaping the approach of policymakers to nuclear weapons cooperation. This has not just been confined to elites scanning public opinion polls to gauge the sentiment of their constituents; decision makers have also been acutely aware of the need to anticipate reactions from the public regarding nuclear-related decisions. The Japanese government's decision to insist in negotiations with the US that Okinawa be free of nuclear weapons following reversion in 1971 is a good example of where a US ally sought to pre-empt a public reaction despite the sympathy of elites themselves towards accommodating US requests. Yet, on nuclear issues within the alliance, Japanese elites operated largely independently from public opinion while remaining acutely conscious of the need to manoeuvre in an atmosphere of extreme secrecy because of the resilient anti-nuclear sentiment among the Japanese population. The Australian government's request to Washington that the country not be involved in directly supporting research and development on the Reagan administration's SDI programme confirmed a view that such cooperation would trigger an unfavourable reaction among the Australian public.

A common unifying theme among US allies has been that, although governments are mindful of public opinion on nuclear issues, they have nevertheless been willing to make decisions that are not always endorsed by their constituents. In this sense, policymakers have aligned their behaviour with both realism and institutionalism. Domestic factors have often been extraneous to alliance dynamics while at the same time alliances have reinforced elite cooperation, including in cases where public opinion has been opposed to specific aspects of nuclear weapons cooperation.

Although none of the cases examined in this book have rivalled the depth of anti-nuclear domestic sentiment in Japan, governments in each case had to contend with significant anti-nuclear sentiment in their respective jurisdictions. The most salient example of governments taking a decision at odds with public sentiment was NATO's decisions regarding LRTNF modernisation from 1979 to 1983. Despite Norwegian public opinion being opposed, the government in Oslo maintained solidarity with other NATO members in backing the deployment. For its part, the West German government confronted similar domestic pressures and focused on ensuring that the arms control offer to Moscow was part of the final NATO decision, even if Chancellor Helmut Schmidt himself did not want to embrace the so-called 'zero option'.

More generally, domestic factors were important across all cases in shaping the approach of US allies to nuclear weapons cooperation. One common theme is that US allies demanded greater consultation and were more active in their bargaining behaviour with Washington when there was greater anti-nuclear pressure at home. This not only included anti-nuclear sentiment in public opinion, but also the philosophical complexion of political parties in government. In general, centre-left governments were more likely than centre-right governments to challenge the US in intra-alliance bargaining on nuclear issues. This was especially apparent in the Norwegian, German, and Australian cases, where although centre-left governments remained committed to the respective alliances, they were more ambivalent about the nuclear dimension that periodically came to the fore on publicly visible issues such as the forward basing of nuclear weapons, transiting of nuclear weapons, or cooperation on SDI.[2]

On the subject of consultation, an important distinction should be made between the perceived need among US allies to ensure that reservations about nuclear commitment were factored into nuclear weapons cooperation, and the need for reassurance and deterrence. Regarding the latter, it is clear that governments of all political shades were willing to demand greater extended nuclear deterrence assurances from the US in circumstances where that ally's security was perceived to be threatened. For example, in the German case there was no perceptible difference between the intensity of reassurance demands from the centre-left government of Helmut Schmidt and the centre-right government of Helmut Kohl. If anything, centre-left governments seemed to believe that if they were taking greater political risks than their centre-right counterparts in supporting nuclear weapons cooperation with the US, there should be a proportionate pay-off in the area of US security assurances. In the case of South Korea, which historically experienced little public pressure on nuclear weapons cooperation, parties on the left and right were equally focused on eliciting extended deterrence reassurances from the US as North Korea's nuclear weapons capability accelerated following its initial nuclear test in 2006.

Importance of the ally for the US

The central consideration in this frame is whether US allies have successfully leveraged their importance to the US to exert influence over nuclear weapons cooperation. For realists, the more valuable an ally is to the US, the more likely it is that abandonment/entrapment pressures will be moderated. For institutionalists, the importance of the ally to the US will be reflected by the ally's capacity to shape collective decisions on nuclear weapons cooperation. Across the cases in the book, the outcomes were mixed. There is evidence to conclude that the US has been willing to compromise on nuclear issues with allies it sees as important to overall US strategy. A particular feature was a US willingness to provide concessions on nuclear weapons cooperation to valued allies where the government in power was confronting domestic pressure. This was pertinent in the case of pro-US centre-left governments and leaders who were concerned with containing the influence of strong anti-nuclear and/or anti-US sentiment within their own parties. With the notable exception of the neutron bomb issue, Washington's approach to nuclear cooperation with West Germany under Helmut Schmidt was very much driven by this logic.

Is deeper nuclear cooperation more likely with countries that are seen as more important to US security than others? And is the US more likely to give important allies what they want? By definition, countries that enjoy any US nuclear guarantees are valuable American allies. There are many states that have security partnerships with the US that do not incorporate arrangements supporting nuclear reassurance or deterrence, so in that sense all of the countries in this book are important to the US. Seen in this light, instances in which the US did not accommodate allied demands are the most significant, and two periods stand out in particular.

First, the absence of US nuclear weapons cooperation with South Korea during the Cold War existed in spite of the very close military relationship between the two countries, which included a significant US conventional force presence on the Korean Peninsula and the stationing of US nuclear weapons on South Korean territory between 1958 and 1991. Despite demands from Seoul for nuclear weapons cooperation, the US refused to include South Korea in the coordination and planning of nuclear operations on the Korean Peninsula; but until the creation of CFC in 1978, this reflected a situation that also pertained to even South Korea's conventional forces. More so than any other ally, the value of (non-democratic) South Korea for the US was largely accidental and contingent on the significance of the inter-Korean conflict for global superpower rivalry. The second period was when Australia proved remarkably unsuccessful during the 1950s and 1960s in its two alliances with the US (via SEATO and ANZUS) in obtaining either the security guarantees that it desired, or the practical cooperation on US regional planning for which it had hoped. During this period, Australia's geography was of little benefit to the US, nor had Australia much to offer of relevance in economic or military terms.

As West Germany's prominence as a political, economic and military actor in Europe grew in the 1960s, the US became more willing to accommodate German positions with respect to nuclear posture, coordination, and strategy. The contrast between West Germany's ability to shape the structure and posture of NATO forces in the 1950s compared to the 1980s is stark, and reflects the steady growth of German power. Similarly, the US willingness to renegotiate its alliance treaty with Japan, and its acceptance of increased political dialogue reflects the growing economic (and, to an extent, military) importance of Japan, even if it was not focused on nuclear weapons. In the case of Norway, the country's geographical significance for US strategy in northern Europe meant that the US was prepared to tolerate Oslo's 'screening' approach to nuclear cooperation, despite Washington's preference for unfettered cooperation in NATO.

As we have seen, the Australian government's requests for greater formal authority over the operation of the joint facilities, while not welcomed, were nevertheless accommodated by Washington. This should not only be seen in the context of the importance of the joint facilities to the US, but also concern within the Reagan administration about the potential spread of the New Zealand 'disease' among allies (like Australia) with centre-left governments in power that might feel tempted to unwind their alliance nuclear commitments in response to public pressure. As the political rather than military importance of US alliances increased over time, so too did the importance of political consensus on nuclear weapons. In that sense, Washington's agreement as early as the 1960s to make changes to the size of US nuclear posture in Europe subject to the NATO consensus rule deliberately reduced the importance of economic or military power of individual NATO allies in determining their influence over nuclear weapons cooperation. Over time, the US expanded the role of allies in the 'inner circle' from the UK and France in the Standing Group, to Italy and Germany as the only non-nuclear permanent members of the NPG after its formation in 1967, to opening membership to all allies who nominally, if not always in practice, have the same weight in shaping alliance decisions on nuclear weapons. And despite Norway hosting key US intelligence facilities and the country's geographical importance to US strategy in northern Europe, there is limited evidence that governments in Oslo sought to leverage this to achieve deeper nuclear weapons cooperation with the US. Norway instead focused on curating the image of a 'loyal ally', especially compared with Denmark, in terms that reflected its behaviour in the alliance rather than specific material contributions.

Access to information

Realism accords little relevance to information about national interest and power, regarding these as self-evident, though access to information can be seen as a form of power that countries use to their benefit. Institutionalism highlights that formal and informal institutions facilitate information sharing and also provide an incentive to release information in order to generate trust in future behaviour. In general, exchange of information is essential for effective alliance management and is a hallmark of a robust alliance. This involves not only the transfer of information about adversary capabilities and intentions, but also sharing information about the capabilities and intentions of the allies themselves. As a general rule, this dimension of US alliances has improved over time. In its postwar alliances, the US sought to heavily restrict access to the role of nuclear weapons in its posture and operational plans, often to allies directly affected. In those alliances that saw greater operational cooperation, the US ability to restrict the flow of information eroded over time. Compared to the early period of the Cold War, US allies today not only feel entitled to a greater share of information, they also have the institutional means in alliance arrangements to bargain for greater access to information.

The path towards increasing NATO nuclear cooperation from the 1960s onwards was laid by the US decision to disseminate more detailed information about US nuclear strategy. Washington was responding to pressure from allies for enhanced information sharing, but it was equally conscious of the need to create trust through increased transparency in order to bind NATO members to the strategy of flexible response. The development of the NPG may have been a compromise by Washington following the demise of the MLF, but it was also a response to demands from US allies for greater information sharing in NATO. As NATO institutions evolved, so too did the 'democratisation' of information flows. Although access to NATO's atomic strike plan was initially confined to the Standing Group, from the late 1970s the NPG ensured that even the smallest NATO members would have access to the operational rationale of nuclear weapons use (though not always the targeting the information itself). The effect was to enable greater involvement by a broader cross-section of NATO members in the nuts and bolts of nuclear planning with the US.

Yet, even within NATO, this has been more important for some US allies than for others. As we have seen, during the Cold War, West Germany remained much more focused than Norway on the details of NATO nuclear planning. Bonn's focus on accessing nuclear targeting information largely remained a corollary of its concerns about NATO strategy during the 1950s and 1960s. Reflecting realist logic, the US sought to restrict both West Germany's and Norway's access to nuclear weapons information in NATO during the 1950s. However, this was gradually undermined by operational cooperation in NATO's military commands, and the Kennedy administration's decision to expand information sharing within NATO regarding US nuclear strategy and plans. As NATO evolved and expanded after the Cold War, new members from eastern Europe have been keen to gain access to information in the nuclear domain even as traditional members have at times been ambivalent about the continued role of nuclear weapons in NATO strategy.

In Asia, the evolution of access to information has been quite different to that of Europe. Significantly, even where strong military alliances exist in which conventional planning is a hallmark of alliance cooperation, this has been no guarantee of information exchange in relation to nuclear weapons cooperation. In the US–ROK alliance, the depth and intimacy of information flows about war planning and operational readiness rivalled NATO during the Cold War, but this did not translate into access to information for South Korea about the strategy and planning for US nuclear weapons stationed on the Korean Peninsula. Despite the transition of the US–ROK alliance to more balanced institutional arrangements in 1978 with the establishment of CFC, nuclear weapons cooperation between the two countries remained very much a US-controlled enterprise up until the advent of bilateral extended deterrence dialogues in 2010.

In explaining the variation in nuclear cooperation among the cases, it is important to note that not all US allies have sought full access to information on operational issues. In the case of Australia, apart from a brief period in the 1950s, governments have been reluctant to engage directly with their US counterparts on the nuclear dimension of extended deterrence. The absence of purpose-built institutions tasked with managing extended deterrence means that the information channels between Canberra and Washington on nuclear policy overall are limited to an extent not evident in the other cases in this book. Apprehensive about seeking a formal commitment that could result in something less than they hope for, Australian policymakers have preferred not to request assurances under the alliance in general and, unlike their Japanese and South Korean counterparts, have avoided structured interactions on extended deterrence in part due to entrapment concerns.

Key findings and implications for the book's hypotheses

An important theme of this book has been that alliances are multidimensional ecosystems of exchange. This is at odds with the traditional literature that portrays them as transactional instruments of external balancing where major alliance partners dominate. Central to our interpretation is the argument that institutionalism yields insights that realism does not in explaining nuclear weapons cooperation between the US and its allies. In this book, we have shown that, as institutions, alliances regularly influence the behaviour of states regarding nuclear weapons cooperation; that material cooperation on US nuclear weapons is used as leverage in intra-alliance debates by the US and its allies; that reassurance from material cooperation and dialogue on nuclear strategy owes more to a perception of US commitment to allies in general, as distinct from specific nuclear guarantees; and that the role of nuclear weapons in addressing strategic and political challenges within US alliances is far wider than can be captured by the traditional realist focus on deterrence and reassurance against external actors. In this sense, the ascendancy of realist accounts in the literature has obscured the importance of institutional interpretations of alliance behaviour in the domain of nuclear policy. Drawing together the empirical case study findings and the book's theoretical framework, our analysis yields four major conclusions of relevance to the theoretical understanding of nuclear weapons cooperation in US alliances.

The first is that the US has frequently and deliberately used its nuclear weapons to shore up confidence about US strategic commitment to allies' security in general, and to promote consensus in alliance relationships. In other words, the US has leveraged nuclear assurances as a proxy for strengthening overall security guarantees in individual alliances. This has a supply-and-demand dimension. As Japanese and South Korean anxieties grew over North Korea's nuclear weapons testing programme after 2006, the Bush and Obama administrations were responsive to requests from Tokyo and Seoul for the public reaffirmation of US extended nuclear deterrence commitments, as well as demonstrations of commitment through the rotation of US nuclear-capable assets into Northeast Asia.

The Trump administration continued this focus on reassurance through maintaining the US extended deterrence dialogues with Tokyo and Seoul, regularly reaffirming the nuclear umbrella, and eschewing nuclear no-first-use while endorsing lower-yield warhead capabilities in the 2018 NPR. While it replaced the permanent presence basing of nuclear-capable aircraft in Guam in 2020 with a more flexible US deterrent posture, this reflected concerns about operational vulnerabilities[3] and hence can be seen as an attempt to strengthen, rather than roll back, the practical demonstrations of US nuclear commitment to the region.

Washington's political use of US nuclear weapons to attain broader alliance objectives is an under-appreciated factor in the literature on alliances. NATO's watershed dual-track decision in 1979 had a military rationale, but its primary intent was to reinforce US strategic commitment to the alliance during a period where anxiety was growing among European allies over decoupling. More recently, in Asia, US agreement to extended deterrence consultation mechanisms with Japan and South Korea was intended to reassure these allies of Washington's commitment to their security in the context of China's military modernisation and North Korea's expanding nuclear weapons capability.

The second finding of the book is that the enhancement of institutional depth in nuclear weapons cooperation has promoted reassurance among the non-nuclear allies of the US and enabled closer political and operational integration of benefits to allies. Information sharing, greater transparency in decision making, and enhanced opportunities for consultation have transformed alliances since they were initially created, and this has also been evident in the area of nuclear weapons cooperation. At the same time, in accordance with institutional theory, this has imposed real constraints on the US ability to disregard allied interests. Both realists and institutionalists predict that alliances mitigate insecurity on the part of members, but realists attribute this to junior partners being reassured by major power security guarantees in formal agreements, and they discount the role of institutions as independent variables. Institutionalists point out that alliances facilitate the sharing of information, foster transparency among member states, and render private commitments more credible through public demonstrations of alliance solidarity. However, it is the political and military interdependencies created by these alliances that ultimately reassure allies about US commitments.

The third finding is that all US allies examined in this book have at times reduced, and in some cases declined, material cooperation that would have visibly linked US nuclear weapons to their own security. This is at odds with realist predictions that junior allies will invariably seek the maximum security commitments from their great power allies. Norway's relationship with Washington was strained during the 1950s because it was a frontline NATO member that sought less, rather than more, US military presence on its territory. It is difficult to find a more loyal US ally than Australia – it has supported the US in every conflict since the First World War – yet Australian decision makers have avoided requesting specific US nuclear commitments as part of the bilateral alliance, or under ANZUS prior to the mid-1980s. This finding also cuts against realist predictions that domestic considerations are extraneous to alliance management, and that junior allies' only interest in alliances is balancing against external threats. In reality, foreign policy elites in democracies cannot fully quarantine decisions from domestic public opinion. For historical reasons, this has been particularly evident in Japan, where governments have successfully gained concessions from Washington over the management of US nuclear weapons within the alliance despite elites in Tokyo attempting to maintain secrecy in relation to allied nuclear deliberations. It also underscores the importance of allied debates about nuclear strategy as a crucial arena in which they negotiate the relative costs and benefits of the alliance. Norway's 'screening' approach to nuclear weapons cooperation with the US reflected sensitivity that pro-alliance public opinion masked an underlying anti-nuclear sentiment among the Norwegian population, but it also mirrored a view on the strategic role of NATO's nuclear forces that placed emphasis on the 'Nordic balance' over operational considerations dominating NATO strategy.

The fourth finding is that, contrary to realist predictions, US allies can exercise a significant degree of influence in cooperation regarding US nuclear weapons. Nuclear weapons are the crown jewels in the US military arsenal, so if there is one area of cooperation with junior allies in which the latter should have little room for manoeuvre according to realist theory, it is in the nuclear domain. Yet, as the cases in this book have illustrated, US allies have not only acted as agents of influence, but they have also often obtained what they were seeking in nuclear-related interactions with Washington. Although it could be argued that a reason for this is the threat that junior allies might defect from an alliance if they were unable to secure the desired reassurances from Washington – France's decision in 1966 to exit NATO's military command is the most prominent example of this in practice – such defections are in fact extremely rare. Over time, alliance defections have become increasingly remote as cooperation in the nuclear realm has deepened and as US allies have reaffirmed their non-proliferation commitments. In the face of popular predictions after the Cold War that NATO would fragment and disintegrate, the alliance has been strengthened and nuclear weapons cooperation has returned as a major preoccupation of NATO deliberations. Even as far back as the conclusion of the NPT, however, US allies achieved success in intra-alliance bargaining on nuclear issues when domestic and strategic challenges loomed large, and when Washington saw a need to maintain alliance cohesion through concessions on nuclear weapons cooperation. In the NATO context, where close integration of conventional and nuclear forces has created mutual dependencies, the political need for consensus has been stronger than in Asian alliances. But even in Asia, greater US willingness to consult and systematically share information on nuclear posture issues with Japan and South Korea has enabled cooperation at the political as well as the operational levels, in the process helping Washington and its allies manage shifting power balances in the region.

Regarding the importance of realism and institutionalism, it is tempting to conclude that 'a bit of both' explains nuclear weapons cooperation between the US and its allies. However, in the light of the book's key findings it is clear that institutional factors and the effect of institutions on national objectives have been more influential than external balancing and the power asymmetries between the US and its allies. Although this is more prominent in the case of NATO, the role and influence of institutions have become more important to alliance management in Asia, even in the case of the US–Australia alliance that remains the least institutionalised of all US alliances. External balancing has undoubtedly loomed large in nuclear weapons cooperation. The assessment of threats, which can be seen as the cognitive engine room of alliances, has been central to the evolution of nuclear weapons cooperation since 1945. Decisions about the deployment of nuclear systems on the territory of US allies, US security guarantees being infused with nuclear reassurances, proposals for nuclear sharing, and the posturing of US strategic forces for extended deterrence are all driven by the need to balance against external threats. Inevitably, as the most powerful ally in material terms, the US has a proportionally greater say than junior allies in determining outcomes in an alliance setting. The US owns the nuclear weapons and is therefore the dominant party in shaping both the hardware and software dimensions of nuclear cooperation. In this respect, it is important not to exaggerate the ability of junior allies to achieve what they are seeking from what are, after all, asymmetric alliances with the US.

While the realist hypothesis appears to provide a persuasive explanation of nuclear weapons cooperation, it does not provide a complete picture of why nuclear weapons cooperation has evolved the way it has. As the case studies have shown, junior allies can and often do exert significant influence on substantive nuclear issues in relation to deployments, doctrine, and strategy. In particular, US allies have been effective in gaining greater access to information regarding nuclear weapons and in bargaining with the US on issues as diverse as shared decision making, explicit public extended deterrence commitments, and demarcating junior allies' involvement in the nuclear dimension of the alliance. Institutions have been central to this, and have become more important over time. As we have seen, the expansion of institutional mechanisms within alliances has not only empowered junior allies through greater modes of transparency and enhanced access to information, but these same mechanisms have also provided the US with the capacity to structure consultations more effectively and build greater trust in alliances in accordance with its policy aims. However, institutionalism cannot fully supplant realism as a framework for explaining nuclear cooperation. While institutionalism provides an indispensable theoretical supplement for explaining alliance behaviour and substantive policy outcomes, the inherent threat-based dynamic of alliances and the concentration of military force to balance against external threats means that realism remains central to explaining how and why alliances exist in the first place. This, in turn, provides the context for the institutionalist factors discussed in this book.

Moreover, the influence that junior allies exert within alliances is not always because of formal institutions as such. As the cases in this book showed, in a number instances influence was attributable to informal bargaining outside alliance modalities in bilateral and multilateral settings. Indeed, in some cases, many of the important agreements with the US that promote a greater role for junior allies owed more to the influence of key individuals in shaping outcomes than to bureaucrats working through institutions behind closed doors to produce outcomes. Charismatic leaders of countries that are small or medium-sized often achieve preferred outcomes by dint of their personal influence, but in the area of nuclear weapons cooperation, those with expertise in the field appear to have been especially influential in their interactions with US counterparts. The influence of West Germany, Australia, Norway, and Japan in nuclear weapons cooperation with the US cannot be understood fully without appreciating the pivotal roles of Helmut Schmidt, Kim Beazley, Johan Jørgen Holst, and Yasuhiro Nakasone, all of whom were respected by their US interlocutors as leading defence experts in their own right.

Finally, some of the elements that were important in explaining nuclear weapons cooperation between the US and its allies were not captured by either hypothesis. Most salient in this respect were domestic factors. With the exception of South Korea, the behaviour of the US and its allies stemmed from how they responded to public opinion specifically within the polity of the junior ally. US allies have been especially conscious of the need to balance frequent anti-nuclear sentiment among their general publics with their alliance obligations and in some cases the preference of elites for more intimate nuclear weapons cooperation with Washington. As noted earlier, managing anti-nuclear and occasionally anti-US sentiment within centre-left governing parties has been a particular challenge. Neither realism nor institutionalism take domestic factors properly into account in their explanation of nuclear weapons cooperation, but a major theme of this book has been that domestic factors remain a key driver of nuclear weapons cooperation between the US and its allies.

Policy implications

The relationship between nuclear weapons and US alliances is a major feature of international security. What are the implications of this book's findings for the understanding (and making) of policy in practice? Scholars occasionally overlook just how complicated managing alliances can be for policymakers. In addition to the vagaries of personalities and domestic political pressures, practitioners must also juggle anxiety over levels of credibility, resolve, burden sharing, and depth of mutual commitment. When nuclear weapons are factored into alliance management, the picture for policymakers becomes even more complicated. From the US perspective, embedding the most powerful weapon in its arsenal into security assurances for allies raises serious challenges. To what extent should allies be involved in the planning process? Should US posture and force structure be subject to negotiation? If the answer is no in certain cases, then how much is enough to reassure nervous allies? For US allies, the challenges are just as daunting. How can US credibility and resolve regarding the nuclear umbrella be measured? How much weight would the US accord to the interests of allies if deterrence failed? And how much scope for independent action should allies sacrifice to achieve closer operational integration with the US? Three major findings of relevance for policy discussions on nuclear weapons cooperation emerge from the analysis of this book.

The first relates to the reasons why nuclear weapons cooperation has become ingrained in NATO, and hence how transferable NATO experiences and policies might be. NATO clearly stands out in terms of nuclear weapons cooperation. That NATO is a multilateral alliance is not a sufficient explanation for this, as both ANZUS and SEATO also had three or more member states during the Cold War. A traditional explanation of NATO's nuclear evolution is that the US sought to address questions about abandonment and relative influence through nuclear 'hardware' (sharing of warheads and the MLF proposal) in the 1950s and 1960s, before finding more success through nuclear 'software' cooperation on policy and planning in the NPG from the 1970s.[4] However, what characterised, and in many ways made necessary, the close cooperation on nuclear weapons in NATO during the 1970s and 1980s was not just policy dialogue (as now occurs in America's Asian alliances) or negotiation of political guidelines alone, but the fact that the nuclear 'hardware' sharing of the 1950s created mutual dependencies that did not exist before, insofar as the US lost, to a considerable extent, the ability to vary its own national nuclear policy and posture without damaging directly the defence capability of its allies that it sought to strengthen at the same time. The dilemma that NATO nuclear 'software' cooperation has had to address, and which meant that it went far beyond the consultation seen in other alliances, is ultimately self-imposed, and directly because of the decisions taken at the 1957 summit on nuclear sharing. The importance of path dependency in this regard cannot be overstated, as NATO would not today incorporate the idea of being a 'nuclear alliance' as part of its identity if it were not for the unexpected consequences of earlier decisions on nuclear sharing.

Second, the material importance of an ally for US security has strong explanatory value for the success or failure of US allies in seeking greater substantiation of US guarantees of nuclear deterrence and use than the US is willing to commit based solely on its own national threat perception. There is little doubt that West Germany managed to achieve a greater US commitment to early nuclear use in NATO than the US would have preferred under flexible response. In contrast, in the 1950s Australia was unable to gain even insights into US plans, let alone additional US nuclear commitments, to the defence of Southeast Asia through either the ANZUS or SEATO alliances.

What really emerges from the analysis of the case studies, however, is how rarely the central policy issues regarding nuclear weapons in US alliances can be framed in the traditional mode of demand and supply of deterrence and reassurance. In practice, the policy objectives that US allies sought to achieve in their cooperation on nuclear weapons were generally highly idiosyncratic. These included the following: West Germany's focus (among a host of factors, not least political burden sharing regarding nuclear deployment), on avoidance of collateral damage through short-range use; Japan's desire to maintain close secrecy and public obfuscation of the extent to which it supported US nuclear operations; Australia's insistence on giving practical effect to sovereignty in relation to the operation of the joint facilities; and Norway's 'screening' of its nuclear cooperation in NATO. Few if any of these objectives arise from factors of threats and power. While the US often was very critical of such demands in the 1950s, over time it began to appreciate that it could usually accommodate them with little cost, while strengthening the political acceptance of broader alliance cooperation within the domestic politics of its allies. The end of the alliance with New Zealand is the single exception, but even in this regard there is a strong argument that the US sacrificed its alliance with Wellington so that it could avoid the same fate in regard to NATO ally Denmark. Overall, these idiosyncratic factors, rather than traditional concerns with abandonment, entrapment or deterrence and reassurance, are representative of most of the dynamics of intra-alliance bargaining on nuclear weapons in practice.

Third, the role of formalised alliance institutions in this regard emerges as a double-edged sword. The success of institutions in NATO, especially the NPG, cannot be separated from the mutual dependencies created by hardware sharing that they were, in many ways, set up to manage in the first place. While they have no doubt enabled the creation of trust through greater transparency and greater detail of nuclear commitments than would otherwise have been possible, the existence of alliance institutions also creates greater potential to disappoint. While in Asia it was Carter's decision to withdraw all US forces from South Korea that caused allied concern, in Europe he achieved much the same disruption merely by cancelling the production of the neutron bomb, and his approach to US–Soviet nuclear arms limitation talks. In SEATO, the US raised expectations about the nature and depth of its commitment that it was never going to fulfil. The military integration achieved in CFC still led to disappointment in South Korea about the restraint the US continued to impose on its ally. The limited scope of institutional arrangements to promote detailed consultation at the political level has exacerbated tensions in the US–ROK alliance, as there is limited evidence that the bilateral SCM and its ancillary institutions have much of a track record in bridging critical policy gaps.[5] And because NATO decided to continue nuclear sharing long after its original strategic rationale had passed, that alliance has in effect set itself a test of political cohesion that is arguably unnecessary, and which it might well fail should a future German government act on repeated calls in the Social Democratic Party to withdraw its commitment to nuclear sharing.[6]

Although a major focus of this book has been on history, these findings have clear relevance for contemporary practitioners. One broad point of relevance is that the book demonstrates that US nuclear weapons cooperation with allies needs to be seen through the prism of underlying relationships, not just the particular condition of alliances under any given US president, or a general strategic effect attributed to nuclear weapons. There can be no doubt that the Trump administration had a disruptive impact on US alliances in Europe and Asia. President Trump's fixation on linking financial contributions from allies (and to a lesser extent personal loyalty from allied leaders) with tangible commitments from the US triggered tensions, and in some cases resulted in decisions by Washington to scale down military commitments. However, this needs to be considered in its historical context. As we have seen, the proposed drawdown in the 1970s of US forces on the Korean Peninsula by the Nixon and Carter administrations involved almost no consultations with Seoul or other US allies in Asia at the time. And there is a well-established track record of US administrations threatening NATO members with reduced military commitments as a result of burden-sharing fatigue in Washington.[7] Despite Trump's hard-edged rhetoric about NATO, the operational-level commitment of the US to the alliance during his administration remained strong on the part of 'the policy establishment in the State Department and the Pentagon where the familiar language of leadership and commitment has prevailed'.[8] This included the nuclear dimension, with the Trump administration continuing all of the Obama-era modernisation initiatives to strengthen extended deterrence and missile defence, in addition to approving new low-yield nuclear options to counter Russian challenges.[9]

Paradoxically for a study that deals with the grim topic of nuclear weapons, the book's policy implications offer some grounds for optimism. One prominent finding is that the US has, over time, chosen to become increasingly dependent on allies for the implementation of its nuclear strategy, which itself reflects an increasing commitment to alliances. Continuing reliance on allies' real estate for the maintenance of early warning and communication facilities, the forward stationing and transit of US nuclear forces, and agreement to vary NATO's nuclear weapons posture only after consensus is reached are all signs that genuine allied cooperation in the nuclear domain remains important to US policymakers. This encompassed the Trump administration, which, despite assertive rhetoric from the White House on burden sharing, maintained close cooperation with allies on nuclear policy, including intensive consultations on the 2018 NPR and carefully amended drafts of the document in response to allied feedback.[10]

The agreement of allies to the terms and conditions of nuclear weapons cooperation furnishes an important element of international legitimacy for US nuclear posture overall, and strengthens US domestic support for nuclear strategy. As the 2009 Congressional Commission on the US Strategic Posture and the subsequent 2010 NPR demonstrated, allied concerns about US administrations either phasing out or not upgrading certain nuclear weapons systems have a tangible impact in Washington. Allied views are taken seriously in Congress and frequently appear as a factor in Congressional support for certain nuclear acquisition programmes (e.g. the B-61 life extension programme) over others.[11] During an era in which perceived inequities in burden sharing across the NATO and Asian alliances with the US have gained a renewed profile, it is worth bearing in mind that the history of alliance nuclear cooperation confirms that no US administration can do everything on its own. To a greater or lesser extent in each case, the US and its allies remain mutually dependent on effective nuclear weapons cooperation. This, perhaps more than anything else, has become the main dynamic of nuclear weapons cooperation in US alliances.

Another important lesson for policymakers is that US alliance partners can often achieve their policy preferences if they are prepared to bargain with Washington. This is good news for junior allies and further challenges the common assumption that in international relations materially weaker allies suffer what they must, while the great powers do what they can. As we have shown, successive administrations in Washington since Eisenhower have proven to be flexible in compromising, including in cases where allied governments that are committed to nuclear weapons cooperation confront significant domestic pressure on specific policy issues. Rather than confirming US benevolence towards allies, this reflects the self-interested premium that Washington places on retaining the commitment of allies to US leadership. Keen to avoid a repetition of New Zealand's defection from ANZUS in the mid-1980s over its opposition to US nuclear strategy, most of the time Washington has been attuned to what it regards as genuine concerns on the part of allies in order to pre-empt smaller issues snowballing into larger grievances. A willingness to compromise on nuclear policy has grown as junior allies have acquired increasing access to institutional channels of influence. In spite of Donald Trump's rhetoric about alliances provoking some soul searching in allied capitals regarding the potential durability of US alliance commitments, there is no evidence to suggest that his administration diluted the depth of nuclear weapons cooperation with allies in Europe and Asia. To the contrary, the administration's pro-nuclear instincts appear to have offset Trump's own ambivalence about the value of US allies.

Nuclear weapons will not be disappearing anytime soon from the armouries of states worldwide. Despite brief periods, including the early post-Cold War era, where their currency has declined, nuclear weapons remain in strong demand. This is not only the case for the dozen or so countries that either possess or aspire to possess their own nuclear arsenals, but also for US allies who see nuclear weapons as integral to the security assurances Washington dispenses as part of its global alliance network. States that made decisions several decades ago to forego the world's most powerful weapon account for a large proportion of the continuing demand for nuclear weapons internationally. For the European and Asian allies of the US, nuclear weapons cooperation is deeply ingrained in their respective relationships with that country. Whether it is a country like Germany, which bases US nuclear weapons on its territory and trains to undertake joint nuclear strike missions with the US, or Australia, which refers abstractly to nuclear deterrence in the context of an existential threat to its security, nuclear weapons continue to cast a long shadow across US alliances. This 'presence' is reinforced by the various institutions that have been created to coordinate nuclear weapons cooperation between the US and its allies.

US alliances have played an important role in their own right in strengthening the role of nuclear weapons in international relations. The demand-side for US nuclear reassurance has remained robust, and US allies have been eager to develop institutional frameworks to formalise nuclear weapons cooperation. Much to the dismay and frustration of nuclear disarmament advocates, even in low-threat environments, US allies are generally unenthusiastic about the prospect of eliminating nuclear weapons. Despite the rhetorical sympathy of some US allies for nuclear disarmament, when it comes to the crunch of renouncing the nuclear umbrella for their own security, these same countries are conspicuously silent. Although concerns about the credibility of US extended nuclear deterrence will no doubt persist, US allies would prefer to continue wrestling with this challenge than confront the prospect of nuclear weapons being taken off the table completely.

Notes

1 A. Gale, 'Japan's Abe to Meet Trump, with North Korea Testing their Ties', *Wall Street Journal*, 15 April 2018, www.wsj.com/articles/japans-abe-to-meet-trump-with-north-korea-testing-their-ties-1523790006
2 In general, West Germany was no exception to this pattern in regard to the behaviour and preferences of the Social Democratic Party (SPD), but at critical junctures it was Conservative parties that posed particular challenges: the ascent to power of the SPD in the mid-1960s reduced tensions with the US on nuclear matters because it ended the reign of Chancellor Adenauer and Minister for Defence Strauss, who had been particular opponents of the concept of flexible response. And in the late 1980s, the Kohl government caused a major crisis in NATO because it was willing to challenge the NATO consensus on short-range nuclear force modernisation. While this partly reflected domestic political pressures, disappointment about the Reagan administration's signature of the INF treaty, as well as different views about the prospect of major change in Soviet policy, also played a role.
3 J. Trevithick, 'The Air Force Abruptly Ends its Continuous Bomber Presence on Guam After 16 Years', *The Drive*, 17 April 2020, www.thedrive.com/the-war-zone/33057/the-continuous-strategic-bomber-presence-mission-to-guam-has-abruptly-ended-after-16-years
4 See D. Schwartz, *NATO's Nuclear Dilemmas* (Washington, DC: Brookings Institution, 1983).
5 This is despite the claim from one former US ambassador to South Korea that 'the SCM and its associated structures have proven both their value, adaptability, and versatility over time'. M. Lippert, 'Here's the Real Value in the US-South Korea Alliance', *Defense One*, 30 October 2018, www.defenseone.com/ideas/2018/10/heres-real-value-us-south-korean-alliance/152445/

6 J. Gotkowska, 'Germany's Future Participation in Nuclear Sharing: A Challenge for NATO?', *RUSI Commentary*, 26 May 2020, https://rusi.org/commentary/germany%E2%80%99s-future-participation-nuclear-sharing-challenge-nato

7 In quintessential Trumpian rhetoric, in March 1974 President Nixon informed an audience of European leaders that they 'cannot have it both ways. They cannot have the US participation and cooperation on the security front and then proceed to have confrontation and even hostility on the economic and political front'. Quoted in T. A. Sayle, *Enduring Alliance: A History of NATO and the Postwar Global Order* (Ithaca, NY: Cornell University Press, 2019), 187.

8 J. Sperling and M. Webber, 'Trump's Foreign Policy and NATO: Exit and Voice', *Review of International Studies*, 45:3 (2019), 524.

9 B. Roberts, 'On Adapting Nuclear Deterrence to Reduce Nuclear Risk', *Daedalus*, 149:2 (2020), 77.

10 F. Rose, 'Is the 2018 Nuclear Posture Review as Bad as the Critics Claim It Is?', *Brookings Institution Policy Brief*, April 2018, www.brookings.edu/wp-content/uploads/2018/04/fp_20180413_2018_nuclear_posture_review.pdf

11 J. Gould and A. Mehta, 'Nuclear Gravity Bomb and Warhead Upgrades Face New Delays', *Defense News*, 4 September 2019, www.defensenews.com/congress/2019/09/04/nuclear-gravity-bomb-and-warhead-upgrades-face-new-delays/

Bibliography

Unless otherwise stated, all URL references were last accessed on 28 January 2021.

Abe, N. 'No First Use: How to Overcome Japan's Great Divide', *Journal for Peace and Nuclear Disarmament*, 1:1 (2018), 145–146.

Ahonen, P. 'Franz Joseph Strauss and the German Nuclear Question, 1956–1962', *Journal of Strategic Studies*, 18:2 (1995), 25–51.

Aishwarya, S. 'USAF Completes Flight Tests of B61–12 Gravity Bombs from F15-E', *Air Force Technology*, 30 August 2017, www.airforce-technology.com/news/newsusaf-completes-testing-of-b61–12-gravity-bombs-on-f-15e-strike-eagle-5913501/

Akihiro, S. *The Self Defense Forces and Postwar Politics in Japan* (Tokyo: JPIC, 2017).

Albinski, H. *The Australian-American Security Relationship: A Regional and International Perspective* (St Lucia: University of Queensland Press, 1982).

Allison, R. *Finland's Relations with the Soviet Union: 1944–1984* (London: Macmillan, 1986).

Amano, Y. 'A Japanese View on Nuclear Disarmament', *Nonproliferation Review*, 9:1 (2002), 132–145.

'Amerikanische Atomwaffen aus Deutschland abziehen', *Frankfurter Allgemeine,* 25 April 2005, www.faz.net/aktuell/politik/atomwaffen-amerikanische-atomwaffen-aus-deutschland-abziehen-1232522.html

Ansell, C. 'Network Institutionalism', in S. Binder, R. Rhodes, and B. Rockman (eds), *The Oxford Handbook of Political Institutions* (Oxford: Oxford University Press, 2008).

Aunesluoma, J., M. Petersson, and C. Silva, 'Deterrence or Reassurance? Nordic Responses to the First Détente, 1953–1956', *Scandinavian Journal of History*, 32:2 (2007), 183–208.

Ayako, K. 'The Sato Cabinet and the Making of Japan's Non-Nuclear Policy', *The Journal of American-East Asian Relations*, 15 (2008), 25–50.

Bacia, H. 'Atomwaffenfrei' *Frankfurter Allgemeine*, 6 May 2010, www.faz.net/aktuell/politik/abruestung-atomwaffenfrei-1979108.html

Ball, D. 'The Strategic Essence', *Australian Journal of International Affairs*, 55:2 (2001), 235–248.

Ball, D. '*Pine Gap*'*: Testimony of Professor Des Ball to the Joint Standing Committee on Treaties*, 9 August 1999.

Ball, D. *Pine Gap: Australia and the US Geostationary Signals Intelligence* (Sydney: Allen and Unwin, 1988).

Ball, D. *A Base for Debate: The US Satellite Station at Nurrungar* (Sydney: Allen and Unwin, 1987).
Ball, D. *A Suitable Piece of Real Estate: American Installations in Australia* (Sydney: Hale and Iremonger, 1980).
Ball, D. and R. Tanter, 'US Signals Intelligence (SIGINT) Activities in Japan: 1945–2015', *Japan Focus: The Asia Pacific Journal*, 14:6 (2016), https://apjjf.org/2016/06/Ball.html
Barclay, G. St J. *Friends in High Places: Australian-American Diplomatic Relations Since 1945* (Melbourne: Oxford University Press, 1985).
Bark, D. and D. Gress, *A History of West Germany: From Shadow to Substance, 1945–1963*, 2nd edition (Cambridge, MA: Blackwell, 1993).
Barnett, M. and R. Duvall, 'Power in International Relations', *International Organization,* 59:1 (2005), 39–75.
Beazley, K. '"America First" and Australia's Strategic Future', in P. Dean, S. Frühling, and B. Taylor (eds), *After American Primacy: Imagining the Future of Australia's Defence* (Melbourne: Melbourne University Press, 2019).
Beazley, K. 'Sovereignty and the US Alliance', in P. Dean, S. Frühling, and B. Taylor (eds), *Australia's American Alliance* (Melbourne: Melbourne University Press, 2016).
Beckley, M. 'The Myth of Entangling Alliances: Reassessing the Security Risks of US Defense Pacts', *International Security,* 39:4 (2015), 7–48.
Bell, B. B. 'The Evolution of Combined Forces Command', Presentation to the 4th Korea Foundation Global Seminar, Washington, DC, 8–11 June 2012, www.brookings.edu/wp-content/uploads/2012/09/69-Bell-Evolution-of-Combined-Forces-Command.pdf.
Bell, R. 'The Challenges of NATO Nuclear Policy', Working Paper 105 (Helsinki: Finnish Institute of International Affairs, 2018).
Bell, S. 'Historical Institutionalism and New Dimensions of Agency: Bankers, Institutions and the 2008 Financial Crisis', *Political Studies*, 65:3 (2017), 724–739.
Bellany, I. *Australia in the Nuclear Age: National Defence and National Development* (Sydney: Sydney University Press, 1972).
Berdal, M. *The United States, Norway and the Cold War, 1954–60* (Basingstoke: Macmillan Press, 1997).
Betts, R. *Nuclear Blackmail and Nuclear Balance* (Washington, DC: Brookings Institution, 1987).
Bird, M. 'Nuclear History Note: US Atomic Demolition Munitions, 1954–1989', *RUSI Journal*, 153:2 (2008), 64–68.
Bisley, N. and B. Taylor, *Conflict in the East China Sea: Would ANZUS Apply?* (Sydney: Australia–China Relations Institute, UTS, 2014).
Bitzinger, R. *Denmark, Norway, and NATO: Constraints and Challenges* (Santa Monica, CA: RAND Corporation, 1989).
Bjerga, K. and K. Skogrand, 'Securing Small State Interests: Norway in NATO', in V. Mastny, S. Holtsmark, and A. Wenger (eds), *War Plans and Alliances in the Cold War: Threat Perceptions in the East and West* (London: Routledge, 2006).
Blaxland, J. 'US-Australian Military Cooperation in Asia', in P. Dean, S. Frühling, and B. Taylor (eds), *Australia's American Alliance* (Melbourne: Melbourne University Press, 2016).

Bogen, O. and M. Hakenstad, 'Reluctant Reformers: The Economic Roots of Military Change in Norway, 1990–2015', *Defence Studies*, 17:1 (2017), 23–37.

Borger, J. 'US Nuclear Weapons: First Low-Yield Warheads Roll Off the Production Line', *Guardian*, 28 January 2019, www.theguardian.com/world/2019/jan/28/us-nuclear-weapons-first-low-yield-warheads-roll-off-the-production-line

Borger, J. 'Five NATO States to Urge Removal of US Nuclear Arms in Europe', *Guardian*, 23 February 2010, www.theguardian.com/world/2010/feb/22/nato-states-us-nuclear-arms-europe

Borresen, J. 'Alliance Naval Strategies and Norway in the Final Years of the Cold War', *Naval War College Review*, 64:7 (2004), 1–20.

Brands, H. 'From ANZUS to SEATO: United States Strategic Policy Towards Australia and New Zealand, 1952–1954', *International History Review*, 9:2 (1987), 250–270.

Brown, A. 'The History of the Radford-Collins Agreement', Royal Australian Navy, Sea Power Centre, www.navy.gov.au/history/feature-histories/history-radford-collins-agreement

Brzezinski, Z. *Power and Principle: Memoirs of the National Security Adviser, 1977–1981* (London: George Weidenfeld and Nicholson, 1983).

Bullard, M. 'Japan's Nuclear Choice', *Asian Survey*, 14:9 (1974), 845–853.

Bunn, E. 'Extended Deterrence and Assurance', in C. Murdock and J. Yeats (eds), *Exploring the Nuclear Posture Implications of Extended Deterrence and Assurance: Workshop Proceedings and Key Takeaways* (Washington, DC: Center for Strategic and International Studies, 2009).

Burr, W. and J. Kimball, *Nixon's Nuclear Specter: The Secret Alert of 1969, Madman Diplomacy, and the Vietnam War* (Lawrence, KA: University Press of Kansas, 2015).

Burt, R. 'Neutron Bomb Controversy Strained Alliance and Caused Splits in the Administration', *New York Times*, 9 April 1978, www.nytimes.com/1978/04/09/archives/neutron-bomb-controversy-strained-alliance-and-caused-splits-in-the.html

Buteux, P. *The Politics of Nuclear Consultation in NATO: 1965–1980* (Cambridge: Cambridge University Press, 1983).

Byong-Chul Lee, 'Don't be Surprised When South Korea Wants Nuclear Weapons', *Bulletin of the Atomic Scientists*, 23 October 2019, https://thebulletin.org/2019/10/dont-be-surprised-when-south-korea-wants-nuclear-weapons/

Calder, K. 'Securing Security Through Prosperity: The San Francisco System in Comparative Perspective', *Pacific Review*, 17:1 (2004), 135–157.

Caldwell, D. 'Permissive Action Links: A Description and Proposal', *Survival*, 29:3 (1987), 224–236.

Camilleri, J. *ANZUS: Australia's Predicament in the Nuclear Age* (Melbourne: Macmillan, 1987).

Cha, V. *Powerplay: The Origins of the American Alliance System in Asia* (Princeton, NJ and Oxford: Princeton University Press, 2016).

Cha, V. *Alignment Despite Antagonism: The US–Korea–Japan Security Triangle* (Stanford, CA: Stanford University Press, 1999).

Chae-Jin Lee, 'The Direction of South Korea's Foreign Policy', *Korean Studies*, 2 (1978), 95–137.

Chalmers, M. and S. Lunn, *NATO's Tactical Nuclear Dilemma*, RUSI Occasional Paper (London: Royal United Services Institute, 2010).

Chanlett-Avery, E. 'The US–Japan Alliance', *Congressional Research Service Report*, RL33740, 13 June 2019, https://fas.org/sgp/crs/row/RL33740.pdf

Chanlett-Avery, E., M. E. Manyin, B. R. Williams, and C. D. Cimino-Isaacs, 'US–Japan Relations in Focus', *Congressional Research Service*, 29 April 2020, https://fas.org/sgp/crs/row/IF10199.pdf

Chernoff, F. *After Bipolarity: The Vanishing Threat, Theories of Cooperation, and the Future of the Atlantic Alliance* (Ann Arbor, MI: University of Michigan Press, 1995).

Choe Sang-hun, 'US and South Korea Make Plans for Defense', *New York Times*, 25 March 2013, www.nytimes.com/2013/03/26/world/asia/us-and-south-korea-sign-plan-to-counter-north.html

Choi, K. and Joon-Sung Park, 'South Korea: Fears of Abandonment and Entrapment', in M. Alagappa (ed.), *The Long Shadow: Nuclear Weapons and Security in 21st Century Asia* (Stanford, CA: Stanford University Press, 2008).

Choi, L. 'The First Nuclear Crisis in the Korean Peninsula, 1975–76', *Cold War History*, 14:1 (2014), 71–90.

Christensen, T. *Worse than a Monolith: Alliance Politics and Problems of Coercive Diplomacy in Asia* (Princeton, NJ and Oxford: Princeton University Press, 2011).

Chubb, D. and I. McAllister, 'Public Attitudes Towards the Future Defence of Australia', in P. Dean, S. Frühling, and B. Taylor (eds), *After American Primacy: Imagining the Future Defence of Australia* (Melbourne: Melbourne University Press, 2019).

Clarke, M., S. Frühling, and A. O'Neil, *Australia's Nuclear Policy: Reconciling Strategic, Economic, and Normative Interests* (Aldershot: Ashgate, 2015).

Cohen, M. and A. O'Neil, 'Doubts Down Under: American Extended Deterrence, Australia, and the 1999 East Timor Crisis', *International Relations of the Asia Pacific*, 15:1 (2015), 27–52.

Cole, W. *Norway and the United States 1905–1955* (Ames, IA: Iowa State University Press, 1989).

Cote, O. 'The Third Battle: Innovation in the US Navy's Silent Cold War Struggle with Soviet Submarines', *Federation of American Scientists*, March 2000, https://fas.org/man/dod-101/sys/ship/docs/cold-war-asw.htm

Crane, M. 'Boosting the US Presence in Northern Australia: Slowly But Surely', *The Strategist*, 21 March 2019, www.aspistrategist.org.au/boosting-the-us-presence-in-northern-australia-slowly-but-surely/

Crouch, C. 'Complementarity', in G. Morgan, J. Campbell, C. Crouch, O. Kaj Pedersen, and R. Whitley (eds), *The Oxford Handbook of Comparative Institutional Analysis* (Oxford: Oxford University Press, 2015).

Cumings, B. *The Korean War: A History* (New York: The Modern Library, 2011).

Cumings, B. 'On the Strategy and Morality of American Nuclear Policy in Korea, 1950 to the Present', *Social Science Japan Journal*, 1:1 (1998), 57–70.

Curran, J. *Fighting with America: Why Saying No to the US Wouldn't Rupture the Alliance* (Sydney: Penguin Random House, 2016).

Curran, J. *Unholy Fury: The US Alliance and the Nixon-Whitlam Crisis* (Melbourne: Melbourne University Press, 2015).

Curtis, G. 'US Policy Towards Japan from Nixon to Clinton: An Assessment', in G. Curtis (ed.), *New Perspectives on US–Japan Relations* (Tokyo: Japan Center for International Exchange, Tokyo, 2000).

Daalder, I. *The Nature and Practice of Flexible Response: NATO Strategy and Theater Nuclear Forces Since 1967* (New York: Columbia University Press, 1991).
Dahl, R. A. 'The Concept of Power', *Behavioural Science*, 2:3 (1957), 201–215.
Danielson, H. 'Military Assistance, Foreign Policy, and National Security: The Objectives of US Military Assistance to Norway, 1950–1965', *Scandinavian Journal of History*, 45:1 (2020), 71–94.
Danilovic, V. 'The Sources of Threat Credibility in Extended Deterrence', *Journal of Conflict Resolution,* 45:3 (2001), 341–369.
Daugherty, L. '"Tip of the Spear": The Formation and Expansion of the Bundeswehr, 1949–1963', *Journal of Slavic Military Studies*, 24:1 (2011), 147–177.
Defence Committee, 'Australia's Strategic Position, 4 February 1963', in S. Frühling (ed.), *A History of Australian Strategic Policy Since 1945* (Canberra: Commonwealth of Australia, 2009).
Defence Committee, 'Strategic Basis of Australian Defence Policy, 11 October 1956', in S. Frühling (ed.), *A History of Australian Strategic Policy Since 1945* (Canberra: Commonwealth of Australia, 2009).
Demetriou, D. 'US–Japan Nuclear Pact Extended Despite Concern Over Tokyo's Plutonium Stockpile', *Telegraph*, 18 July 2018, www.telegraph.co.uk/news/2018/07/18/us-japan-nuclear-pact-extended-despite-concern-tokyos-plutoniumstockpile/
Dennis, P. 'Major and Minor: The Defense of Southeast Asia and the Cold War', in K. Neilson and R. Haycock (eds), *The Cold War and Defense* (New York: Praeger, 1990).
Denyer, S. 'Japan-South Korea Ties "Worst in Five Decades" as US Leaves Alliance Untended', *Washington Post*, 9 February 2019, www.washingtonpost.com/world/asia_pacific/japan-south-korea-ties-worst-in-five-decades-as-us-leaves-alliance-untended/2019/02/08/f17230be-2ad8–11e9–906e-9d55b6451eb4_story.html?noredirect=on&utm_term=.2981e3dd2dfc
Department of Defence, *Defence White Paper 2016* (Canberra: Commonwealth of Australia, 2016).
Department of Defence, *Defending Australia in the Asia-Pacific Century: Force 2030* (Canberra: Commonwealth of Australia, 2009).
Department of Defence, 'Draft Presentation to the Congressional Commission on the Strategic Posture of the United States', 12 February, 2009.
Department of Defence, *Strategic Review 1993* (Canberra: Defence Centre Publishing, 1993).
Department of Defence, *The Defence of Australia 1987: Presented to Parliament by the Minister for Defence, the Honourable Kim Beazley MP* (Canberra: Australian Government Publishing Service, 1987).
Department of Defense, 'The Guidelines for US–Japan Defense Cooperation (April 27, 2015)', https://archive.defense.gov/pubs/20150427__GUIDELINES_FOR_US-JAPAN_DEFENSE_COOPERATION.pdf
Department of Defense, 'Charts re. Reporting on North Korean Military Strength, June 8, 1979, Top Secret', *US National Security Archive,* https://nsarchive2.gwu.edu//dc.html?doc=3696533-Document-06-Charts-re-Reporting-on-North-Korean
Department of Foreign Affairs, *Uranium, the Joint Facilities, Disarmament and Peace* (Canberra: Australian Government Publishing Service, 1984).
Department of Foreign Affairs and Trade, 'Australia and Nuclear Weapons', www.dfat.gov.au/international-relations/security/non-proliferation-disarmament-arms-control/nuclear-issues/Pages/australia-and-nuclear-weapons

Department of Foreign Affairs and Trade, 'AUSMIN Joint Communique, 12 August 2014', www.dfat.gov.au/geo/united-states-of-america/ausmin/Pages/ausmin-joint-communique-2014

Department of State, 'State Department Telegram (195214) to US Embassy South Korea: "ROK Nuclear Fuel Reprocessing Plans", 16 August 1975, Secret', https://nsarchive2.gwu.edu//dc.html?doc=5798497-National-Security-Archive-Doc-03-State

Department of State, 'Paper prepared by the National Security Staff, no date', in *Foreign Relations of the United States, 1969–1976*, Vol. 41: *Western Europe; NATO, 1969–1972*, https://history.state.gov/historicaldocuments/frus1969–76v41/d52

Department of State, 'Memorandum of Conversation: Secretary Schlesinger's Meeting with Deputy Prime Minister Barnard of Australia, January 9, 1974', in *Foreign Relations of the United States: 1969–1976,* Vol. E-12: *Documents on East and Southeast Asia, 1973–1976*, https://history.state.gov/historicaldocuments/frus1969–76ve12/d45

Department of State, 'Letter from President Nixon to Korean President Park, Washington, November 29, 1971', in *Foreign Relations of the United States: 1969–1976*, Vol. XIX, Part 1: *Korea, 1969–1972*, https://history.state.gov/historicaldocuments/frus1969–76v19p1/d115

Department of State, 'Minutes of a National Security Council Meeting, Washington DC, October 14, 1970', in *Foreign Relations of the United States, 1969–1976,* Vol. 41: *Western Europe; NATO, 1969–1972*, https://history.state.gov/historicaldocuments/frus1969–76v41/d49

Department of State, 'Memorandum from Laurence E. Lynn, Jr., of the National Security Council Staff to the President's Assistant for National Security Affairs (Kissinger), Washington, February 26, 1970', in *Foreign Relations of the United States: 1969–1976*, Vol. XIX, Part 1: *Korea, 1969–1972*, https://history.state.gov/historicaldocuments/frus1969–76v19p1/d53

Department of State, 'Memorandum from President Nixon to the President's Assistant for National Security Affairs (Kissinger), Washington, November 24, 1969', in *Foreign Relations of the United States: 1969–1976*, Vol. XIX, Part 1: *Korea, 1969–1972*, https://history.state.gov/historicaldocuments/frus1969–76v19p1/d45

Department of State, 'Telegram from the Embassy in Japan to the Department of State, Tokyo, June 5, 1968, 0700Z', in *Foreign Relations of the United States: 1964–1968*, Vol. 29, Part 2; *Japan*, Office of the Historian, Washington, DC, 2006, https://history.state.gov/historicaldocuments/frus1964–68v29p2/d123

Department of State, 'Addendum INR Contribution to NIE 4–65 Likelihood of Further Nuclear Proliferation', 4 November 1965, https://nsarchive2.gwu.edu/NSAEBB/NSAEBB155/prolif-11b.pdf

Department of State, 'Letter from Johnson to Wilson, December 23, 1965', in *Foreign Relations of the United States, 1964–1968,* Vol. 13: *Western Europe Region*, https://history.state.gov/historicaldocuments/frus1964–68v13/d121

Department of State, 'Memorandum from the Joint Chiefs of Staff to Secretary of Defense McNamara, JCSM-900–65, Washington, December 23, 1965', in *Foreign Relations of the United States: 1964–1968*, Vol. 29, Part 2: *Japan*, https://history.state.gov/historicaldocuments/frus1964–68v29p2/d65

Department of State, 'Memorandum of Conversation: Problems of the NATO Alliance, Washington DC, October 16, 1963', in *Foreign Relations of the United States, 1961–1963*, Vol. 13: *Western Europe and Canada*, https://history.state.gov/historicaldocuments/frus1961–63v13/d215

Department of State, 'Circular Telegram from the Department of State to Certain Missions, Washington DC, 9 May 1962', in *Foreign Relations of the United States, 1961–1963*, Vol. 13: *Western Europe and Canada*, https://history.state.gov/historicaldocuments/frus1961–63v13/d137

Department of State, 'Despatch from the Embassy in Norway to the Department of State, 29 July 1960, Subject: Norway and U.S. Leadership', in *Foreign Relations of the United States, 1958–60, Western Europe*, Vol. 7, Part 2, https://history.state.gov/historicaldocuments/frus1958–60v07p2/d301

Department of State, 'National Security Council Report: Statement of US Policy Toward Scandinavia, 6 April 1960, Subject: General Considerations', in *Foreign Relations of the United States, 1958–60, Western Europe*, Vol. 7, Part 2, https://history.state.gov/historicaldocuments/frus1958–60v07p2/d301

Department of State, 'National Security Council Report: Statement of US Policy on France, November 4, 1959', in *Foreign Relations of the United States, 1958–1960, Western Europe*, Vol. 7, Part 2, https://history.state.gov/historicaldocuments/frus1958–60v07p2/d145

Department of State, 'Memorandum of Discussion at the 334th Meeting of the National Security Council, Washington, August 8, 1957', in *Foreign Relations of the United States: 1955–1957*, Vol. XXIII, Part 2: *Korea, 1955–1957*, https://history.state.gov/historicaldocuments/frus1955–57v23p2/d239

Department of State, 'Memorandum of Discussion at the 326th Meeting of the National Security Council, Washington, June 13, 1957', in *Foreign Relations of the United States: 1955–1957*, Vol. XXIII, Part 2: *Korea, 1955–1957*, https://history.state.gov/historicaldocuments/frus1955–57v23p2/d221

Department of State, 'Memorandum of Discussion at the 297th Meeting of the National Security Council, Washington, September 20, 1956', in *Foreign Relations of the United States: 1955–1957*, Vol. XXIII, Part 2: *Korea, 1955–1957*, https://history.state.gov/historicaldocuments/frus1955–57v23p2/d169

Department of State, 'Memorandum of Conversation: US Embassy France Telegram 1135 to Department of State, 16 September 1954', RG 59, Central Decimal Files 1950–1954, 740.5/9–1654.

'Description of Consultation Arrangements Under the Treaty of Mutual Security and Cooperation with Japan, June 1960, https://nsarchive2.gwu.edu/nukevault/ebb291/doc01.pdf

Dibb, P. *Into the Wilderness of Mirrors: Australia and the Threat from the Soviet Union in the Cold War and Russia Today* (Melbourne: Melbourne University Press, 2018).

Die Bundesregierung, *Weissbuch zur Sicherheitspolitik und zur Zukunft der Bundeswehr: 2016*, www.bmvg.de/resource/blob/13708/015be272f8c0098f1537a491676bfc31/weissbuch2016-barrierefrei-data.pdf

Dietl, R. 'In Defence of the West: General Lauris Norstad, NATO Nuclear Forces and Transatlantic Relations: 1956–1963', *Diplomacy and Statecraft*, 17:2 (2006), 347–392.

Dingman, R. 'Atomic Diplomacy During the Korean War', *International Security*, 13:3 (1988/89), 50–91.

Djelic, M. 'Institutional Perspectives – Working towards Coherence or Irreconcilable Diversity?' in G. Morgan, J. Campbell, C. Crouch, O. Kaj Pedersen, and R. Whitley (eds), *The Oxford Handbook of Comparative Institutional Analysis* (Oxford: Oxford University Press, 2015).

Doran, M. 'Federal Government Spends $1.1 Billion on Northern Territory Airbase, Expanding Reach into the Indo-Pacific', *ABC News Online*, 21 February 2020, www.abc.net.au/news/2020–02–21/federal-government-spends-1.1-billion-on-top-end-air-base/11986904

Dorling, P. 'B-1 Bombers Coming to Australia to Deter Beijing's South China Sea Ambitions: US', *Sydney Morning Herald*, 15 May 2015, www.smh.com.au/world/b1-bombers-coming-to-australia-to-deter-beijings-south-china-sea-ambitions-us-20150515-gh23zl.html

Dower, J. 'The San Francisco System: Past, Present, Future in US–Japan–China Relations', *Japan Focus: The Asia-Pacific Journal*, 12:8 (2014), https://apjjf.org/2014/12/8/John-W.-Dower/4079/article.html

Duffield, J. 'International Security Institutions', in D. Marsh and G. Stoker (eds), *Theory and Methods in Political Science* (Basingstoke: Palgrave Macmillan, 2010).

Dyndal, G. L. 'How the High North Became Central to NATO Strategy: Revelations from the NATO Archives', *Journal of Strategic Studies*, 34:4 (2011), 557–585.

Edwards, P. *Permanent Friends? Historical Reflections on the Australia-American Alliance*, Lowy Institute for International Policy, Paper No. 8 (2005).

Edwards, P. with G. Pemberton, *Crises and Commitments: The Politics and Diplomacy of Australia's Involvement in Southeast Asian Conflicts, 1948–1965* (Sydney: Allen and Unwin in association with the Australian War Memorial, 1992).

Egeland, K. 'Spreading the Burden: How NATO Became a "Nuclear' Alliance"', *Diplomacy and Statecraft*, 31:1 (2020), 143–167.

Egeland, K. 'Oslo's 'New Track: Norwegian Nuclear Disarmament Diplomacy, 2005–2013', *Journal for Peace and Nuclear Disarmament*, 2:2 (2019), 468–490.

Elias Mikalsen Gronning, B. 'Operational and Industrial Military Integration: Extending the Frontiers of the Japan-US Alliance', *International Affairs*, 94:4 (2018), 755–772.

Ellsberg, D. *The Doomsday Machine: Confessions of a Nuclear War Planner* (New York: Bloomsbury, 2017).

Emmott, R. and J. Chalmers, 'Trump Troop Pullout Would Still Leave Hefty US Footprint in Europe', *Reuters*, 9 June 2020, www.reuters.com/article/us-usa-germany-military-analysis/trump-troop-pullout-would-still-leave-hefty-u-s-footprint-in-europe-idUSKBN23F29P

Endicott, J. *Japan's Nuclear Option: Political, Technical, and Strategic Factors* (New York: Praeger, 1975).

Envall, H. 'What Kind of Japan? Tokyo's Strategic Options in a Contested Asia', *Survival*, 6:4 (2019), 117–130.

Epstein, J. 'Horizontal Escalation: Sour Notes of a Recurrent Theme', *International Security*, 8:3 (1983–84), 19–31.

Fearon, J. 'Signalling Foreign Policy Interests: Tying Hands Versus Sinking Costs', *Journal of Conflict Resolution*, 41:1 (1997), 68–90.

Federation of American Scientists, 'DF-5', https://fas.org/nuke/guide/china/icbm/df-5.htm

Fifield, A. 'South Korea's Defense Minister Suggests Bringing Back Tactical US Nuclear Weapons', *Washington Post*, 4 September 2017, www.washingtonpost.com/

world/south-koreas-defense-minister-raises-the-idea-of-bringing-back-tactical-us-nuclear-weapons/2017/09/04/7a468314–9155–11e7-b9bc-b2f7903bab0d_story.html?utm_term=.6757fc92bc40

Fifield, A. 'No American Strike in North Korea Without My Consent, Says South's President', *Washington Post*, 17 August 2017, www.washingtonpost.com/world/asia_pacific/no-american-strike-on-north-korea-without-my-consent-says-souths-president/2017/08/17/775290e8–8332–11e7–82a4–920da1aeb507_story.html

Flitton, D. 'Australia, Japan in Nuclear Rift', *Sydney Morning Herald*, 4 September 2009, www.smh.com.au/national/australia-japan-in-nuclear-rift-20090903-f9yw.html

Ford, G. 'Japan-US Joint Announcement to the Press (by Prime Minister Takeo Miki and President Gerald R. Ford, Washington DC, August 6, 1975', in *Public Papers of the Presidents: Gerald Ford, 1975*, Book II (Washington, DC: US Government Printing Office, 1976).

Forland, A. 'Norway's Nuclear Odyssey: From Optimistic Proponent to Nonproliferator', *The Nonproliferation Review*, 4:2 (1997), 1–16.

'Founding Act on Mutual Relations, Cooperation and Security between NATO and the Russian Federation, Signed in Paris, 27 May 1997', www.nato.int/cps/en/natohq/official_texts_25468.htm?

'France and Germany Agree on Truce over Nuclear Arms Control Committee as NATO Works on Deterrence and Defense Posture Review', *Arms Control Now*, 3 October 2011, www.armscontrol.org/blog/2011-10-03/france-germany-agree-truce-over-nuclear-arms-control-committee-nato-works-deterrence

Frankel, B. 'Restating the Realist Case: An Introduction', *Security Studies*, 5:3 (1996), 9–20.

Freedman, L. and J. Michaels, *The Evolution of Nuclear Strategy*, 4th edition (Houndmills: Palgrave Macmillan, 2019).

French, H. 'South Korea's President-Elect Rejects Use of Force Against North Korea', *New York Times*, 17 January 2003, www.nytimes.com/2003/01/17/world/threats-responses-korean-peninsula-south-korea-s-president-elect-rejects-use.html

Frühling, S. 'A Nuclear-armed Australia? Contemplating the Unthinkable Option', *Australian Foreign Affairs*, 4 (2018), 71–91.

Frühling, S. 'Is ANZUS Really an Alliance? Aligning the US and Australia', *Survival*, 60:5 (2018), 199–218.

Frühling, S. 'Wrestling with Commitment: Geography, Alliance and the ANZUS Treaty', in P. Dean, S. Frühling, and B. Taylor (eds), *Australia's American Alliance* (Melbourne: Melbourne University Press, 2016).

Frühling, S. 'The Fuzzy Limits of Self-Reliance: US Extended Deterrence and Australian Strategic Policy', *Australian Journal of International Affairs*, 67:1 (2013), 18–34.

Frühling, S. 'Never Say Never: Considerations About the Possibility of Australia Acquiring Nuclear Weapons', *Asian Security*, 6:2 (2010), 146–169.

Frühling, S. and A. O'Neil, 'Institutions, Informality, and Influence: Explaining Nuclear Cooperation in the Australia–US Alliance', *Australian Journal of Political Science*, 55:2 (2020), 135–151.

Frühling, S. and A. O'Neil, 'Nuclear Weapons, the United States, and Alliances in Europe and Asia: An Institutional Perspective', *Contemporary Security Policy*, 38:1 (2017), 4–25.

Fuhrmann M. and T. Sechser, 'Signalling Alliance Commitments: Hand-Tying and Sunk Costs in Extended Nuclear Deterrence', *American Journal of Political Science*, 58:4 (2014), 919–935.

Fujita, N. 'US Analyst: Japan's Nuke Stance Obstructs Arms Control', *The Asahi Shimbun*, 26 April 2018.

Gaddis, J. L. *Strategies of Containment: A Critical Appraisal of Postwar American National Security Policy* (Oxford: Oxford University Press, 1982).

Gaffney, H. 'Euromissiles as the Ultimate Evolution of Theater Missile Forces in Europe', *Journal of Cold War Studies*, 16:1 (2014), 180–199.

Gale, A. 'Japan's Abe to Meet Trump, with North Korea Testing Their Ties', *Wall Street Journal*, 15 April 2018, www.wsj.com/articles/japans-abe-to-meet-trump-with-north-korea-testing-their-ties-1523790006

Garthoff, R. 'The NATO Decision on Theater Nuclear Forces', *Political Science Quarterly*, 98:2 (1983), 197–214.

Gavin, F. 'The Myth of Flexible Response: United States Strategy in Europe During the 1960s', *The International History Review*, 23:4 (2001), 847–875.

George, A. and A. Bennett, *Case Studies and Theory Development in the Social Sciences* (Cambridge, MA: MIT Press, 2005).

German, R. 'Norway and the Bear: Soviet Coercive Diplomacy and Norwegian Security Policy', *International Security*, 7:2 (1982), 55–82.

'Germany Raises No-first-use Issue at NATO Meeting', *Arms Control Association* (November 1998), www.armscontrol.org/act/1998–11/press-releases/germany-raises-first-use-issue-nato-meeting

Gerzhoy, G. 'Alliance Coercion and Nuclear Restraint: How the United States Thwarted West Germany's Nuclear Ambitions', *International Security*, 39:4 (2015), 91–129.

GlobalSecurity.org, 'Globus III', www.globalsecurity.org/space/systems/globus-iii.htm

Gordon, P. *France, Germany and the Western Alliance* (Boulder, CO: Westview Press, 1995).

Gormley, D. 'Securing Nuclear Obsolescence', *Survival* 48:3 (2006), 127–148.

Gotkowska, J. 'Germany's Future Participation in Nuclear Sharing: A Challenge for NATO?', *RUSI Commentary*, 26 May 2020, https://rusi.org/commentary/germany%E2%80%99s-future-participation-nuclear-sharing-challenge-nato

Gould, J. and A. Mehta, 'Nuclear Gravity Bomb and Warhead Upgrades Face New Delays', *Defense News*, 4 September 2019, www.defensenews.com/congress/2019/09/04/nuclear-gravity-bomb-and-warhead-upgrades-face-new-delays/

Green, M. and K. Furukawa, 'Japan: New Nuclear Realism', in M. Alagappa (ed.), *The Long Shadow: Nuclear Weapons and Security in 21st Century Asia* (Stanford, CA: Stanford University Press, 2008).

'Guidelines for Japan-US Defense Cooperation: Report by the Subcommittee for Defense Cooperation, Submitted to and Approved by the Japan-US Security Consultative Committee, November 27 1978', https://japan2.usembassy.gov/pdfs/wwwf-mdao-defense-guidelines1978.pdf

Guthrie-Shimizu, S. 'Japan, the United States, and the Cold War: 1945–1960', in M. Leffler and O. Arne Westad (eds), *The Cambridge History of the Cold War*, Vol. 1: *Origins* (Cambridge: Cambridge University Press, 2010).

Gwertzman, B. 'Shultz Ends US Vow to Defend New Zealand', *New York Times*, 28 June 1986, www.nytimes.com/1986/06/28/world/shultz-ends-us-vow-to-defend-new-zealand.html

Haberman, C. 'Japan Formally Drops Military Spending Cap', *New York Times*, 25 January 1987, www.nytimes.com/1987/01/25/world/japan-formally-drops-military-spending-cap.html

Haftendorn, H. 'NATO and the Arctic: Is the Atlantic Alliance a Cold War Relic in a Peaceful Region Now Faced with Non-military Challenges?', *European Security*, 20:3 (2011), 337–361.

Haftendorn, H. *NATO and the Nuclear Revolution: A Crisis of Credibility, 1966–67* (Oxford: Oxford University Press, 1996).

Halperin, M. 'The Nuclear Dimension of the U.S.-Japan Alliance', *NAPSNet Special Reports*, 21 December 2000, https://nautilus.org/napsnet/napsnet-special-reports/the-nuclear-dimension-of-the-u-s-japan-alliance/

Hampton, M. 'NATO at the Creation: US Foreign Policy, West Germany and the Wilsonian Impulse', *Security Studies*, 4:3 (1995), 627–651.

Han, Yong-Sup 'The Sunshine Policy and Security on the Korean Peninsula: A Critical Assessment and Prospects', *Asian Perspective*, 26:3 (2002), 37–69.

Harrison, S. *Korean Endgame: A Strategy for Reunification and US Disengagement* (Princeton, NJ: Princeton University Press, 2002).

Hasegawa, T. 'The Soviet Factor in US–Japanese Defense Cooperation, 1978–1985', *Journal of Cold War Studies*, 15:2 (2013), 72–103.

Hayden, B. *Hayden: An Autobiography* (Sydney: HarperCollins, 1996).

Hayes, P. *Pacific Powderkeg: American Nuclear Dilemmas in Korea* (New York: Lexington Books, 1991).

Hayes, P. 'American Nuclear Hegemony in Korea', *Journal of Peace Research*, 25:4 (1988), 351–364.

Hayes, P. and Chung-in Moon, 'Park Chung-hee, the CIA and the Bomb', *Global Asia*, 6:3 (2011), 46–58.

Healy, M. 'NATO Cancels War Games to Shift Scenarios', *Los Angeles Times*, 20 May 1990, www.latimes.com/archives/la-xpm-1990–05–20-mn-179-story.html

Heginbotham, E. and R. Samuels, 'Active Denial: Redesigning Japan's Response to China's Military Challenge', *International Security*, 42:4 (2018), 128–169.

Heuser, B. 'The Development of NATO's Nuclear Strategy', *Contemporary European History*, 4:1 (1994), 37–66.

Heuser, B. and K. Stoddart, 'Difficult Europeans: NATO and Tactical/Non-strategic Nuclear Weapons in the Cold War', *Diplomacy and Statecraft*, 28:3 (2017), 454–476.

Higgins, A. 'On a Tiny Norwegian Island, America Keeps an Eye on Russia', *New York Times*, 13 June 2017, www.nytimes.com/2017/06/13/world/europe/arctic-norway-russia-radar.html

Higgott, R. 'International Political Institutions', in S. Binder, R. Rhodes, and B. Rockman (eds), *The Oxford Handbook of Political Institutions* (Oxford: Oxford University Press, 2008).

'Highlights from our Interview with Donald Trump on Foreign Policy', *New York Times*, 26 March 2016, www.nytimes.com/2016/03/27/us/politics/donald-trump-interview-highlights.html

Holst, J. 'The Nordic Region: Changing Perspectives in International Relations', *Annals of the American Academy of Political and Social Science*, 512 (1990), 8–15.

Holst, J. 'The Pattern of Nordic Security', *Daedalus*, 113:2 (1984), 195–225.

Holst, J. 'A Nuclear Weapon-free Zone in the Nordic Area: Conditions and Options – A Norwegian View', *Bulletin of Peace Proposals*, 14:4 (1983), 227–238.

Holst, J. 'Norwegian Security Policy for the 1980s', *Cooperation and Conflict*, 17:4 (1982), 207–236.

Hong-nam, J. *America's Commitment to South Korea: The First Decade of the Nixon Doctrine* (Cambridge: Cambridge University Press, 2009).

Honkanen, K. *The Influence of Small States on NATO Decision-making* (Stockholm: FOI, 2002).

Hornung, J. *Modelling a Stronger US–Japan Alliance: Assessing US Alliance Structures* (Washington, DC: Centre for Strategic and International Studies, 2015).

Hughes, C. 'Japan's "Resentful Realism" and Balancing China's Rise', *Chinese Journal of International Politics*, 9:2 (2016), 109–150.

Hughes, L. 'Why Japan Will Not Go Nuclear (Yet); International and Domestic Constraints on the Nuclearization of Japan', *International Security*, 31:4 (2007), 67–96.

Humphrey, H. and J. Glenn, *US Troop Withdrawal from the Republic of Korea: A Report to the US Senate Committee on Foreign Relations* (Washington, DC: US Government Printing Office, 1978).

Huth, P. 'The Extended Deterrent Value of Nuclear Weapons', *Journal of Conflict Resolution*, 34:2 (1990), 270–290.

Huth, P. *Extended Deterrence and the Prevention of War* (New Haven, CT: Yale University Press, 1988).

Huth P. and B. Russett, 'Testing Deterrence Theory: Rigor Makes a Difference', *World Politics*, 42:4 (1990), 466–501.

Huth P. and B. Russett, 'What Makes Deterrence Work? Cases from 1900–1980', *World Politics*, 36:4 (1984), 496–526.

Hymans, J. 'Veto Players, Nuclear Energy, and Nonproliferation: Domestic Institutional Barriers to a Japanese Bomb', *International Security*, 36:2 (2011), 154–189.

Hymans, J. *The Psychology of Nuclear Proliferation: Identity, Emotions, and Foreign Policy* (Cambridge: Cambridge University Press, 2006).

ICAN [International Campaign to Abolish Nuclear Weapons], 'Norway', www.icanw.org/norway

In-Bum Chun, 'Korean Defense Reform: History and Challenges', *Brookings Institution Report*, 31 October 2017, www.brookings.edu/research/korean-defense-reform-history-and-challenges/

Jacobsen, A. 'Scandinavia, SIGINT and the Cold War', *Intelligence and National Security*, 16:1 (2001), 209–242.

Jackson, G. 'Actors and Institutions', in G. Morgan, J. Campbell, C. Crouch, O. Kaj Pedersen, and R. Whitley (eds), *The Oxford Handbook of Comparative Institutional Analysis* (Oxford: Oxford University Press, 2015).

Jackson, V. *On the Brink: Trump, Kim, and the Threat of Nuclear War* (Cambridge: Cambridge University Press, 2019).

Jackson, V. *Rival Reputations: Coercion and Credibility in US–North Korea Relations* (Cambridge: Cambridge University Press, 2016).

Jansen, M. *The Making of Modern Japan* (Cambridge, MA: Harvard University Press, 2000).

'Japan Abstains as Nuclear Arms Ban Treaty Talks Start at UN', *Japan Times*, 28 March 2017. www.japantimes.co.jp/news/2017/03/28/national/japan-abstains-talks-start-u-n-nuclear-arms-ban-treaty/

'Japan Officially Gave US Consent to Bring in Nuclear Weapons Ahead of Okinawa Reversion Accord: Document', *The Japan Times*, 14 August 2017, www.japantimes.co.jp/news/2017/08/14/national/history/japan-officially-gave-u-s-consent-bring-nukes-ahead-okinawa-reversion-accord-document/

'Japanese Defence Policy', *Survival*, 13:1 (1971), 2–8.

Jeong, A. 'North Korea Test-Fires Projectiles, Aims to Pressure US on Sanctions Relief', *Wall Street Journal*, 28 November 2019, www.wsj.com/articles/north-korea-test-fires-projectiles-aims-to-pressure-u-s-on-sanctions-relief-11574939934

Jervis, R. 'Deterrence Theory Revisited', *World Politics*, 31:2 (1979), 289–324.

Johnson, C. *Blowback: The Costs and Consequences of American Empire* (New York: Metropolitan Books, 2000).

Johnson, J. 'South Korean Plans to Kill Kim Likely to Reinforce North's View that Nukes Are Needed', *Japan Times*, 11 September 2016, www.japantimes.co.jp/news/2016/09/11/asia-pacific/south-korean-military-floats-plan-decapitation-strikes-decimate-norths-leadership-report/#.WYuuIHcjFPM

Johnson, L. 'Remarks at the State Dinner at Parliament House, Kuala Lumpur, Malaysia, October 30, 1966', in *Public Papers of the Presidents, 1966, Book II*, available at: www.presidency.ucsb.edu/ws/index.php?pid=27971#axzz1n4DpGsuo

Jones, D. 'Post-INF Treaty Attitudes in East Asia', *Asian Survey*, 30:5 (1990), 481–492.

Jones, M. 'Targeting China: US Nuclear Planning and "Massive Retaliation" in East Asia, 1953–1955', *Journal of Cold War Studies*, 10:4 (2008), 37–65.

Jones, M. 'The Radford Bombshell: Anglo-Australian-US Relations, Nuclear Weapons and the Defence of South East Asia, 1954–1957', *Journal of Strategic Studies*, 27:4 (2004), 636–662.

Jorgensen-Dahl, A. 'The Soviet–Norwegian Maritime Disputes in the Arctic: Law and Politics', *Ocean Development and International Law*, 21:4 (1990), 411–429.

Kaplan, L. *The Long Entanglement: NATO's First 50 Years* (Westport, CT: Praeger, 1999).

Katz, J. and K. Quealy, 'Which Country is America's Strongest Ally? For Republicans, It's Australia', *New York Times*, 3 February 2017, www.nytimes.com/interactive/2017/02/03/upshot/which-country-do-americans-like-most-for-republicans-its-australia.html

Katzenstein, P. *Cultural Norms and National Security: Police and Military in Postwar Japan* (Ithaca, NY: Cornell University Press, 1996).

Kaufmann W. (ed.), *Military Policy and National Security* (Princeton, NJ: Princeton University Press, 1956).

Keller, P. 'Germany in NATO: The Status Quo Ally', *Survival*, 54:3 (2012), 95–110.

Keohane, R. *After Hegemony: Cooperation and Discord in the World Political Economy* (Princeton, NJ: Princeton University Press, 1984).

Keohane, R. 'The Big Influence of Small Allies', *Foreign Policy*, 2 (1971), 161–182.

Keohane, R. and L. Martin, 'The Promise of Institutionalist Theory', *International Security*, 20:1 (1995), 39–51.

Kim, D. 'How to Keep South Korea from Going Nuclear', *Bulletin of the Atomic Scientists*, 9 March 2020, https://thebulletin.org/2020/03/how-to-keep-south-korea-from-going-nuclear/

Kim, D., N. Wright, and K. Lee, 'The United States Needs a Gray-Zone Strategy Against North Korea', *Foreign Policy*, 14 May 2019, https://foreignpolicy.com/2019/05/14/the-united-states-needs-a-gray-zone-strategy-against-north-korea-missile-test-nuclear/

Kim, H. 'The Sato Government and the Politics of Okinawa Reversion', *Asian Survey*, 13:110 (1973), 1021–1035.

Kim, Hyung-A. 'Heavy and Chemical Industrialisation, 1973–1979: South Korea's Homeland Security Measures', in Hyung-A Kim and C. Sorensen (eds), *Reassessing the Park Chung Hee Era, 1961–1979: Development, Political Thought, Democracy, and Cultural Influence* (Seattle, WA: University of Washington Press, 2011).

Kim, J. 'Military Considerations for OPCON Transfer on the Korean Peninsula', *Council on Foreign Relations Blog*, 20 March 2020, www.cfr.org/blog/military-considerations-opcon-transfer-korean-peninsula

Kim, Seung-Young, 'Security, Nationalism, and the Pursuit of Nuclear Weapons and Missiles: The South Korean Case, 1970–82', *Diplomacy and Statecraft*, 12:4 (2001), 53–80.

Kim, Sung-han and S. Snyder, 'Denuclearizing North Korea: Time for Plan B', *Washington Quarterly*, 42:4 (2020), 75–90.

Kim, T. *The Supply Side of Security: A Market Theory of Military Alliances* (Stanford, CA: Stanford University Press, 2016).

Kissinger, H. *The White House Years* (London: George Weidenfeld and Nicholson, 1979).

Kissinger, H. *Nuclear Weapons and Foreign Policy* (New York: Harper, 1957).

Knudsen, O. 'Norway: Domestically Driven Foreign Policy', *Annals of the American Academy*, 512 (1990), 101–115.

Koalitionsvertrag 19. Legislaturperiode (signed Berlin 12 March 2018), www.bundesregierung.de/resource/blob/975226/847984/5b8bc23590d4cb2892b31c987ad672b7/2018-03-14-koalitionsvertrag-data.pdf?download=1

Kohl, W. *French Nuclear Diplomacy* (Princeton, NJ: Princeton University Press, 1971).

Komine, Y. *Negotiating the US–Japan Alliance: Japan Confidential* (London and New York: Routledge, 2017).

Komine, Y. 'Whither a "Resurgent Japan": The Nixon Doctrine and Japan's Defense Buildup', *Journal of Cold War Studies*, 16:3 (2014), 88–128.

Komine, Y. 'Okinawa Confidential, 1969: Exploring the Linkage between the Nuclear Issue and the Base Issue', *Diplomatic History*, 27:4 (2013), 807–840.

Krasner, S. 'Structural Causes and Regime Consequences: Regimes as Intervening Variables', *International Organization*, 36:2 (1982), 185–205.

Kristensen, H. 'Declassified: US Nuclear Weapons at Sea', *Federation of American Scientists Blog*, 3 February 2016, https://fas.org/blogs/security/2016/02/nuclear-weapons-at-sea/

Kristensen, H. 'When the Boomers Went to South Korea', *Federation of American Scientists Blog*, 4 October 2011, https://fas.org/blogs/security/2011/10/ssbnrok/

Kristensen, H. 'Japan, TLAM/N, and Extended Deterrence', *Federation of American Scientists Blog*, 2 July 2009, available at: https://fas.org/blogs/security/2009/07/tlam/

Kristensen, H. 'Japan Under the US Nuclear Umbrella', *Nautilus Institute for Security and Sustainability*, 21 July 1999, https://nautilus.org/supporting-documents/japan-under-the-us-nuclear-umbrella/

Kristensen, H. and R. Norris, 'A History of US Nuclear Weapons in South Korea', *Bulletin of the Atomic Scientists*, 73:6 (2017), 349–357.

Kristensen, H., R. Norris, and M. McKinzie, *Chinese Nuclear Forces and US Nuclear War Planning* (Washington, DC: Federation of American Scientists and the Natural Resources Defense Council, 2006).

Kroenig, M. *The Logic of American Nuclear Strategy: Why Strategic Superiority Matter*s (Oxford: Oxford University Press, 2018).

Kruger, D. 'Institutionalizing NATO's Military Bureaucracy: The Making of an Integrated Chain of Command', in S. Mayer (ed.), *NATO's Post-Cold War Politics: The Changing Provision of Security* (Houndmills: Palgrave Macmillan, 2014).

Kugler, R. 'The Great Strategy Debate: NATO's Evolution in the 1960s', *RAND Note*, N-3252-FF/RC, 1991.

Kupchan, C. 'NATO and the Persian Gulf: Examining Intra-Alliance Behavior', *International Organization,* 42:2 (1988), 317–346.

Kurosaki, A. 'Public Opinion, Party Politics and Alliance: The Influence of Domestic Politics on Japan's Reliance on the US Nuclear Umbrella, 1964–8', *The International History Review*, 42:4 (2020), 774-793.

Kurosaki, A. 'Nuclear Energy and Nuclear Weapon Potential: A Historical Analysis of Japan in the 1960s', *Nonproliferation Review*, 24:1/2 (2017), 47–65.

Lake, D. 'Beyond Anarchy: The Importance of Security Institutions', *International Security*, 26:1 (2001), 129–160.

Landler, M. 'As Next Trump-Kim Summit Nears, Japan Worries US Will Leave it in the Dark', *New York Times*, 23 January 2019, www.nytimes.com/2019/01/23/world/asia/shinzo-abe-north-korea-trump.html

Landler, M. 'US Resists Push by Allies for Tactical Nuclear Cuts', *New York Times*, 22 April 2010, www.nytimes.com/2010/04/23/world/europe/23diplo.html

Lanoszka, A. 'Alliances and Nuclear Proliferation in the Trump Era', *The Washington Quarterly*, 41:4 (2019), 85–101.

Lanoszka, A. *Atomic Assurance: The Alliance Politics of Nuclear Proliferation* (Ithaca, NY: Cornell University Press, 2018).

Larsen, J. *The Future of US Non-strategic Nuclear Weapons and Implications for NATO Drifting Toward the Foreseeable Future: A Report Prepared in Accordance with the Requirements of the 2005–06 Manfred Worner Fellowship for NATO Public Diplomacy Division* (Brussels: NATO, 31 October 2006).

Layne, C. 'This Time It's Real: The End of Unipolarity and the Pax Americana', *International Studies Quarterly,* 56:1 (2012), 203–213.

Leah, C. 'Deterrence Beyond Down Under: Australia and US Security Guarantees Since 1955', *Journal of Strategic Studies*, 39:4 (2016), 521–534.

Leah, C. and R. Lyon, 'Three Visions of the Bomb: Australian Thinking About Nuclear Weapons and Strategy', *Australian Journal of International Affairs*, 64:4 (2010), 449–477.

Lee, D. 'Australia and Allied Strategy in the Far East, 1952–1957', *Journal of Strategic Studies*, 16:4 (1993), 516–522.

Lee Jae-bong, 'US Deployment of Nuclear Weapons in 1950s South Korea and North Korea's Nuclear Development: Toward Denuclearisation of the Korean Peninsula', *Japan Focus: The Asia Pacific Journal*, 7:3 (2009), https://apjjf.org/-Lee-Jae-Bong/3053/article.pdf

Leeds, B. 'Alliance Reliability in Times of War: Explaining State Decisions to Violate Treaties', *International Organization*, 57:4 (2003), 801–827.

Legge, J. M. 'Theater Nuclear Weapons and the NATO Strategy of Flexible Response', *RAND Corporation Paper*, R-2964-FF, March 1983.

Lieber, K. and D. Press, *The Myth of the Nuclear Revolution: Power Politics in the Atomic Age* (Ithaca, NY: Cornell University Press, 2020).

'Letter Sent by the Minister for External Affairs to the Acting Secretary-General of the United Nations Concerning Resolution 1664, 15 March 1962', tabled in *Commonwealth Parliamentary Debates* (House of Representatives), 5 April 1962.

Levy, J. and W. Thompson, 'Hegemonic Threats and Great Power Balancing in Europe, 1495–1999', *Security Studies*, 14(1), 2005, 1–33.

Lewis, J. 'Extended Deterrence Policy Committee', *Arms Control Wonk*, 19 October 2010, www.armscontrolwonk.com/archive/203057/extended-deterrence-policy-committee/

Lippert, M. 'Here's the Real Value in the US–South Korea Alliance', *Defense One*, 30 October 2018, www.defenseone.com/ideas/2018/10/heres-real-value-us-south-korean-alliance/152445/

Lodgaard, S. 'Norway and NATO at 50', *Perceptions: Journal of International Affairs*, 41:1 (1999), http://sam.gov.tr/pdf/perceptions/Volume-IV/march-may-1999/SVERRE-LODGAARD.pdf

Lodgaard, S. 'A Nuclear Weapon Free Zone in the North? A Reappraisal', *Bulletin of Peace Proposals*, 11:1 (1980), 33–39.

Lodgaard, S. and N. Petter Gleditsch, 'Norway – the Not So Reluctant Ally', *Cooperation and Conflict*, 12:4 (1977), 209–219.

Lowe, P. *Contending with Nationalism and Communism: British Policy Towards Southeast Asia, 1945–65* (Houndmills: Palgrave Macmillan, 2009).

Lowndes, V. 'The Institutional Approach', in D. Marsh and G. Stoker (eds), *Theory and Methods in Political Science* (Basingstoke: Palgrave Macmillan, 2010).

Lowy Institute for International Policy, 'Importance of the US Alliance', https://lowyinstitutepoll.lowyinstitute.org/australia-us-relations/

Lund, J. *Don't Rock the Boat: Reinforcing Norway in Crisis and War* (Santa Monica, CA: RAND Corporation, 1989).

Lunde Saxi, H. 'British and German Initiatives for Defence Cooperation: The Joint Expeditionary Force and the Framework Nations Concept', *Defence Studies*, 17:2 (2017), 171–197.

Lundestad, G. 'The Evolution of Norwegian Security Policy: Alliance with the West and Reassurance in the East', *Scandinavian Journal of History*, 17:2–3 (1992), 227–256.

Lutsch, A. 'Merely 'Docile Self-Deception'? German Experiences with Nuclear Consultation in NATO', *Journal of Strategic Studies*, 39:4 (2016), 535–558.

Lyon, R. 'Australia: Back to the Future?', in M. Alagappa (ed.), *The Long Shadow: Nuclear Weapons and Security in 21st Century Asia* (Stanford, CA: Stanford University Press, 2008).

McArdle Kelleher, C. *Germany and the Politics of Nuclear Weapons* (New York and London: Columbia University Press, 1975).
McCalla, R. 'NATO's Persistence After the Cold War', *International Organization,* 50:3 (1996), 445–475.
Macintyre, T. *Anglo-German Relations During the Labour Governments, 1964–1970* (Manchester: Manchester University Press, 2007).
McManus, R. 'Making It Personal: The Role of Leader-Specific Signals in Extended Deterrence', *The Journal of Politics*, 80:3 (2018), 982–995.
McMillan, S. *Neither Confirm Nor Deny: The Nuclear Ships Dispute Between New Zealand and the United States* (Sydney: Allen and Unwin, 1987).
McNamara, R. 'Speech to NATO Council, Athens, 5 May 1962', in P. Bobbit, L. Freedman, and G. Treverton (eds), *US Nuclear Strategy: A Reader* (Houndmills: Macmillan Press, 1989).
March, J. and J. Olsen, 'Elaborating the "New Institutionalism"', in S. Binder, R. Rhodes, and B. Rockman (eds), *The Oxford Handbook of Political Institutions* (Oxford: Oxford University Press, 2008).
Mattox, G. 'NATO Enlargement and the United States: A Deliberate and Necessary Decision?', in C. David and J. Lévesque (eds), *The Future of NATO: Enlargement, Russia, and European Security* (Montreal: McGill-Queen's University Press, 1999).
Mayer, S. 'Introduction: NATO as an Organization and Bureaucracy', in S. Mayer (ed.), *NATO's Post-Cold War Politics: The Changing Provision of Security* (Houndsmills: Palgrave Macmillan, 2014).
Mearsheimer, J. 'A Realist Reply: The False Promise of International Institutions', *International Security,* 20:1 (1995), 82–93.
Mearsheimer, J. 'A Strategic Misstep: The Maritime Strategy and Deterrence in Europe', *International Security*, 11:2 (1986), 3–57.
Meier, O. 'France and Germany Agree on Truce over Nuclear Arms Control Committee as NATO Works on Deterrence and Defense Posture Review', *Arms Control Now*, 3 October 2011, www.armscontrol.org/blog/2011–10–03/france-germany-agree-truce-over-nuclear-arms-control-committee-nato-works-deterrence
Meier, O. 'NATO Revises Nuclear Policy', *Arms Control Association*, December 2010, www.armscontrol.org/act/2010–12/nato-revises-nuclear-policy
'Memoranda of Conversations between James R. Schlesinger and Park Chung-hee and Suh Jyong-chul, August 26, 1975', History and Public Policy Program Digital Archive, Gerald R. Ford Presidential Library, National Security Adviser Presidential Country Files for East Asia and the Pacific, Box 9, Korea (11), obtained by Charles Kraus, http://digitalarchive.wilsoncenter.org/document/114633.pdf?v=240ba63526da6f1f845710c0d685600f
Memorandum from Allan Griffith to Peter Lawler, 'Australian Nuclear Policy', 16 May 1967, NAA [National Archives of Australia]: A1209, 1965/6470, A1209.
Messemer, A. 'Konrad Adenauer: Defence Diplomat on the Backstage', in J. Gaddis, P. Gordon, E. May, and J. Rosenberg (eds), *Cold War Statesmen Confront the Bomb: Nuclear Diplomacy Since 1945* (Oxford: Oxford University Press, 1999).
Mills Rodrigo, C. 'Prime Minister Says US Won't Deploy Missiles in Australia', *The Hill*, 5 August 2019, https://thehill.com/policy/defense/456150-prime-minister-says-us-wont-deploy-missiles-in-australia

Ministry of Defense, 'The Guidelines for Japan-US Defense Cooperation (September 23, 1997)', www.mod.go.jp/e/d_act/us/anpo/19970923.htmlwww
Ministry of Defense, *Defence of Japan 2013*, www.mod.go.jp/e/publ/w_paper/2013.htmlwww
Ministry of Defense, 'National Defense Program Guidelines for FY 2014 and Beyond (Summary)', www.mod.go.jp/e/d_act/d_policy/national.html
Ministry of Foreign Affairs, *Setting the Course for Norwegian Foreign and Security Policy*, Meld. St. 36 (2016–2017), report to the Storting (White Paper), www.regjeringen.no/contentassets/0688496c2b764f029955cc6e2f27799c/en-gb/pdfs/stm201620170036000engpdfs.pdf
Mochizuki, M. 'Three Reasons Why Japan Will Likely Continue to Reject Nuclear Weapons', *Washington Post*, 6 November 2017, https://www.washingtonpost.com/news/monkey-cage/wp/2017/11/06/japan-is-likely-to-retain-its-non-nuclear-principles-heres-why/
Moller, J. E. 'Trilateral Defence Cooperation in the North: An Assessment of Interoperability between Norway, Sweden and Finland', *Defence Studies*, 19:3 (2019), 235–256.
Montgomery, M. 'US, Japan Extend Nuclear Agreement', *Arms Control Today*, September 2018, www.armscontrol.org/act/2018–09/news-briefs/us-japan-extend-nuclear-agreement
Morgan, P. 'The State of Deterrence in International Politics Today', *Contemporary Security Policy*, 33:1 (2012), 85–107.
Morgan, P. *Deterrence Now* (Cambridge: Cambridge University Press, 2003).
Morgan, R. 'Australians View Terrorism and War as the Most Important Problems Facing the World After Terrorist Incidents and Rising Global Tensions', 14 July 2017, www.roymorgan.com/findings/7263-issues-facing-the-world-terrorism-verbatims-mid-2017–201707141606
Muller, H. 'Flexible Responses: NATO Reactions to the US Nuclear Posture Review', *Nonproliferation Review*, 18:1 (2011), 103–124.
Munroe, T. and J. Kim, 'US Flies B-52 Over South Korea After North's Nuclear Test', *Reuters*, 11 January 2016, www.reuters.com/article/us-northkorea-nuclear/u-s-flies-b-52-over-south-korea-after-norths-nuclear-test-idUSKCN0UN0Y420160111
Nakanishi, T. 'US Policy and Japan', *The Washington Quarterly*, 10:1 (1987), 81–97.
'National Defense Program Outline, October 29 1976', http://worldjpn.grips.ac.jp/documents/texts/docs/19761029.O1E.html
'NATO Deterrence and Defence Posture Review, 20 May 2012', www.nato.int/cps/en/natohq/official_texts_87597.htm
'NATO Leaders: Lord Ismay', www.nato.int/cps/en/natohq/declassified_137930.htm
'NATO's Nuclear Forces in the New Security Environment', *NATO/OTAN Handbook* (Brussels: NATO Office of Information and Press, Brussels, 2001).
'NATO's Nuclear Weapons: The Rationale for No-first-use', *Arms Control Association* (July 1999), www.armscontrol.org/act/1999–07/features/natos-nuclear-weapons-rationale-first-use
Neubauer, S. 'The Plan to Deploy US Troops to Norway: How Oslo and Moscow Could Respond', *Foreign Affairs*, 9 November 2016, www.foreignaffairs.com/articles/norway/2016–11–09/plan-deploy-us-troops-norway

Neukirch, R. 'Westerwelle legt sich mit Clinton an', *Der Spiegel*, 25 February 2010, www.spiegel.de/politik/deutschland/streit-ueber-atomwaffen-abruestung-westerwelle-legt-sich-mit-clinton-an-a-680122.html

Njolstad, O. 'Atomic Intelligence in Norway During the Cold War', *Journal of Strategic Studies*, 29:4 (2006), 653–673.

Norris, R., W. Arkin, and W. Burr, 'Where They Were: How Much Did Japan Know?', *Bulletin of the Atomic Scientists* (January–February 2000), 11–13, 78–79.

Norwegian Ministry of Foreign Affairs, *Setting the Course for Norwegian Foreign and Security Policy*, Meld. St. 36 (2016–2017), report to the Storting (White Paper), www.regjeringen.no/contentassets/0688496c2b764f029955cc6e2f277 99c/en-gb/pdfs/stm201620170036000engpdfs.pdf

O'Hanlon, M. 'Stopping a North Korean Invasion: Why Defending South Korea Is Easier than the Pentagon Thinks', *International Security*, 22:4 (1998), 135–170.

O'Malley, N. 'US Bid for Multi-billion Dollar Nuclear Aircraft Carrier Strike Group in Perth', *Sydney Morning Herald*, 1 August 2012, www.smh.com.au/politics/federal/us-bid-for-multibillion-dollar-nuclear-aircraft-carrier-strike-group-in-perth-20120801–23emq.html

O'Neil, A. *Asia, the US and Extended Nuclear Deterrence: Atomic Umbrellas in the Twenty-First Century* (London and New York: Routledge, 2013).

O'Neil, A. 'Australia and the South Pacific Nuclear Free Zone Treaty: A Reinterpretation', *Australian Journal of Political Science*, 39:3 (2004), 567–583.

Oberdorfer, D. *The Two Koreas: A Contemporary History* (Reading, MA: Addison-Wesley, 1997).

Oberdorfer, D. 'How to Make a Japanese Brouhaha', *Washington Post*, 20 March 1983, www.washingtonpost.com/archive/opinions/1983/03/20/how-to-make-a-japanese-brouhaha/0e508dd9–105b-4673–98aa-1e63fe8eae08/

Office of the Assistant to the Secretary of Defense, 'History of the Custody of Deployment of Nuclear Weapons: July 1945 through September 1977', February 1978, https://nsarchive2.gwu.edu//dc.html?doc=6532113-National-Security-Archive-Doc-01-Office-of-the

Office of the Secretary of Defense, *Nuclear Posture Review* (2018) https://media.defense.gov/2018/Feb/02/2001872886/-1/-1/1/2018-NUCLEAR-POSTURE-REVIEW-FINAL-REPORT.PDF

Ole Sandnes, H. *The 1970–1974 Combat Aircraft Analysis* (Trondheim: Tapir Academic Press, 2010).

Olsen, E. 'The Maritime Strategy in the Western Pacific', *Naval War College Review*, 40:4 (1987), 38–49.

Orvik, N. 'Scandinavia, NATO, and Northern Security', *International Organization*, 20:3 (1966), 380–396.

Osgood, R. *NATO: The Entangling Alliance* (Chicago, IL: University of Chicago Press, 1962).

Ota, M. 'Conceptual Twist of Japanese Nuclear Policy: Its Ambivalence and Coherence Under the US Nuclear Umbrella', *Journal for Peace and Nuclear Disarmament*, 1:1 (2018), 193–208.

Ota, M. 'Japan warned US over reductions to nuclear arsenal and sought flexible deterrence, 2009 memo reveals', *Japan Times*, 4 April 2018, www.japantimes.co.jp/news/2018/04/04/national/politics-diplomacy/japan-warned-u-s-reductions-nuclear-arsenal-sought-flexible-deterrence-2009-memo-reveals/

Papayoanou, P. 'Intra-Alliance Bargaining and US Bosnia Policy', *Journal of Conflict Resolution,* 41:1 (1997), 91–116.

'Parliamentary Statement by the Prime Minister on the Joint Facilities, 22 November 1988', https://pmtranscripts.pmc.gov.au/sites/default/files/original/00007438.pdf

Payne, K. 'US Nuclear Weapons and Deterrence: Realist Versus Utopian Thinking', *Air & Space Power Journal* (July–August 2015), 63–71.

Payne, K. *Deterrence in the Second Nuclear Age* (Lexington, KY: The University Press of Kentucky, 1996).

Pedlow, G. 'The Evolution of NATO's Command Structure: 1951–2009', https://shape.nato.int/resources/21/Evolution%20of%20NATO%20Cmd%20Structure%201951–2009.pdf

Pedlow, G. 'The Evolution of NATO Strategy, 1949–1969', in G. Pedlow (ed.), *NATO Strategy Documents, 1949–1969* (Brussels: NATO, 1997).

Pemberton, G. *All the Way: Australia's Road to Vietnam* (Sydney: Allen and Unwin, 1987).

Peng, T. 'China's Changing Japan Policy in the Late 1960s and Early 1970s and the Impact on Relations with the United States', *Journal of American-East Asian Relations*, 15 (2008), 147–171.

Petersen, N. 'Footnoting' as a Political Instrument: Denmark's NATO Policy in the 1980s', *Cold War History*, 12:2 (2012), 295–317.

Petersen, N. 'The Security Policies of Small NATO Countries: Factors of Change', *Cooperation and Conflict*, 13 (1988), 145–162.

Petersson, M. and H. Lunde Saxi, 'Shifted Roles: Explaining Danish and Norwegian Alliance Strategy 1949–2009', *Journal of Strategic Studies*, 36:6 (2013), 761–788.

Pollack, J. 'Denuclearization of the Korean Peninsula: Reviewing the Precedents', *Arms Control Wonk*, 10 June 2018, www.armscontrolwonk.com/archive/1205354/denuclearization-of-the-korean-peninsula-reviewing-the-precedents/

Pollack, J. and M. Reiss, 'South Korea: The Tyranny of Geography and the Vexations of History', in K. Campbell, R. Einhorn, and M. Reiss (eds), *The Nuclear Tipping Point: Why States Reconsider Their Nuclear Choices* (Washington, DC: Brookings Institution, 2004).

Pressman, J. *Warring Friends: Alliance Restraint in International Politics* (Ithaca, NY: Cornell University Press, 2008).

Przystup, J. 'The Enduring Relevance of the US–Japan Alliance', *INSS Strategic Forum*, July 2019, https://inss.ndu.edu/Portals/68/Documents/stratforum/SF-300.pdf?ver=2019-07-23-142433-990

Putnam, R. 'Diplomacy and Domestic Politics: The Logic of Two Level Games', *International Organization,* 42:3 (1988), 427–460.

Pyne, C. 'Ministerial (Defence) Statement: Australia-United States Joint Facilities', *Commonwealth Parliamentary Debates* (House of Representatives), 20 February 2019.

Quackenbush, S. *Understanding General Deterrence: Theory and Application* (New York: Palgrave Macmillan, 2011).

Quester, G. 'Japan and the Nuclear Non-Proliferation Treaty', *Asian Survey*, 10:9 (1970), 765–778.

Rafferty, K. 'An Institutional Reinterpretation of Cold War Alliance Systems: Insights for Alliance Theory', *Canadian Journal of Political Science*, 36:2 (2003), 341–362.

Ramstad, E. 'Firing Drill Increases Tensions in Korea', *Wall Street Journal*, 20 December 2010, www.wsj.com/articles/SB10001424052748704138604576029240348016046

Rapp-Hooper, M., *Shields of the Republic: The Triumph and Peril of America's Alliances* (Cambridge, MA: Harvard University Press, 2020).

Rapp-Hooper, M. 'Decoupling is Back in Asia: A 1960s Playbook Won't Save These Problems', *War on the Rocks*, 7 September 2017, https://warontherocks.com/2017/09/decoupling-is-back-in-asia-a-1960s-playbook-wont-solve-these-problems/

Reiss, M. *Without the Bomb: The Politics of Nuclear Nonproliferation* (New York: Columbia University Press, 1988).

Reiter, D. 'Learning, Realism, and Alliances: The Weight of the Shadow of the Past', *World Politics,* 46:2 (1994), 490–526.

Reiter, E. and H. Gärtner (eds), *Small States and Alliances* (Heidelberg and New York: Physica-Verlag, 2001).

Review of Australia's Defence Capabilities: Report to the Minister for Defence by Mr Paul Dibb (Canberra: Australian Government Publishing Service, 1986).

Reynolds, W. *Australia's Bid for the Atomic Bomb* (Melbourne: Melbourne University Press, 2000).

Reynolds, W. 'The Wars that were Planned: Australia's Forward Defence Posture in Asia and the Role of Tactical Nuclear Weapons, 1945–1967', *Australian Journal of International Affairs*, 53:3 (1999), 295–309.

Richelson, J. *Spying on the Bomb: American Nuclear Intelligence from Nazi Germany to Iran to North Korea* (New York: W. W. Norton, 2006).

Risse-Kappen, T. *Cooperation Among Democracies: The European Influence on US Foreign Policy* (Princeton, NJ: Princeton University Press, 1995).

Riste, O. *The Norwegian Intelligence Service: 1945–1970* (London: Frank Cass, 1999).

Roberts, B. 'On Adapting Nuclear Deterrence to Reduce Nuclear Risk', *Daedalus*, 149:2 (2020), 69–83.

Roberts, B. 'Deterrence and Détente on the Korean Peninsula', *Council on Foreign Relations Blog*, 22 April 2019, www.cfr.org/blog/deterrence-and-detente-korean-peninsula

Roberts, B. *The Case for U.S. Nuclear Weapons in the 21st Century* (Stanford, CA: Stanford University Press, 2016).

Roberts, B. 'Extended Deterrence and Strategic Stability in Northeast Asia', *NIDS Visiting Scholar Paper Series*, 1 (2013), www.nids.mod.go.jp/english/publication/visiting/pdf/01.pdf

Roehrig, T. *Japan, South Korea, and the United States Nuclear Umbrella: Deterrence After the Cold War* (New York: Columbia University Press, 2017).

Roman, P. 'Curtis LeMay and the Origins of NATO Atomic Targeting', *Journal of Strategic Studies,* 16:1 (1993), 46–74.

Rose, F. 'Is the 2018 Nuclear Posture Review as Bad as the Critics Claim It Is?', *Brookings Institution Policy Brief*, April 2018, www.brookings.edu/wp-content/uploads/2018/04/fp_20180413_2018_nuclear_posture_review.pdf

Rosenbaum, D. 'US to Pull A-Bombs from South Korea', *New York Times*, 20 October 1991, www.nytimes.com/1991/10/20/world/us-to-pull-a-bombs-from-south-korea.html

Rost Rublee, M. *Nonproliferation Norms: Why States Choose Nuclear Restraint* (Athens, GA and London: University of Georgia Press, 2009).

Rothstein, R. *Alliances and Small Powers* (New York and London: Columbia University Press, 1968).
Ruggie, J. 'Multilateralism: The Anatomy of an Institution', *International Organization,* 46:3 (1992), 561–598.
Ruhle, M. 'NATO and Extended Deterrence in a Multinuclear World', *Comparative Strategy*, 28:1 (2009), 110–116.
Rynning, S. 'The Divide: France, Germany and Political NATO', *International Affairs,* 93:2 (2017), 267–289.
Samuels, R. *Securing Japan: Tokyo's Grand Strategy and the Future of East Asia* (Ithaca, NY: Cornell University Press, 2007).
Samuels, R. *'Rich Nation, Strong Army': National Security and the Technological Transformation of Japan* (Ithaca, NY: Cornell University Press, 1994).
Samuels R. and J. Schoff, 'Japan's Nuclear Hedge: Beyond "Allergy" and Breakout', *Political Science Quarterly*, 130(3), 2015, 473–503.
Sanders, E. 'Historical Institutionalism', in S. Binder, R. Rhodes, and B. Rockman (eds), *The Oxford Handbook of Political Institutions* (Oxford: Oxford University Press, 2008).
Sayle, T. A. *Enduring Alliance: A History of NATO and the Postwar Global Order* (Ithaca, NY: Cornell University Press, 2019).
Scaparotti, C. M. and C. B. Bell, *Moving Out: A Comprehensive Assessment of European Military Mobility* (Washington, DC: Atlantic Council, 2020).
Schelling, T. *Arms and Influence* (New Haven, CT: Yale University Press, 1966).
Schelling, T. *The Strategy of Conflict* (Cambridge, MA: Harvard University Press, 1960).
Schmemann, S. 'Kohl Sets Stage for NATO Fight by Laying Out New Arms Policy', *New York Times*, 28 April 1989, www.nytimes.com/1989/04/28/world/kohl-sets-stage-for-nato-fight-by-laying-out-new-arms-policy.html
Schmidt, G. 'From London to Brussels: Emergence and Development of a Politico-Administrative System', in S. Mayer (ed.), *NATO's Post-Cold War Politics: The Changing Provision of Security* (Houndmills: Palgrave Macmillan, 2014).
Schmidt, H. 'The 1977 Alastair Buchan Memorial Lecture', *Survival*, 20:1 (1978), 3–4.
Schnabel, J. and R. Watson, *The Joint Chiefs of Staff and National Policy,* Vol. III: *1950–1951, The Korean War, Part One* (Washington, DC: Office of the Chairman of the Joints Chiefs of Staff, 1998).
Schofield, J. *Strategic Nuclear Sharing* (Houndmills: Palgrave Macmillan, 2014).
Schrafstetter, S. 'The Long Shadow of the Past: History, Memory and Debate Over West Germany's Nuclear Status, 1954–69', *History and Memory*, 16:1 (2004), 118–145.
Schroeder, P. 'Alliances, 1815–1945: Weapons of Power and Tools of Management', in K. Knorr (ed.), *Historical Dimensions of National Security Problems* (Lawrence, KS: University of Kansas Press, 1976).
Schulte, P. 'Tactical Nuclear Weapons in NATO and Beyond: A Historical and Thematic Examination', in T. Nichols, D. Stuart, and J. D. McCausland (eds), *Tactical Nuclear Weapons and NATO* (Carlisle: USAWC SSI, 2012).
Schwartz, D. *NATO's Nuclear Dilemmas* (Washington, DC: Brookings Institution, 1983).
Schweller, R. and D. Priess. 'A Tale of Two Realisms: Expanding the Institutions Debate', *Mershon International Studies Review*, 41:1 (1997), 1–32.

Sechser, T. 'Goliath's Curse: Coercive Threats and Asymmetric Power', *International Organization,* 64:4 (2010), 627–660.

Secretary of Defense J. Schlesinger, *The Theater Nuclear Force Posture in Europe: A Report to the United States Congress in Compliance with Public Law 93–365* (1 April 1975).

Seth, M. *A Concise History of Modern Korea: From the Late Nineteenth Century to the Present*, 2nd edition (Lanham, MD: Rowman and Littlefield, 2016).

Shea, J. 'How the Harmel Report Helped Build the Transatlantic Security Framework', *The New Atlanticist*, 29 January 2018, www.atlanticcouncil.org/blogs/new-atlanticist/how-the-harmel-report-helped-build-the-transatlantic-security-framework/

Shepsle, K. 'Rational Choice Institutionalism', in S. Binder, R. Rhodes, and B. Rockman (eds), *The Oxford Handbook of Political Institutions* (Oxford: Oxford University Press, 2008).

Shultz, G., W. Perry, H. Kissinger, and S. Nunn, 'A World Free of Nuclear Weapons', *Wall Street Journal*, 4 January 2007, www.wsj.com/articles/SB116787515251566636

Skogrand, K. and R. Tamnes, *Fryktens Likevekt: Atombomben, Norge og verden 1945–1970* (Oslo: Tiden Norsk Forlag, 2001).

Skylar Mastro, O. 'Conflict and Chaos on the Korean Peninsula: Can China's Military Help Secure North Korea's Nuclear Weapons?', *International Security*, 43:2 (2018), 84–116.

Smeltz, D., K. Friedhoff, and L. Wojtowicz, 'South Koreans See Improved Security, Confident in US Security Guarantee', Chicago Council on Global Affairs, 18 January 2019, www.thechicagocouncil.org/research/public-opinion-survey/south-koreans-see-improved-security-confident-us-security-guaranteewww

Smith, M. 'To Neither Use Them Nor Lose Them: NATO and Nuclear Weapons Since the Cold War', *Contemporary Security Policy*, 25:3 (2004), 524–544.

Smith, M. *NATO Enlargement During the Cold War* (Houndmills: Palgrave, 2000).

Smith, S. *Japan Rearmed: The Politics of Military Power* (Cambridge, MA: Harvard University Press, 2019).

Smith, S. 'Ministerial Statement (Defence): Full Knowledge and Concurrence', *Commonwealth Parliamentary Debates* (House of Representatives), 26 June 2013.

Snyder, G. *Alliance Politics* (Ithaca, NY: Cornell University Press, 1997).

Snyder, G. *Deterrence by Denial and Punishment*, Research Monograph (1) (Princeton, NJ: Center of International Studies, Woodrow Wilson School, Princeton University, 1959).

Snyder, S. *South Korea at the Crossroads: Autonomy and Alliance in an Era of Rival Powers* (New York: Columbia University Press, 2018).

Solingen, E. *Nuclear Logics: Contrasting Paths in East Asia and the Middle East* (Princeton, NJ and Oxford: Princeton University Press, 2007).

Solomon, J., J. Barnes, and A. Gale, 'North Korea Warned: US Flies Stealth Bombers Over Peninsula in Show of Force', *Wall Street Journal*, 29 March 2013, www.wsj.com/articles/SB10001424127887323501004578389162106323642

Sperling, J. and M. Webber, 'Trump's Foreign Policy and NATO: Exit and Voice', *Review of International Studies*, 45:3 (2019), 511–526.

Spohr, K. *The Global Chancellor: Helmut Schmidt and the Reshaping of the International Order* (Oxford: Oxford University Press, 2016).

Spohr Readman, K. 'Conflict and Cooperation in Intra-Alliance Nuclear Politics: Western Europe, the United States and the Genesis of NATO's Dual-Track Decision, 1977–79', *Journal of Cold War History,* 13:2 (2011), 39–89.

Spohr Readman, K. 'Germany and the Politics of the Neutron Bomb', *Diplomacy and Statecraft*, 21:2 (2010), 259–285.

Steinbruner, J. *The Cybernetic Theory of Decision: New Dimensions of Political Analysis* (Princeton, NJ: Princeton University Press, 1974).

Stewart, P. and I. Ali, 'Exclusive: Inside Trump's Standoff with South Korea Over Defense Costs', *Reuters*, 11 April 2020, www.reuters.com/article/us-usa-southkorea-trump-defense-exclusiv/exclusive-inside-trumps-standoff-with-south-korea-over-defense-costs-idUSKCN21S1W7

Stewart, P. and A. Doyle, 'Norway Renews NATO Spending Pledge and Trump's Defense Chief Visits', *Reuters*, 15 July 2018, www.reuters.com/article/us-norway-usa-mattis/norway-renews-nato-spending-pledge-as-trumps-defense-chief-visits-idUSKBN1K40LJ

Stiles, M. 'Upset Over a US Missile Defense System, China Hits South Korea Where it Hurts, in the Wallet', *Los Angeles Times*, 28 February 2018, www.latimes.com/world/asia/la-fg-china-south-korea-tourism-20180228-htmlstory.html

Stokes, B. and K. Devlin, 'Views of the US and President Trump', *Pew Research Centre: Global Attitudes and Trends*, 12 November 2018, www.pewresearch.org/global/2018/11/12/views-of-the-u-s-and-president-trump/

Strauss, J. 'What Did We Want? Debates within the Australian Nuclear Disarmament Movement in the 1980s', *Labour History*, 115 (2018), 145–165.

Stueck, W. 'The Korean War', in M. Leffler and O. Arne Westad (eds), *The Cambridge History of the Cold War*, Vol. 1: *Origins* (Cambridge: Cambridge University Press, 2010).

Sukin, L. 'Credible Nuclear Commitments Can Backfire: Explaining Domestic Support for Nuclear Weapons Acquisition in South Korea', *Journal of Conflict Resolution*, 64:6 (2020), 1011–1042.

Sungjoo, H. 'South Korea and the United States: The Alliance Survives', *Asian Survey*, 20:11 (1980), 1075–1086.

Tai Young Kwon and Young Sun Song, 'The First ROK Defense White Paper: Its Significance and Important Contents', *Korean Journal of Defense Analysis*, 1:1 (1989), 193–211.

Takubo, M. 'The Role of Nuclear Weapons: Japan, the US, and "Sole Purpose"', *Arms Control Today*, 5 November 2009, www.armscontrol.org/act/2009_11/Takubo

Tamnes, R. 'The High North: A Call for a Competitive Strategy', in J. Andreas Olsen (ed.), *Security in Northern Europe: Deterrence, Defence and Dialogue* (London: Routledge, 2018).

Tamnes, R. *The United States and the Cold War in the High North* (Aldershot: Dartmouth, 1991).

Tange, Sir Arthur *Defence Policy-Making: A Close-Up View, 1950–1980*. Ed. P. Edwards (Canberra: ANU Press, 2008).

Terriff, T. *The Nixon Administration and the Making of US Nuclear Strategy* (Ithaca, NY: Cornell University Press, 1995).

'The Alliance's New Strategic Concept Agreed by the Heads of State and Government Participating in the Meeting of the North Atlantic Council, 7–8 November 1991', www.nato.int/cps/en/natohq/official_texts_23847.htm

'The Fallout: South Korean Public Opinion Following North Korea's Third Nuclear Test', *Asan Institute for Policy Studies Brief*, 24 February 2013, http://en.asaninst.org/contents/issue-brief-no-46-the-fallout-south-korean-public-opinion-following-north-koreas-third-nuclear-test/

Thomas, J., Z. Cooper, and I. Rehman, *Gateway to the Indo-Pacific: Australian Defense Strategy and the Future of the Australia-US Alliance* (Washington, DC: CSBA, 2013).

Tidwell, A. 'The Role of "Diplomatic Lobbying" in Shaping US Foreign Policy and Its Effects on the Australia-US Relationship', *Australian Journal of International Affairs*, 71:2 (2017), 184–200.

Tillett, A. 'North Korea Threatens Australia with "Disaster" Over Opposition to Nuke Program', *Australian Financial Review*, 15 October 2017, www.afr.com/news/north-korea-threatens-australia-with-disaster-over-opposition-to-nuke-program-20171015-gz14zj

Tow, W. 'ANZUS: Regional Versus Global Security in Asia', *International Relations of the Asia Pacific*, 5:1 (2005), 197–216.

Tow, W. *Encountering the Dominant Player: US Extended Deterrence Strategy in the Asia-Pacific* (New York: Columbia University Press, 1991).

Townshend, A., D. Santoro, and B. Thomas-Noone, 'Revisiting Deterrence in an Era of Strategic Competition: Outcomes Report from the Inaugural US–Australia Indo-Pacific Deterrence Dialogue', US Studies Centre, University of Sydney, 8 February 2019, www.ussc.edu.au/analysis/revisiting-deterrence-in-an-era-of-strategic-competition

Trachtenberg, D. 'US Extended Deterrence: How Much Strategic Force is Too Little?' *Strategic Studies Quarterly,* 6:2 (2012), 62–92.

Trachtenberg, M. *The Cold War and After: History, Theory, and the Logic of International Politics* (Princeton, NJ: Princeton University Press, 2012).

Trevithick, J. 'The Air Force Abruptly Ends its Continuous Bomber Presence on Guam After 16 Years', *The Drive*, 17 April 2020, www.thedrive.com/the-war-zone/33057/the-continuous-strategic-bomber-presence-mission-to-guam-has-abruptly-ended-after-16-years

Tsuruoka, M. 'The NATO vs. East Asian Models of Extended Nuclear Deterrence? Seeking a Synergy Beyond Dichotomy', *Asan Forum,* 4:3 (2016), www.theasanforum.org/the-nato-vs-east-asian-models-of-extended-nuclear-deterrence-seeking-a-synergy-beyond-dichotomy/

Tuschhoff, C. *Deutschland, Kernwaffen und die NATO 1949–1967* (Baden-Baden: Nomos, 2002).

Tuschhoff, C. 'Alliance Cohesion and Peaceful Change in NATO', in H. Haftendorn, R. Keohane, and C. Wallander (eds), *Imperfect Unions: Security Institutions Over Time and Space* (Oxford: Oxford University Press: 1999).

Umetsu, H. 'The Birth of Anzus: America's Attempt to Create a Defense Linkage between Northeast Asia and the Southwest Pacific', *International Relations of the Asia-Pacific* 4:1 (2004), 171–196.

United Nations, 'First Committee: Nuclear Cluster, Statement by Norway to the United Nations, 21 October 2019', www.un.org/disarmament/wp-content/uploads/2019/10/statement-by-norway-nw-oct-21–19.pdf

Urnes Johnson, A. K., K. Hove, and T. Lillekvelland, 'Country Survey: Military Expenditure and Defence Policy in Norway 1970–2013', *Defence and Peace Economics*, 28:6 (2017), 669–675.

US Congress, *John S. McCain National Defense Authorization Act for Fiscal Year 2019*, www.congress.gov/bill/115th-congress/house-bill/5515/text
US Embassy and Consulate in Korea, 'Joint Statement of the 2016 United States-Republic of Korea Foreign and Defense Ministers' Meeting, Washington DC, October 19, 2016', https://kr.usembassy.gov/joint-statement-2016-united-states-republic-korea-foreign-defense-ministers-meeting/
US Space Command, 'Background Paper on Australian Implementing Arrangement – Deputy Commander Controversy, April 19, 1990', https://nsarchive2.gwu.edu//NSAEBB/NSAEBB235/20.pdf
Van Dassen, L. and A. Wetter, 'Nordic Nuclear Non Proliferation Policies: Different Traditions and Common Objectives', in G. Herolf, A. Bailes, and B. Sundelius (eds), *The Nordic Countries and the European Defence Policy* (Oxford: Oxford University Press and SIPRI, 2006).
Van de Velde, J. 'Japan's Nuclear Umbrella: US Extended Nuclear Deterrence for Japan', *Journal of Northeast Asian Studies*, 7:4 (1988), 16–39.
Vogel, E. 'Japanese-American Relations After the Cold War', *Daedalus*, 121:4 (1992), 35–60.
Waldahl, R. 'Norwegian Attitudes Toward Defense and Foreign Policy Issues', in G. Flynn and H. Rattinger (eds), *The Public and Atlantic Defense* (New York: Rowman and Littlefield, 1985).
Wallander, C. 'Institutional Assets and Adaptability: NATO After the Cold War', *International Organization*, 54:4 (2000), 705–735.
Walsh, J. 'Surprise Down Under: The Secret History of Australia's Nuclear Ambitions', *Nonproliferation Review*, 5:1 (1997), 1–20.
Walt, S. 'US Strategy After the Cold War: Can Realism Explain It? Should Realism Guide It?', *International Relations*, 32:1 (2018), 3–22.
Walt, S. 'Why Alliances Endure or Collapse', *Survival*, 39:1 (1997), 156–179.
Walt, S. *The Origins of Alliances* (Ithaca, NY: Cornell University Press, 1987).
Waltz, K. *Theory of International Politics* (Long Grove, IL: Waveland Press, 1979).
Watts, R. '"Rockets' Red Glare": Why Does China Oppose THAAD in South Korea, and What Does it Mean for US Policy?', *Naval War College Review*, 71:2 (2018), 79–107.
Weber, S. 'Shaping the Postwar Balance of Power: Multilateralism in NATO', *International Organization*, 46:3 (1992), 633–680.
Weede, E. 'Extended Deterrence by Superpower Alliance', *Journal of Conflict Resolution*, 27:2 (1983), 231–254.
Weinraub, B. 'NATO Voices Concern Over Plans to Limit Cruise Missile Range', *New York Times*, 13 October 1977, www.nytimes.com/1977/10/13/archives/nato-voices-concern-over-plans-to-limit-cruise-missile-range.html
Welfield, J. 'Japan and Nuclear China: Japanese Reactions to China's Nuclear Weapons', *Canberra Papers on Strategy and Defence*, no. 9 (Canberra: Australian National University Press, 1970).
Wheeler, M. 'NATO Nuclear Strategy, 1949–1990', in G. Schmidt (ed.), *A History of NATO: The First Fifty Years*, Vol. 3 (Houndmills: Palgrave Macmillan, 2001).
White House Office of the Press Secretary, 'Joint Vision for the Alliance of the United States of America and the Republic of Korea, June 16, 2009', https://obamawhitehouse.archives.gov/the-press-office/joint-vision-alliance-united-states-america-and-republic-korea

Williams, M. 'The 2018 Nuclear Posture Review: Reception by US Allies in the Asia-Pacific', *CSIS Next Generation Nuclear Network*, 23 May 2018, https://nuclearnetwork.csis.org/2018-nuclear-posture-review-reception-u-s-allies-asia-pacific/

Wirtz, J. 'Conclusions', in Jeffrey Knopf (ed.), *Security Assurances and Non-Proliferation* (Stanford, CA: Stanford University Press, 2012).

Wit, J., D. Poneman and R. Gallucci, *Going Critical: The First North Korean Nuclear Crisis* (Washington, DC: Brookings Institution Press, 2004).

Wither, J. 'Svalbard: NATO's Arctic 'Achilles' Heel', *RUSI Journal*, 163:5 (2018), 28–37.

Wood, J. 'Persuading a President: Jimmy Carter and American Troops in Korea', Unpublished Paper, 1996, https://nsarchive2.gwu.edu//NSAEBB/NSAEBB431/docs/intell_ebb_002.PDF

Woolf, A. and E. Chanlett-Avery, 'Redeploying US Nuclear Weapons to South Korea; Background and Implications in Brief', *Congressional Research Service Report*, R44950, 14 September 2017, https://crsreports.congress.gov/product/pdf/R/R44950/3

Work, C. 'Alternative Futures for the US–ROK Alliance: Will Things Fall Apart?', *38 North*, May 2020, www.38north.org/2020/05/cwork050720/

Wuthnow, J. 'US Minilateralism in Asia and China's Responses: A New Security Dilemma?', *Journal of Contemporary China*, 28:115 (2019), 133–150.

Yamazaki, M. 'Nuclear Energy in Postwar Japan and Anti-Nuclear Movements in the 1950s', *Historia Scientiarum*, 19:2 (2009), 132–145.

Ye Hee Lee, M. 'More than Ever, South Koreans Want Their Own Nuclear Weapons', *Washington Post*, 13 September 2017, www.washingtonpost.com/news/worldviews/wp/2017/09/13/most-south-koreans-dont-think-the-north-will-start-a-war-but-they-still-want-their-own-nuclear-weapons/?utm_term=.e8776cdfa10a

Yennie Lindgren, W. and N. Graeger, 'The Challenges and Dynamics of Alliance Policies: Norway, NATO and the High North', in M. Wesley (ed.), *Global Allies: Comparing US Allies in the 21st Century* (Canberra: ANU Press, 2017).

Yoshihara, T. and J. Holmes, 'Thinking About the Unthinkable: Tokyo's Nuclear Option', *Naval War College Review*, 63:2 (2009), 59–78.

Yoshii, M. 'The Creation of the "Shock Myth": Japan's Reactions to America's Rapprochement with China, 1971–72', *Journal of American East Asian Relations*, 15 (2008), 131–146.

Yost, D. 'The US Debate on NATO Nuclear Deterrence', *International Affairs*, 87:6 (2011), 1401–1438.

Yost, D. 'US Extended Deterrence in NATO and North-East Asia', in B. Tertrais (ed.), *Perspectives on Extended Deterrence*, recherches & documents 03/2010, 15–36 (Paris: Fondation pour la recherche stratégique, 2010).

Yost, D. 'Assurance and US Extended Deterrence in NATO', *International Affairs* 85:4 (2009), 755–780.

Yost, D. 'The History of NATO Theater Nuclear Force Policy: Key Findings from the Sandia Conference', *Journal of Strategic Studies,* 15:2 (1992), 228–261.

Young Jang, Se. 'The Evolution of US Extended Deterrence and South Korea's Nuclear Ambitions', *Journal of Strategic Studies*, 39:4 (2016), 502–520.

Zagare, F. 'Deterrence Is Dead. Long Live Deterrence', *Conflict Management and Peace Science*, 23:2 (2006) 115–120.

Zagare, F. 'Rationality and Deterrence,' *World Politics,* 42:2 (1990), 238–260.

Zakheim, D. 'The United States and the Nordic Countries During the Cold War', *Cooperation and Conflict*, 33:2 (1998), 115–129.

Zapfe, M. 'NATO's Spearhead Force', *CSS Analyses in Security Policy*, 174 (2015), https://css.ethz.ch/content/dam/ethz/special-interest/gess/cis/center-for-securities-studies/pdfs/CSSAnalyse174-EN.pdf

Index